The Data Collection Toolkit
Everything You Need to Organize, Manage, and Monitor Classroom Data

by

Cindy Golden, Ed.D.
University of West Florida
Pensacola

Baltimore • London • Sydney

Paul H. Brookes Publishing Co.
Post Office Box 10624
Baltimore, Maryland 21285-0624
USA

www.brookespublishing.com

Typeset by Progressive Publishing Services, York, Pennsylvania.
Manufactured in the United States of America by
Versa Press, Inc., East Peoria, Illinois.

Cover image © istockphoto/artursfoto.
Clip art © istockphoto.

Library of Congress Cataloging-in-Publication Data

Names: Golden, Cindy, author.
Title: The data collection toolkit : everything you need to organize, manage, and monitor classroom
    data / Cindy Golden.
Description: 1 | Baltimore : Paul H. Brookes Publishing Co., 2017. | Includes bibliographical
    references and index.
Identifiers: LCCN 2017020801 (print) | LCCN 2017042519 (ebook) | ISBN 9781681252537 (pdf) |
    ISBN 9781681252520 (epub) | ISBN 9781598579246 (paperback)
Subjects: LCSH: Special education—United States. | Special education—United States—
    Administration. | Students with disabilities—Education—United States. | Educational evaluation—
    Data processing. | Classroom management. | BISAC: EDUCATION / Decision-Making & Problem
    Solving. | EDUCATION / Evaluation. | EDUCATION / Aims & Objectives.
Classification: LCC LC3981 (ebook) | LCC LC3981 .G574 2017 (print) | DDC 371.9—dc23
LC record available at https://lccn.loc.gov/2017020801

British Library Cataloguing in Publication data are available from the British Library.

2021

10   9   8   7   6   5   4   3

Contents

About the Author v

About the Forms and Tools vi

Introduction: Becoming a Classroom Detective vii

I   **Preparing for Data Collection** 1

1   The Step-by-Step Process of Data Collection: What You Need to Know 3

2   Determining the Specific Issue and Defining the Target Behavior or Focus 11

II   **Collecting Your Data** **23**

3   Academic Data and Progress Monitoring 25

4   Behavioral Data 41

5   IEP Data 71

6   Establishing Your Data Collection System 83

III   **Data Analysis and Follow-Up** **103**

7   Analyzing Data 105

8   Data-Based Decision Making 125

IV   **Your Classroom Data Toolkit** 135

A   Academic and Progress Monitoring Forms 137

B   Behavior Forms 159

C IEP Forms 207

D Organizational Tools: Establishing a Data Collection System 217

References... 235

Appendix A Building Your Data Collection Notebook: Handouts,
Embellishments, and Extras..................................... 237

Appendix B Answers to Quick Quizzes 243

Index 245

About the Author

Cindy Golden, Ed.D., has more than 30 years' experience working with students with disabilities. She serves as an adjunct faculty member for the University of West Florida and as an autism consultant for Florida State University's Center for Autism and Related Disabilities. Before retiring from public education, Dr. Golden served as the assistant director and principal/psychologist of an educational and therapeutic program serving students with severe emotional and behavioral needs and autism. In the past, she served as a special education supervisor in a metro Atlanta school system, supervising the countywide autism and emotional/behavioral disorders programs, and she worked as a school psychologist for students with neurodevelopmental disabilities. Dr. Golden served 13 years of her career in the classroom, where she was elected Teacher of the Year twice.

Dr. Golden has an undergraduate degree in special education from the University of West Florida, master's and educational specialist degrees in school psychology from Georgia State University, and a certificate in educational leadership and an educational specialist degree from Kennesaw State University. She has a doctoral degree in inclusive education with a focus on autism from Kennesaw State University. Dr. Golden authored *The Special Educator's Toolkit: Everything You Need to Organize, Manage, and Monitor Your Classroom* (Paul H. Brookes Publishing Co., 2012), served as a contributing author to *Understanding Children with Autism Spectrum Disorders: Educators Partnering with Families* (Sage, 2012), and has been featured in a Q & A article in *Scholastic Instructor Magazine* and on an hour-long back-to-school show on Autism Spectrum Radio. She was the author of several popular blogs for parents and teachers of children with special needs and has written numerous online articles. Dr. Golden is considered an expert in the field of special education and is a popular speaker at local, state, regional, national, and international conferences, along with being a sought-after trainer of educators across the country.

About the Forms and Tools

Purchasers of *The Data Collection Toolkit: Everything You Need to Organize, Manage, and Monitor Classroom Data* are granted permission to download, print, and photocopy the forms, data sheets, Quick-Graphs, and other materials included in this book for educational or professional purposes. These materials are included with the print and e-book and are also available for download at **http://www.brookespublishing.com/downloads,** with (case sensitive) key-code 46ldCiB46.

Introduction
Becoming a Classroom Detective

In many respects, the world of the detective is parallel to the world of the educator. They both hypothesize, gather documentation, test their theories, map out timelines, look for evidence, persevere when there seems to be no clear answer, reinvestigate if necessary, and gather information by interviewing those involved. Their problems or cases are different, but they both require the "cold, hard facts," called *data,* in order to solve the case or find the answer to the issue affecting the student.

Data are evidence. Though teaching in a classroom is a softer science than working a crime scene, educators are required to deal in evidence and should use objective facts to inform their teaching practices and educational decisions. There are cases to be solved and questions to be answered, such as "Why is a student's behavior occurring?" "Is the academic intervention actually working?" and "Is the student making progress?"

Teachers need to collect data to confirm a hypothesis, to answer questions that may arise about a certain situation or student, and to solve a problem that may come up in the classroom. The mounds of raw data that the busy teacher collects will require organization. The teacher will need a way to present the data easily so that others can understand the findings.

In researching the detective lifestyle, I found several steps to be very important in helping a detective solve a case. I am going to call this list Detective Skills 101. When a detective is presented with a problem or issue that needs to be solved, he or she needs to tackle several steps. Likewise, the educator takes a similar course of action when collecting data to solve a classroom challenge. Consider how each step a detective takes to solve a case is also relevant to educators who are collecting data to resolve problems in their classrooms.

1. *Determine the problem.* What is the specific issue or problem to be solved? What objective, observable details are most relevant to the case?

   How this applies to the classroom: You must first determine the challenging behavior or learning issue at hand in order to decide which intervention to implement and how to effectively collect data to monitor progress. When addressing a challenging behavior, observe it objectively without an emotional connection or reaction so that it can be defined in neutral terms. Having a good understanding of the problem is a first step to solving it.

2. *Understand the terms.* The detective investigating the issues of a case must have a complete understanding of all that is involved in the case and be able to describe precisely what happened in clear terms.

   How this applies to the classroom: Is the behavior or the learning challenge operationally defined (e.g., defined in concise, observable, and measurable terms) (Cooper,

Heron, & Heward, 2007)? Two neutral observers working with the student should be able to understand exactly what the issue is and identify the behavior. This will ensure that the data taken will be precise and accurate.

3. *Nail down the timeline of events.* One of the first things a detective will do is to map out a timeline of events, which can uncover new leads and offer clues that can help solve the case.

    How this applies to the classroom: When and where the behavior or the issue happens is important. Does it occur in only one setting, during one activity, or in interactions with one person? Does it occur during a certain time of day? By investigating the preceding circumstances for a behavior or academic difficulty, the teacher can uncover potential issues that are impacting the behavior and look for solutions.

4. *Remain alert.* A detective must take in information gained from all five senses. Evidence may be seen, felt, or heard. Remaining alert to the details ensures that nothing is overlooked.

    How this applies to the classroom: When doing an observation, be sure to note everything. What did you hear, see, and experience in the classroom or learning environment? Did you observe the noise level, the organization of the learning environment, and the tone of verbal communication? What can you learn from forms of nonverbal communication? Were there any smells, bright lights, or distractions that could be causing sensory or visual stimulation issues for students? Be sure to acutely observe what is going on when the problem or issue occurs.

5. *Interview people, and request information from those in the environment.* A detective must continue to investigate by interviewing those involved in the case and gathering information. Those with firsthand knowledge will provide evidence that may be vital. What about getting background and historical information on those involved? This information may lead the detective down the path to solving the case.

    How this applies to the classroom: Have you reviewed the background information on the student and the issue? Have you read the individualized education program (IEP) or reviewed academic records? Maybe a conference with the parent, administrators, or other teachers involved with the student is in order. What about talking to the student? When appropriate, absolutely question and talk to the student so you can get firsthand information about his or her perspectives, needs, and experiences in the classroom.

6. *Treat everything as evidence, and follow every lead.* Detectives comb through the strangest things looking for clues that will help to answer questions and solve the case. Anything and everything can be used as evidence until it is shown to be unimportant.

    How this applies to the classroom: Have you considered everything that you saw or learned in the classroom and not overlooked what may seem like insignificant details? Carefully analyze all information gained during an observation, through review of background information and records, or during a conference.

7. *Document and take note of the facts.* Consider the classic depiction of detectives. They usually wear a trench coat and a hat and carry a tablet of paper to document everything they learn. Detectives deal in facts—not opinions.

    How this applies to the classroom: Have you collected permanent products from the student, such as work samples and other items? Have you documented your interviews and observations right away (since you are human and will probably not remember all the details later)?

8. *Persevere, and do not give up too soon.* There are some cold cases in criminal investigations that were solved years after the crime was committed. Someone did not give up and continued to investigate.

   How this applies to the classroom: Are there learning or behavioral issues that you have just accepted as "the way it is" because nothing has worked before? Have you given up too soon on a behavior change and just decided to manage or contain the behavior?

9. *Search the scene thoroughly, and do not be afraid to revisit the scene several times.* Detectives frequently must go back to the scene of the crime more than once, each time with fresh eyes and a new perspective, to ensure no evidence was missed.

   How this applies to the classroom: Have you collected sufficient data in the learning environment? Is it the right kind of data? Have you considered having a second or third set of eyes review the same behavior in order to get a different perspective or to make sure the data are accurate, valid, and reliable?

10. *Formulate a hypothesis, and test out theories.* Detectives always formulate a theory or a hypothesis. This provides a place to start, even though the hypothesis may change as the evidence points and guides in different directions. Investigating is a fluid process.

    How this applies to the classroom: Have you used the process of data analysis to get an idea of what is affecting the behavior or issue? Have you brainstormed a possible solution or at least some ideas of how to begin solving the issue? Have you tried things that did not work? If so, have you followed up with a new approach?

This book will help you to become a detective in the classroom in order to help your students learn and to solve challenging behaviors; it breaks down the overwhelming task of collecting data into manageable steps. For many teachers, data collection can seem intimidating, particularly on top of numerous classroom responsibilities. The mounds of raw data that the busy teacher collects will require organization. These data will also need a way to be easily presented so that others can understand the findings.

Without the appropriate skills or easy-to-use tools for collecting and analyzing educational data, teachers may not know where to begin. That is where this book comes in. This book is complete with practical tips and helpful tools that will assist you in creating an effective and efficient data collection system in your classroom, whether you work in a school or homeschool environment.

In addition to breaking down the task of data collection, this book provides a one-of-a-kind data collection tool called a Quick-Graph! Quick-Graphs are self-graphing data collection tools that lighten the load by allowing you to create visual graphs while collecting raw data, taking care of two steps in one. As you read, you will also encounter quizzes, other types of printable data sheets, handouts, and true-life stories that make the information real.

The book is organized into four sections:

- *Section I: Preparing for Data Collection* provides the basics of classroom data collection and takes you step-by-step through all you need to know to begin effectively collecting data in your classroom.

- *Section II: Collecting Your Data* is about the process of collecting and graphing a variety of data—academic data, behavioral data, and IEP data for students with special needs—to help the students in your class. This section introduces you to Quick-Graphs, helpful data collection forms that allow you to create visual graphs while collecting raw data. You will learn ways to determine which type of data you will need to answer specific target questions and solve problems in your classroom, as well as how to create and organize an efficient and effective data collection system.

- *Section III: Data Analysis and Follow-Up* discusses how to actually use the data you have collected to maximize the benefits for your students. You will learn how to analyze trends and patterns in the data and use the information you have collected to make intervention and teaching decisions that will have a measurable impact on your students' learning and success.

- *Section IV: Your Classroom Data Toolkit* presents photocopiable/printable handouts and Quick-Graphs, with detailed instruction for use. These tools can be used in any classroom, homeschool, or other environment that requires data collection.

Each chapter in Sections I, II, and III is designed to build on your prior learning and provide you with the tools you need to use classroom data effectively. The following features are provided in each chapter:

- Mission (or objective)

- Questions to Investigate

- Definitions of Terms and Abbreviations

- Eyewitness Account

- Quick Quiz

Each chapter opens with a broader "mission"—an objective or end goal for what readers will learn about data collection—before focusing on specific questions that will be investigated and answered in the chapter. These focused questions help frame the discussion and organize the most pertinent information. The beginning of the chapter also provides you with all the facts you need to understand the content that follows, providing clear, simple, operational definitions of key terms that you will encounter as you read.

Other useful features include Eyewitness Accounts that present real, firsthand challenges that educators face in collecting data in their classroom and numerous handouts that can be used in the classroom or for training purposes. These handouts can be placed in a notebook in the classroom for reference or distributed at staff trainings so that staff members can create their own data collection notebooks. Just as the traditional detective carries a notebook or sketchpad to take notes and collect evidence, an educator or other school professional can use his or her data collection notebook to record and organize important classroom data. (Appendix A: Building Your Data Collection Notebook: Handouts, Embellishments, and Extras contains photocopiable cover pages, handouts, and forms to include in a notebook or binder of your choice; see the About the Forms and Tools page for instructions on downloading printable copies.) Finally, each chapter ends with a Quick Quiz that allows you to review relevant concepts you have learned about data collection. Answers to the Quick Quizzes are included in Appendix B.

Are you ready to start thinking like a classroom detective? Let's get started!

REFERENCE

Cooper, J. O., Heron, T. E., & Heward, W. L. (2007). *Applied behavior analysis* (2nd ed.). Upper Saddle River, NJ: Prentice Hall.

To my mom, who has selflessly fed me, cleaned my house, walked my dogs, and even edited my work; without her, I could not have finished this book—I love you, Mama

Preparing for Data Collection

What does data collection involve? Why do educators collect data, and what steps need to be followed to ensure these data are meaningful and can be used effectively? Section I introduces you to the basics of classroom data collection. It takes you step by step through the process of collecting data (Chapter 1) and explains in depth how to prepare for data collection by first determining a specific issue or problem and then defining a related target behavior or focus (Chapter 2).

The Step-by-Step Process of Data Collection

What You Need to Know

 MISSION: To learn the facts about classroom data collection, investigate why data are important, and introduce the basic steps of the data collection process

QUESTIONS TO INVESTIGATE

- Why should I collect data in my classroom?
- Is collecting classroom data actually going to make a difference?
- In what environments can data be collected?
- What are the basic steps to data collection in any environment?
- After collecting data, what should I do next?
- Does the data collection process work the same way for RTI and MTSS?

DEFINITIONS OF TERMS AND ABBREVIATIONS

Analysis   The examination and interpretation of data.

BCBA   Board Certified Behavior Analyst; a person who has extensive training in the field of behavior analysis and is certified by passing a test and undergoing hours of supervised field experiences. He or she is experienced in dealing with behavioral challenges.

BIP   Behavior intervention plan; an individual plan of interventions used to target specific behavioral challenges.

Data   Systematically collected information about a student's academic and/or behavioral performance. Data can be qualitative (typically presented in narrative form as a description) or quantitative (typically presented as numbers).

FBA   Functional behavioral assessment; a problem-solving process in which a behavior is measured and examined in a methodical manner so that the function of the behavior can be determined and appropriate interventions can be implemented. It involves observation and the collection and analysis of data.

MTSS   Multi-tiered system of supports; a global framework of supports created and measured to meet the needs of all students.

RTI   Response to intervention; a type of multi-tiered system of supports (MTSS). RTI is a tiered approach to providing and measuring the effectiveness of varying levels of interventions for all students.

Target behavior   The behavior or skill on which you are focusing. It is the specific behavior you are going to observe and measure. The target behavior should be defined in clear terms so that all individuals involved in the observation or measurement of the behavior understand exactly what to look for. For example, "inappropriate behavior" is not a target behavior but "talking out in class" is.

Task analysis   Systematically breaking down a complicated task into discrete steps that can be easily observed. For example, "making a sandwich" is an everyday task that can be broken down into small, discrete steps that can be taught, observed, and measured.

Visual analysis   Presenting summarized data in graph or chart format so that anyone can easily determine trends, patterns, and discrepancies.

Your mission in this chapter is to acquire a foundational understanding of the data collection process—to learn the basic steps for collecting evidence in the classroom to solve learning and behavior issues so that students can succeed. Many educators are intimidated by the prospect of collecting data, and new teachers in particular may not know where to begin. Consider the following Eyewitness Account from a new teacher.

 Eyewitness Account

As a first-year fourth-grade general education teacher, I was eager to get started in my new classroom. I was a little nervous about the first faculty meeting, as it is a half-day workshop before the school year starts, but mostly I looked forward to the experience. During this workshop, the principal began by talking about the classroom setup, scheduling, and the fun things the school planned to do during the school year. I was confident and happy, as these were the reasons I went into teaching. I thought to myself, "I have this covered." The principal then began talking about progress monitoring, inclusion of students with IEPs [individualized education programs], and the mandated requirements of data collection, and I suddenly felt much more nervous than excited. At a break in the meeting, the special education teacher approached me in order to let me know that my classroom will include some of her students who have IEPs, FBAs [functional behavioral assessments], and BIPs [behavior intervention plans]. She said that the BCBA [Board Certified Behavior Analyst] for the county would be working with me on designing and monitoring interventions for these students. I walked away with my head spinning. How was I going to handle all of this in addition to the curriculum and management of the classroom? I didn't even have a clear understanding of all of the acronyms!

—*Jeannette Torres,*
First-Year Fourth-Grade Teacher

Jeanette is struggling. She has the training to be a terrific first-year teacher, and she is excited about many aspects of her chosen career. She feels prepared, but she is overwhelmed by some of the details of her new job. Data collection is one of those details. Although Jeannette is a general education teacher, she is still required to collect data in her classroom. Some teachers might be wondering why data collection is important, which is the first question explored in this chapter.

WHY SHOULD I COLLECT DATA IN MY CLASSROOM?

Data are collected for a variety of reasons. Let me share a personal example. I recently had back pain and did not want to go to the doctor. I thought, "I'm relatively bright, and I solve problems on a daily basis. Unless there is a medical reason for my pain, I can figure this one out, and if I can't, then I'll go to the doctor." So, as only a special educator/psychologist would do, I gathered a little informal data. I began with my target question: "Why has my back begun to hurt on a daily basis?" I then began charting my back pain, my timeline of activities, my sleep schedule, and objects I interacted with in my environment. After I had collected 4 days' worth of baseline data, I began to test my theories by implementing some interventions. I tested four theories with a combination of interventions, which involved manipulating items and activities in my environment while collecting data. I started a stretching routine; changed pillows; monitored shoe-heel height; and changed the hard, straight-backed, no padding, old wooden chair that I sat in for hours while working on the computer. Do you know what I found? The cause of the pain was the hard, straight-backed, no padding, old wooden chair! I changed chairs and had no more pain. Problem solved! This is only one reason for collecting data in everyday life.

So, to simplify, there are three reasons for collecting data in any environment:

1. To answer a question

2. To provide evidence to support or refute a theory

3. To measure progress

Educators want to do their jobs to the best of their ability. All educators struggle to find the time to do everything required of them. However, as Heward (2000) noted, they need to remember that "when practiced most effectively and ethically, special education is also characterized by the use of research-based teaching methods, the application of which is guided by direct and frequent measures of student performance" (p. 37). Data collection is therefore an essential responsibility when educating students with special needs or challenges. It is also an essential duty of general educators such as Jeannette and is beneficial for all students.

IS COLLECTING CLASSROOM DATA ACTUALLY GOING TO MAKE A DIFFERENCE?

Jeanette's eyes probably glazed over as she thought about all that she had to learn and do to collect data, and she most likely asked herself if data collection was going to have any real impact. You might be wondering, "Is learning about data collection actually going to make a difference in what I do in my classroom, how I teach, the interventions I use, and how much progress my students will make?" The answer is yes.

There is only one way to determine whether the interventions that you implement, the ways that you teach, and the classroom activities that you conduct have a positive impact on your students: by measuring student progress. Witt, VanDerHeyden, and Gilbertson (2004) stated that an intervention is considered "fatally flawed" if data are not collected on the intervention when it is being used with a student. They also said that the intervention is flawed if one of the following elements is missing: definition of the presenting problem, measurement of baseline performance, a goal for the intervention, and ongoing measurement of performance. This book covers each of these elements and shows how to implement them in the classroom.

IN WHAT ENVIRONMENTS CAN DATA BE COLLECTED?

Now that you understand that data collection is important and required, it is time to consider where data should be collected. As was the case with Jeanette, data often need to be collected in a general education classroom that includes students with a variety of special needs. Teachers such as Jeanette are responsible for implementing accommodations and modifications to the curriculum as outlined by each student's IEP. If data are required, then these teachers may also be responsible for collecting them in their classrooms. In addition, data can be collected in special education classrooms, whether the classroom is a pull-out or self-contained setting (Fisher & Frey, 2013; Jimenez, Mims, & Browder, 2012; Lane & Ledford, 2014). Your students' academic functioning, social functioning, and behaviors do not stop once they walk out the classroom door. Can data be collected on the bus, in the hallway, at the media center, on the playground, and in the gym? Should data be collected in these settings? If applicable and appropriate, then of course!

As a psychologist, I completed hundreds of psychological evaluations on students. If the presenting question was to rule out behaviors that may or may not be typical of a student with autism spectrum disorder, I would have been remiss if I observed the student only in the classroom setting. In a classroom, everything is controlled. Peer groups are usually structured, tasks are outlined, and informal communication is limited. The adults in the classroom typically create a structured environment and guide interactions. Thus, the ritualistic behaviors or social-communication challenges of a student who is possibly functioning on the autism spectrum may not be visible due to the controlled surroundings.

The student observations that I most disliked doing were those in which the student was quiet, reading silently, or taking a long test and therefore had no chance to interact with people around him or her. These observations were not very helpful. However, if that same student were placed on a playground with peers, I might see a very different child. I could observe peer interactions, verbal communication, nonverbal communication, responses to sensory input, gross and fine motor skills, and more. Because the child may behave, respond, and interact differently in settings outside the classroom, data collected only in the classroom environment may lead to results that are skewed, inaccurate, and incomplete.

Data should be collected in whatever environments the student participates, whether in the classroom, on the playground, in the cafeteria, on the bus, or in a homeschool environment. Specifics about the data collection—how, when, and where it is done, and who does it—may differ, but the same data sheets can be used, and the methods for determining the target behavior, analyzing and interpreting the data, and graphically depicting the summary of data are generalizable to all settings. This book presents several data forms, provides general steps to creating a data collection system, details methods of data analysis, and gives examples of how to discuss the data with others. This information can be applied to a variety of environments, including classrooms, homeschool settings, faith-based schools, private schools, private therapeutic settings, and more.

WHAT ARE THE BASIC STEPS TO DATA COLLECTION IN ANY ENVIRONMENT?

The best way to make a complicated and overwhelming task such as data collection easier is to create a task analysis of it. You may already have a good understanding of the five steps for collecting data in the classroom, but it never hurts to revisit them. Each of the steps is discussed in more detail in the upcoming chapters. See Figure 1.1 for a visual summary of the steps to data collection: define target, select method, implement collection, analyze and graph, and make decisions. Figure 1.1 is available in Appendix A as a full-page photocopiable handout for your data collection notebook; see also the About the Forms and Tools page at the beginning of this book for instructions on downloading a printable copy.

Steps to Data Collection

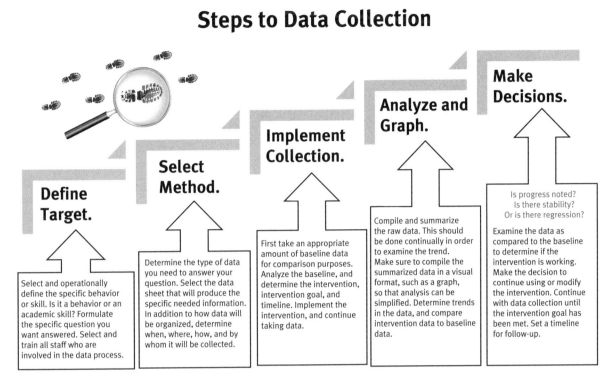

Define Target.

Select and operationally define the specific behavior or skill. Is it a behavior or an academic skill? Formulate the specific question you want answered. Select and train all staff who are involved in the data process.

Select Method.

Determine the type of data you need to answer your question. Select the data sheet that will produce the specific needed information. In addition to how data will be organized, determine when, where, how, and by whom it will be collected.

Implement Collection.

First take an appropriate amount of baseline data for comparison purposes. Analyze the baseline, and determine the intervention, intervention goal, and timeline. Implement the intervention, and continue taking data.

Analyze and Graph.

Compile and summarize the raw data. This should be done continually in order to examine the trend. Make sure to compile the summarized data in a visual format, such as a graph, so that analysis can be simplified. Determine trends in the data, and compare intervention data to baseline data.

Make Decisions.

Is progress noted? Is there stability? Or is there regression?

Examine the data as compared to the baseline to determine if the intervention is working. Make the decision to continue using or modify the intervention. Continue with data collection until the intervention goal has been met. Set a timeline for follow-up.

Figure 1.1. Steps to data collection.

Step 1: Define Target

This is the beginning of the entire process—the point at which you set the course. Pretend that you are going on a vacation. It's time for a road trip! You get the car packed, gas it up, make sure everyone is buckled in, and head out—but without a map or an idea of how to reach your final destination. You might accidently head in the opposite direction. You may end up eventually reaching your destination, but it is going to take a long, long time (and someone will inevitably get carsick from all the twists and turns)! It is the same scenario when collecting data. The focus questions and defined target behavior map out what you hope to accomplish by collecting data; they point you in the right direction so you will know exactly what you are measuring and can collect information purposefully with a set goal in mind.

First, you select and operationally define the specific behavior or skill. Is it a behavior or an academic skill? Formulate the specific question you want answered, then select and train all staff who are involved in the data collection process. Targeted questions are needed to ensure that the interventions make a difference in the classroom. Data collection will be useful if your questions are focused on the changes you want to see or the behaviors you want to investigate (Love, Stiles, Mundry, & DiRanna, 2008).

Step 2: Select Method

In this step, you will not only select the type(s) of data to be collected (i.e., data that, when analyzed, will answer your presenting question) but will also select the data collection tools you will use; how, when, and where the data will be collected; and who will be responsible for the data collection. This step is important because there is nothing like getting to the end of a 12-week data collection process, with mounds of data, only to realize that none of it addresses the initial issue! In other words, you wasted your time because the data did not answer the question at all. Therefore, you must determine the type of data you need to answer your question.

There are a variety of data collection tools to gather many types of information. For example, behaviors that have an observable beginning and ending point, with enough time between behaviors to distinguish between events, can be measured using an event or frequency recording data tool (Lane & Ledford, 2014). A behavior that lasts for an extended period of time can be measured using a duration data collection format. To select the tool or method that will best assist you, just think backward: What kind of answer are you hoping that the data will provide? Chapters 3, 4, and 5 will help you determine the type of data you need to answer your question. They contain data sheets to help you organize and track your data.

Step 3: Implement Collection

You have set your course and selected your tools. Now, it's time to collect your data! You should be consistent when collecting data. If you are not, your data may not be accurate, and this, in turn, will not help you to answer your question or address the issue at hand. When collecting data to determine the effectiveness of an intervention, you must first take an appropriate amount of baseline data for comparison purposes. Analyze the baseline data, and determine the intervention, intervention goal, and timeline. Then, implement the intervention, and continue taking data to see how the intervention is working.

Step 4: Analyze and Graph

You have your data—sometimes hundreds of pages of information—but the data will not be useful to you unless they are summarized, analyzed, and put into a visual format. Even if you are gifted in the ability to memorize numbers, internally visualize them, make comparisons among them, and see the trends or gaps in your head, you will still need to organize the data in a way that is easy for others to understand. So, graph it! You will easily be able to see trends, anomalies, and variances in the data, and that will lead you to make effective decisions about the implementation of interventions.

Step 5: Make Decisions

Data are not useful until they are used to make improvements. Do the data collected answer the question you initially presented? Do they show you if the interventions being implemented are working or if any progress has been made? Use the data to answer the initial question. Compare the summary of the data to that original issue, and make decisions based on the data.

Remember that data collection and the use of data in decision making are not only important for students receiving special education services but also for students in all tiers of response to intervention (RTI). Research studies stress the importance of using data to monitor student progress and the impact of the interventions implemented (Fisher & Frey, 2013; Kurz, Elliott, & Roach, 2015). A study by Jimenez, Mims, and Browder (2012) indicated a need for educator training in how to make data-based decisions for students with special needs, but the same research study also indicated that educators can master the data-based decision-making system with relative ease and, I will add, with the right training. Decisions about the use of interventions in the classroom should be immersed in evidence.

AFTER COLLECTING DATA, WHAT SHOULD I DO NEXT?

The answer to the final focus question is one word—analyze! Collecting raw data is nothing but a waste of time without conducting an analysis and then presenting the results in a visual format so that those individuals involved can understand the data and analysis. Many times, as a psychologist, I looked at the data in a student's folder only to be dismayed at the stack of anecdotal information that I was going to have to wade through in order to make sense of the student's issue. There have also been times that I have been given a stack of daily point sheets with no explanation of their meaning. How was I going to determine baseline or postintervention progress? I was not there when the data were collected, so I did not understand the context, specifics of the type of data, parameters of the collection process, or even the exact presenting issue.

In the late 1980s, when I began my career, teachers were saying (just as they are today) that analysis and use of data in the classroom are very difficult and complicated (Grigg, Snell, & Lloyd, 1989). Teachers know they need to do it, but data collection seems so intimidating and cumbersome that teachers may procrastinate on actually using the data they have collected. They can end up with stacks of data on their desks. So, let's break data analysis down to its two parts so that the task seems more manageable.

The first part is the analysis itself. Do you need to determine the rate of a behavior, percentage of correct responses, intensity level of an outburst, or the level of prompting required for independent completion of a task? Determine what you need to know, then analyze the data to answer that question.

The second part of data analysis involves presenting the data in a visual format that can be understood by everyone working with the student. If it takes a BCBA to understand the collected data, then a teacher is not going to be able to explain the findings to a parent at an IEP meeting or use the data meaningfully in the classroom. Educators should visually present the data in order to make a difficult topic easy to understand. That is what this book is about—making the complicated task of data collection simple and providing a means of presenting data to others.

DOES THE DATA COLLECTION PROCESS WORK THE SAME WAY IN RTI AND MTSS?

The data collection process described in this book is absolutely in line with RTI and MTSS. MTSS is a framework of supports that is created to meet the needs of every student. Kansas MTSS (2008) defined it as "a coherent continuum of evidence-based, system-wide practices to support a rapid response to academic and behavioral needs, with frequent data-based monitoring for instructional decision-making to empower each student to achieve to high standards" (p. 1). RTI is also a tiered approach to making sure that all students' needs are met. Batsche et al. (2006) defined RTI as "the practice of providing high quality instruction and interventions matched to student need, monitoring progress frequently to make decisions about changes in instruction or goals, and applying child response data to important educational decisions" (p. 3). Data are key to both RTI and MTSS. Does data collection work the same way in both programs? Yes. You or your school may utilize different data collection materials or comprehensive systems for classroom, school, or districtwide MTSS, RTI, or other tiered interventions, but the same basic principles are in place. Analysis of the data is key in order to monitor the progress of the student and the effectiveness of the interventions.

REVIEW OF THE FACTS AND A PEEK AHEAD

To wrap up, you should do the following when designing a data collection system in the classroom:

- Determine the presenting issue or the specific question to answer.

- Establish preintervention baseline levels by collecting data before an intervention is implemented.

- Create a visual or graphic representation of the summary of the collected data.

- Follow up postintervention using data to make decisions.

I hope this chapter has helped you to understand the importance of data collection and introduced you to the basics of what you need to know about collecting data to answer questions, solve problems, and implement interventions within the classroom. The good news is that the data collection procedures in this book are in line with RTI and MTSS and that the same basic data collection processes can work in a variety of settings. The Quick Quiz at the end of this chapter will test your newfound knowledge and assess what you have learned.

In the next chapter, you will learn more about preparing to collect data to address both behavioral and academic concerns, with an emphasis on how to determine the specific issue or problem that data will help to solve.

QUICK QUIZ

Use this short five-question quiz to review the chapter material, or use it for training purposes. It is a helpful way to check for understanding of the concepts and vocabulary. The answers to the Quick Quiz questions can be found in Appendix B.

1. What is the first step in data collection?
    a. Determining the target behavior or question to be answered
    b. Determining which data sheet to use
    c. Determining where you will collect the data

2. Systematically breaking down a complicated task is called what?
    a. Target analysis
    b. Task analysis
    c. Task examination

3. After analyzing the data, what is the next step?
    a. Graph and file the data for future use.
    b. Show it to the student.
    c. Determine if the intervention is working and what the next step should be.

4. Is it ever appropriate to collect data in a homeschool environment?
    a. Yes
    b. No

5. What does BCBA stand for?
    a. Board Certified Brain Analyst
    b. Board Certified Behavior Analyst
    c. Biologically Certified Brain Analysis

CHAPTER 2

Determining the Specific Issue and Defining the Target Behavior or Focus

---

✳ **MISSION:** To provide in-depth information about how to begin the data collection process, including how to determine the specific issue or behavior in question so that the correct type of data can be collected

QUESTIONS TO INVESTIGATE

- Why do I need to determine the specific issue?
- How do I define a target behavior?
- Is data collection only for behavior problems, or is it for other issues, too?

DEFINITIONS OF TERMS AND ABBREVIATIONS

Baseline data   The initial, quantifiable information gathered about a student's academic and/or behavioral performance. Baseline data are gathered so that comparisons can be made after interventions are implemented.

Generalization   The movement of a specific skill learned in one environment to a more broadly based, naturally occurring environment.

Neutral observer   A person who observes a student but has no preconceived opinions that would slant the observation.

Observation   A time period when the behavior of a student is watched in order to gather information about his or her performance.

Operationally defined   A skill or behavior is stated in terms that can be observed so that everyone involved understands what to look for during an observation.

Progress monitoring   A data-based, objective approach to examining the effectiveness of interventions. It is an ongoing system of measuring student progress.

Replacement behavior   A desired behavior that is more appropriate than the behavior the student is currently exhibiting but serves the same function for the student.

This chapter explains everything you need to know to get started with the data collection process, particularly how to determine the specific issue or target behavior that you will focus on when collecting information. As shown in the Eyewitness Account, without a clearly defined issue, problem, or behavior, data collection is challenging, and teachers ultimately have a more difficult time helping their students.

 Eyewitness Account

As a school psychologist for an elementary school, I had been asked to collect data and recommend interventions for a boy in third grade who was having "terrible behavioral issues all day long." The referral for the observation did not provide a great deal of specific details except to say that the student was "so disruptive that the other students could not concentrate, and the teacher was devoting an inordinate amount of time to the one student." The classroom was fortunate enough to also have a teacher's aide who assisted the student. Prior to observing the student, I spoke with both staff members in addition to the principal in an attempt to get specific information about the behavior, but all three professionals gave different accounts of what was happening. One stated that the child "throws tantrums and is rebellious." Another said that he was "disruptive and defiant." The last staff member just said that the student was "out of control." With only this information to go on, all I knew was that the child has "tantrums and is disruptive, defiant, and out of control." I didn't have a clear picture of exactly what was going on in the classroom. Because it was so difficult to determine the exact issue, I knew it would also be difficult to recommend successful interventions and collect data.

—Lisa Grand,
Elementary School Psychologist

It is difficult to make recommendations of any kind if you do not know the exact issue. It is like trying to pick up a wet fish—something slippery and hard to grip. In this chapter, you will learn how to determine the specific target behavior as well as how to operationally define the issue so that everyone knows how to collect data and the type of data to collect. This process ensures that the data collected are useful in addressing the issue at hand.

WHY DO I NEED TO DETERMINE THE SPECIFIC ISSUE?

Collecting data and making intervention recommendations on a loosely defined behavior or issue is like being asked to find something without knowing what you are looking for. It does not make sense. Consider the difficulties faced by Lisa Grand. Exactly what issue is occurring in the classroom? What is the specific behavior at hand that prompted the need for data collection? Like a detective analyzing words and information conveyed in an interview, Lisa had to try to piece together the words her colleagues used to describe the student's behavior, and she did not have much to go on. Her colleagues had described the student in these terms:

- Disruptive
- Prone to throwing tantrums
- Rebellious
- Defiant
- Out of control
- Exhibiting terrible behavioral issues

Can you tell what the target behavior is from this list? You probably can imagine what it *might* look like, but one specific, overarching behavior is difficult to determine.

In this case, the school psychologist needed to collect data in order to determine an appropriate intervention. She had many questions about which types of data were appropriate to collect to measure the student's challenging behaviors. However, those questions could not be adequately addressed and answered until the behavior was specifically defined.

HOW DO I DEFINE A TARGET BEHAVIOR?

Recall the five basic steps for collecting data in the classroom (see Figure 1.1):

1. Define target.

2. Select method.

3. Implement collection.

4. Analyze and graph.

5. Make decisions.

Defining the target behavior is the initial step in the data collection process, and it is essential in setting you on the right course in collecting information. But how are behaviors accurately and precisely defined and described?

Behavior looks different to everyone. The definition of the behavior, and most especially the determination of the behavior's intensity, can vary greatly among those observing the behavior in question. What does a tantrum look like to you? To me, a person who has been involved with students with severe emotional and behavioral challenges, a tantrum looks much different than it does to a kindergarten teacher in a general education classroom. The behavior also looks much different to a general education teacher of high school students than it does to a preschool teacher. Behavior is subjective unless it is appropriately defined.

In order to effectively define the target behavior, all members of the education team must have a common vocabulary, and the target behavior must be described using specific terms. As discussed in Chapter 1, a target behavior is the specific behavior or skill that you plan to observe and measure, stated in precise terms so that everyone involved in the observation or measurement of the behavior understands exactly what to look for. As an example, "inappropriate behavior" is not a target behavior, but "calling out in class" is. Operationally defining the behavior that you would like to change ensures consistent observations and a collective understanding of the behavior.

Operationally Defining the Target Behavior

In order to operationally define a behavior, you must ensure it is observable and measurable. The behavior must have a beginning and an ending so that it is quantifiable.

Consider this example. Which of these behavioral concerns is operationally defined?

1. Arturo has tantrums several times a day.

2. Arturo's behavior involves hitting himself or others, kicking, throwing objects, biting himself or others, screaming, and making verbal threats of harm.

The behavioral concern that is operationally defined is Option 2. Even though you are not in the classroom observing Arturo, you can still visualize what his behaviors look like. If you walk into the classroom and observe the students, you will be able to recognize these behavioral concerns without having to ask the teacher. Here is another example related to following directions in the classroom. Which behavior is operationally defined?

1. When presented with a written task, Liza will sit and not begin the task. Instead, she will put her head on her desk, refuse to get out needed materials, get up and wander around the room, or talk to others.

2. Liza refuses to do assignments.

In this case, the answer is Option 1. Again, you can recognize the exact issues immediately. They are stated clearly enough for a neutral observer to recognize the concern and are specific enough to allow data collection to occur.

Defining and Determining a Replacement Behavior

Have you ever heard of the Dead Man Test? In 1965, Ogden Lindsley (1991), an American psychologist who is credited with developing precision teaching, said, "If a dead man can do it, it ain't behavior, and if a dead man can't do it, then it is behavior." Put another way, the behavior being observed must be an action by a living person that others can witness and describe. The Dead Man Test can help teachers determine which active behaviors to look for in the classroom when collecting data. Consider the following examples.

Teachers in different situations were asked about behavioral concerns in their classrooms. The teachers indicated they wished for their students to stop doing certain things (e.g., getting up out of their seats, screaming out in class, throwing themselves on the floor, throwing objects in class) and they wanted to design a system for the classroom in order to collect data. When questioned about the behaviors they wanted to see occur instead, they gave the following responses:

*   Ann will not get out of her seat.

*   Bubba will not scream in class.

*   Cindy will not throw herself on the floor.

*   David will not throw objects in class.

How do these behaviors measure up to the Dead Man Test? Because each example focuses on the *absence* of a behavior, the sentences could indeed describe a dead man. Dead men do not get out of their seats, scream, throw themselves on the floor, or throw objects. By focusing on what they wanted students to stop doing, the teachers neglected to describe the actions they hoped to witness. So, these examples are not actual behaviors and most certainly are not good choices for a target behavior on which to collect data. How can you collect data on someone *not* doing something? It is not possible.

It is less helpful to describe behaviors as something negative or something teachers want the student to do less often. Instead, behaviors should be stated as something positive that teachers want the student to do more often. For example, instead of "Bubba will not scream in class," the desired behavior can be "Bubba will raise his hand for permission before speaking out during class." Instead of "Cindy will not throw herself on the floor," the behavior can be "Cindy will use her words to ask for a break when frustrated." These behaviors are measurable and objective, and observers can easily collect data on them. They are considered replacement behaviors, or the behaviors that teachers want to see more often.

Target behaviors are actions you want to alleviate or decrease, and replacement behaviors are actions you want to increase. Both behaviors should be stated in measurable terms and should pass the Dead Man Test. When deciding on an appropriate replacement behavior, the teacher typically observes and collects data on the target behavior to complete an FBA. The goal of the FBA is to determine the function of the behavior for the student and the environmental conditions that make the behavior more likely to

Table 2.1. How the target behavior, function, and replacement behavior are linked

Target behavior (Behavior the teacher wants to decrease)	Function (What the student gets from the behavior)	Replacement behavior (Behavior the teacher wants to increase; it serves the same function as the target behavior)
Calls out in class when has questions during seatwork	Seeks attention from teacher	Raises hand or uses a visual cue to request assistance
Throws desk items on floor when frustrated	Escapes task	Uses a cue card to request a break when frustrated
Refuses to complete work	Escapes task due to academic frustration	Raises hand or uses visual cue to request assistance with task

occur. The function of the behavior will then guide the teacher in selecting an appropriate replacement behavior. See Table 2.1 for examples of replacement behaviors that have the same function as the challenging behavior. Note that in these examples, the teachers have already completed FBAs and have determined the functions of the target behaviors through careful observation and data collection.

Do you see the difference between the replacement behavior and the target behavior? The target behavior has passed the Dead Man Test. No dead men can call out, throw items, or refuse to do anything. The replacement behavior is an appropriate, positive replacement for the challenging target behavior, and it serves the same function or purpose as the inappropriate behavior. Data can easily be collected on either the target behavior or the replacement behavior because both involve observable actions.

Exercise: Define Luis's Target Behavior

To review the material covered so far, consider how to define the target behavior for Luis, the subject of an observation. An observer was called in to help with Luis's disruptive behaviors. The teacher reported that she had difficulty teaching with Luis in the classroom. The teacher did not provide specific details about the behaviors, just that they were disruptive to others. The observer collected baseline data on what she saw in the classroom. Her observation write-up is depicted in Figure 2.1.

Student: Luis

Observation time: 9:30 a.m.–10:15 a.m.

Setting: Fifth-grade general education classroom

Subject: Math

Luis is of average height and weight and looks to be in adequate health. He was sitting in the front row with approximately 20 other students in the class. The teacher and a paraprofessional roamed the classroom assisting students with a math seatwork assignment. The students were provided with an explanation of the task (for approximately 5 minutes). During the explanation, Luis had his head on his desk. Eighteen of the other twenty students in the classroom were on task for the explanation. Luis was given three verbal prompts and one physical prompt (touch) to pick his head up and pay attention. He complied with each prompt for approximately 10 seconds. When the students were asked to complete the worksheet based on the explanation provided by the teacher, 20 out of 20 of the other students initially complied with the task and began the worksheet within 5 seconds of the verbal directive. After initially complying, Luis put his head back down on his desk, saying that he was not doing the assignment. After 3, 4, and 5 minutes, the paraprofessional verbally asked him to pick his head up and begin the task. Luis got up from his desk and went to the pencil sharpener. He then roamed the room for about 3 minutes before stopping and looking at a poster on the wall. Luis then stopped by a student's desk and began talking to him. He was again reminded to begin work. He began to get frustrated and sat back down at the desk, cursing and putting his head down. Luis was reminded again to get to work, and he ripped up the worksheet, threw it on the floor, and got up to leave the room, slamming the door and saying that he was going to the bathroom.

Figure 2.1. Observation write-up for Luis.

Your tasks are as follows:

1. Determine the target behavior.
2. Operationally define the behavior.
3. Determine a replacement behavior.

After reading the write-up, you may have hypothesized about the function of Luis's behaviors and may even have some ideas for interventions, but take the time to tackle the three tasks step by step. First, determine one target behavior to focus on. To do so, brainstorm some possibilities for the target behavior. In this scenario, possible target behaviors include

- Physical aggression
- Noncompliance
- Verbal aggression
- Inattention
- Work incompletion
- Leaving the classroom
- Being out of his area

What would you say is the most significant concern that was consistent through the entire observation period? Yes, the student was aggressive (both physically and verbally), wandered out of his area, was inattentive, did not complete his work, and actually left the classroom, but the overarching behavior was noncompliance, with escape from the frustrating task as the probable function. The other behaviors were part of the description of noncompliance.

During this observation, the observer took some cursory frequency data. Notice the difference in the frequency of noncompliance versus other behaviors:

- Physical aggression: / /
- Noncompliance: ⧺⧺⧺ / / / /
- Verbal aggression: /
- Inattention: difficult to measure
- Work incompletion: /
- Left classroom: /
- Out of his area (within classroom): /

Do you see how important baseline data can be? These data may not be the only type collected, but gathering cursory data during an initial observation can help to determine the target behavior. Sometimes behavioral challenges are so complex that without quantifying the observational information, you will have trouble deciding what to focus on. Table 2.2 lists the target and replacement behaviors determined from the observation.

Table 2.2.   Target and replacement behaviors determined from Luis's observation

Target behavior	Noncompliance
Operational definition of target behavior	The student exhibits noncompliance that is characterized by one or more of the following behaviors: wandering around the room, talking to others, putting his head on his desk, ripping up his assignments, cursing, leaving the classroom, slamming the door, and verbally refusing to do assignments.
Replacement behavior (assuming that the function is to escape the task due to difficulty understanding it)	The student will request assistance when frustrated with assignments by raising his hand or placing a red card on his desk to indicate that he needs assistance.

Student Observation Form

Student: _____   Page 1

Date		Time period	
School			
Class or environment			
Teacher			
Observer			
Referral question or concern			

- -

_____

_____

_____

_____

_____

_____

_____

_____

_____

_____

Figure 2.2.   Student Observation Form.   *(continued)*

Student Observation Form

_____
_____
_____
_____
_____
_____
_____
_____
_____
_____
_____
_____
_____

Possible target behaviors	Initial baseline data
Operational definition of chosen target	

Possible replacement behaviors:_____

Figure 2.2. *(continued)*

The other details are listed in the operational description of the behavior, so this information is certainly not wasted.

The information in Table 2.2 paints a picture that is much more defined and detailed. You can now clearly visualize the scene, understand the potential reason for the behavioral issue, and come up with a possible solution or intervention for the problem behavior.

As this exercise illustrates, initial observations and the collection of baseline data are helpful and often necessary to determine the target behavior, operationally define the behavior, and determine a replacement behavior. The Student Observation Form (see Figure 2.2) can assist you with these processes. You can add this photocopiable form to your data collection notebook to help you conduct student observations; see also the About the Forms and Tools page at the beginning of this book for instructions on downloading a printable copy.

The Student Observation Form has two pages, so you may wish to print it on the front and back of one piece of paper. The form has a place to record possible target behaviors, initial baseline data, the operational definition of the chosen target behavior, possible replacement behaviors, and other basic student information.

IS DATA COLLECTION ONLY FOR BEHAVIOR PROBLEMS, OR IS IT FOR OTHER ISSUES, TOO?

This chapter discusses problem behavior, but data collection and the process of determining the issue at hand can apply to other areas. You can collect data to measure a number of things, including the following:

- Overall progress in a classroom

- On-task behavior

- Work completion

- Individual academic progress in specific subject areas

- Mastery of discrete steps in a task analysis

- Generalization of a learned task to a natural environment

Teachers sometimes wonder whether they are teaching effectively. They can use pre- and postassessments to find out whether their instructional strategies are working and are teaching the skill or objective intended (Stronge, Ward, & Grant, 2011).

Consider an academic objective, such as mastery of the use of timelines. After implementing the timeline activity, the teacher can collect postactivity data. If the data show that the students still do not understand the concept, then this teaching activity was likely not effective, and the teacher may want to modify it for next year.

On-task behavior and work completion are not only considered to be behavioral in nature, but they can also reveal information about the academic environment. Table 2.3 provides a solid operational definition of off-task behavior and a replacement behavior that is easy to observe. Though off-task behavior and incomplete work may not be

Table 2.3. Example of an operational definition and replacement behavior for off-task behavior in the classroom

Target behavior	Off-task behavior
Operational definition of target behavior	Off-task behavior is characterized by inattention to work, wandering around the room, sitting at her desk without doing an activity, talking to peers instead of completing directed tasks, and fumbling with objects in her desk instead of completing directed tasks.
Replacement behavior (assuming that the function is to escape the task due to difficulty understanding it)	The student will complete the task, answer questions when posed of her, make eye contact with others when appropriate, and remain in her area.

significant behavioral issues that affect the classroom, they certainly will have an impact on the student's academic success.

Individual progress on academic subjects, mastery of discrete tasks, and the generalization of mastered tasks to a natural environment are all considered to fall in the academic domain. The measurement of individual progress in academic areas certainly requires the collection of data, but what should the target or focus objective look like?

Consider the following objective: "Becky will use appropriate phonemic awareness skills to sound out unfamiliar words." A data collection tool can be developed to measure whether Becky meets this objective so that the observer can note whether Becky appropriately uses her phonemic awareness skills to sound out unfamiliar words she encounters. Collecting data allows the observer to quantify and measure Becky's progress.

If you are teaching students with autism and using discrete trial training (DTT), then you understand the need for data collection. DTT uses task analysis to break down a skill into smaller chunks or steps. You need to measure the student's progress on each discrete step, You must teach each step to mastery (based on data) before teaching the next step. This procedure continues until the student learns the skill in its entirety.

Finally, measuring the generalization of learned skills certainly requires a data collection process. Consider the following scenario:

Larry is able to recognize and correctly name the color orange if presented with an orange flash card in the classroom and asked, "What color is the card?" The teacher noted on the data collection form that he exhibits mastery of this task at 98% in the classroom using the flash cards, but the teacher noticed that when Larry saw someone wearing a solid orange shirt in the hallway, he was not able to correctly answer, "What color is that shirt?" Has Larry really mastered the skill of recognizing and naming the color orange?

A student has not truly mastered a skill until he or she is able to execute it successfully in several different environments, with different types of materials and with several different people. To measure whether the skill has been truly mastered, you must collect data across a variety of settings in order to determine if the student has generalized the use of the skill into a more naturalized environment.

REVIEW OF THE FACTS AND A PEEK AHEAD

You should now have a solid grasp on the concepts of determining a target behavior, operationally defining the target behavior, and determining an appropriate replacement behavior for the target behavior. These are all important initial steps in the data collection process. You have also learned how data can be used to address academic issues. Section I introduced you to the basic steps of data collection and prepared you to begin collecting classroom data to systematically answer and solve concrete questions and problems. In Section II, you will acquire the tools you need to start collecting a variety of data and to design your personalized data collection system.

QUICK QUIZ

1. Which behavior is operationally defined?
   a. Max is off-task.
   b. Max is inattentive.
   c. Max will wander the room, play with items in his desk, and not complete tasks.

2. What is a desired student behavior that is taught to take the place of a behavior that should be decreased?
   a. Discrete behavior
   b. Target behavior
   c. Replacement behavior

3. Data that are initially collected so that a comparison can be made after interventions have been implemented are called _____.
   a. Proactive data
   b. Baseline data
   c. Discrete data

4. Is it appropriate to collect data during an initial observation?
   a. Yes
   b. No

SECTION **II**

Collecting Your Data

The information in this section will move you closer to the development of a model data collection program in your special education classroom, general education classroom, private school setting, homeschool setting, or therapeutic setting. Now that you are acquainted with the first step for collecting data in the classroom—define target—it's time to learn how to determine the appropriate tools and methods to use in your data collection process. Among the tools introduced in the following chapters are a series of helpful data sheets called Quick-Graphs. As the name implies, these data sheets are fast and efficient to use. The Quick-Graphs make it easy not only to record data but also to graph the data for a visual representation to be used in meetings and shared with parents and colleagues. I am sure you have a myriad of data collection forms in folders in your classroom desk, but what makes these data sheets different is that they allow you to easily create an instant graph and a visual summary of data. Blank photocopiable versions of these data sheets are provided in Section IV: Your Classroom Data Toolkit; see also the About the Forms and Tools page at the beginning of this book for instructions on downloading printable copies of the forms.

The data collection process in any classroom is multifaceted and can seem complicated and intimidating. It is like a multipiece puzzle that teachers must put together in order to measure progress and to facilitate optimal learning. Teachers must collect data to measure student progress in several areas, including the following:

- Speech
- RTI
- Social skills
- Adaptive behavior
- Behavior
- IEPs

Regardless of where you teach, you will need to collect data to measure progress. Whether you need to collect data to measure progress in communication skills, math skills, toileting skills, reading skills, or behavior, the data can generally be categorized into one of three areas: academic data, behavioral data, and IEP data.

Academic data collection can include RTI/MTSS progress monitoring and can be tied to specific teaching techniques, such as DTT. Behavioral data can also be collected as a part of RTI/MTSS progress monitoring, as a way to assess social skills, or as part of FBA requirements. Tracking progress on IEP goals and objectives is a vital part of any data collection system. You may need to collect data on speech-language goals, occupational therapy goals, functional skills, vocational skills, physical therapy goals, and more. Chapters 3–5 give an overview of data collection in each of these three areas. Chapter 6 provides tips for creating a data collection system, discussing the use of technology in data collection, organizing classroom data, and managing your time so that you can fit data collection into your busy schedule. After reading these chapters, you will be better equipped to determine the appropriate method of data collection and to record and graph many kinds of classroom data for a variety of purposes.

CHAPTER 3

Academic Data and Progress Monitoring

 MISSION: To learn to record and graph academic data and how to select appropriate methods for monitoring progress

QUESTIONS TO INVESTIGATE

- What are some ways to collect academic data and monitor progress?

DEFINITIONS OF TERMS AND ABBREVIATIONS

CBA Curriculum-based assessment; the observation and collection of data on a student's academic abilities using everyday curriculum content. Instructional decisions will be made based on the collected data.

DTT Discrete trial training; the procedure of using a task analysis to break down a skill into smaller chunks or steps. Each step is then taught to mastery (based on data) before the next step is taught. This procedure continues until the student learns the skill in its entirety.

Prompt A cue that is used to encourage a response, such as asking, "What do you drink with?" while pointing to a cup (a gestural prompt). Another example would be for the teacher to clap hands (as a modeling prompt) while asking the student to "clap your hands like this."

Rubric A structured set of guidelines to ensure the consistent evaluation of student behavior.

Qualitative data Data that are typically presented as a narrative description of a behavior.

Quantitative data Data that are typically presented as a number or count.

Task analysis A method that breaks a complex task down into consecutive steps and allows for more discrete data collection.

Chapters 3–8 present dozens of forms for collecting data. Blank photocopiable versions of each form, along with step-by-step instructions for completing them, are provided in Section IV: Your Classroom Data Toolkit. See also the About the Forms and Tools page at the beginning of this book for instructions on downloading printable copies of the forms.

Academic data collection is an important part of general education, special education, and the RTI/MTSS process. The following lists describe some of the educator's roles and responsibilities when collecting academic data.

In the general education setting, data collection is used

- To quantify a student's academic levels in order to provide specific information to parents

- To establish an academic baseline for progress monitoring

- To document academic progress in specific areas such as reading and math

- To document academic challenges so that appropriate interventions can be put into place to assist the student

In the special education setting, data collection is used

- To quantify academic performance levels that may be required for an evaluation due to specific learning challenges (which, in turn, may lead to eligibility for special education services)

- To gather academic progress data in order to determine mastery of specific goals or objectives on an IEP

- To assess the appropriateness of an academic intervention being used in the classroom

In the RTI/MTSS process, data collection is used

- To document academic baseline performance levels and progress in specific areas

- To determine appropriate academic interventions for a student in the RTI/MTSS process

- To determine the most appropriate academic materials or teaching techniques designed to meet specific student needs

The Eyewitness Account provides firsthand insight into one common challenge with collecting academic data.

 Eyewitness Account

I am having a hard time this year supporting my third graders, several of whom are struggling academically. A few students do not appear to be making progress on the more global assessments used by the school system, but these assessments are not helping me identify exactly where my students need further instruction and support. I want to implement interventions that will make a difference and create a learning environment where my students can succeed; however, I need more precise data to help me do so. Is there a different way to collect and analyze academic data that is easy to implement but will help me pinpoint exactly where my students need to improve?

—Ms. Henley,
Third-Grade Teacher

Ms. Henley's issue is quite common. Global academic assessment tools, such as the state-wide assessments given by the school system where she works, may not yield data that are discrete enough to be used in making specific decisions regarding instructional interventions. For example, if a student is having a difficult time with multistep math equations, a simple right/wrong assessment tool will not provide specific data about the step that gives the student the most trouble. Yes, a global evaluation tool may tell Ms. Henley that the student only correctly completed 5 out of 10 problems, but how will that clarify how to help the student? What is it about the process that the student is unable to understand? What type of intervention will be the most effective? The data need to be more specific. For example, if the student's work is assessed using an evaluation tool that measures correct/incorrect completion of each discrete step, then Ms. Henley will be able to determine exactly where to intervene. More appropriate data collection tools lead to more appropriate instructional interventions.

WHAT ARE SOME WAYS TO COLLECT ACADEMIC DATA AND MONITOR PROGRESS?

Academic data collection can take several forms and can involve several methods. This chapter specifically looks at academic data collection in the following areas:

- Progress monitoring of academic levels
- Rubrics
- Task analysis
- Yes/no data
- Prompt-level data

Progress Monitoring of Academic Levels

In order for teacher observations to effectively monitor progress, they must be quantified. In many school systems, RTI/MTSS and academic progress monitoring are being assessed, and the data are kept by larger programs that are, many times, countywide and Internet based. Curriculum-based assessment (CBA), or curriculum-based measurement (CBM), is one way that educators determine how students are progressing in academic areas. Gickling, Shane, and Croskery (1989) described CBA as the systematic assessment and collection of data about "the instructional needs of a student based upon the ongoing performance within the existing course content in order to deliver instruction as effectively as possible" (pp. 344–345). *CBA* is a broad term that encompasses basic assessments used to measure progress and develop instructional strategies used in the classroom. This chapter focuses on tools to assist with basic assessments in areas such as reading fluency, reading comprehension, math computation, spelling, and writing.

In basic CBA, a baseline level of academic performance is determined, and probes are consistently and intermittently used to measure progress. However, there may be times when you need to measure and graph a student's basic academic skills using informal observation tools. For example, you may need to monitor progress on knowledge of grade-level sight words; timed single-digit math computation assessments; grade-level spelling words; functional or survival words; number, letter, or color recognition; and so forth. Progress in all of these skills can be tracked and graphed using a simple progress monitoring data sheet, the Academic Progress Monitoring Quick-Graph. A graph is created at the same time the data are entered—combining two tasks into one! The form can be modified to fit the needs of your classroom. See Form 1A in Section IV: Your Classroom Data Toolkit for a blank photocopiable Academic Progress Monitoring Quick-Graph that you can customize (see also the About the Forms and Tools page at the beginning of this book for instructions on downloading a printable copy). You may want to familiarize yourself with Section IV's Form 1A completion steps before looking at the example completed version presented in this chapter.

Figure 3.1 is a completed Academic Progress Monitoring Quick-Graph for a sixth-grade student, Jasmine, in the area of reading comprehension. Jasmine's reading comprehension was assessed through a 10-question pretest, and baseline data collected on Jasmine's performance shows low percentages in test scores (45%–55%). The intervention determined for Jasmine was to teach her to identify keywords in the passage. The dashed vertical line in Figure 3.1 represents implementation of this intervention, and the solid horizontal line represents Jasmine's goal for mastery—a score of 80% on the 10-question test. Following the intervention, the teacher continued to plot and graph Jasmine's test scores. As you can see, Jasmine's scores reached and surpassed the goal line, indicating that the intervention was effective and resulted in measurable progress.

Rubrics

Rubrics are a great way to assess progress and levels of mastery in subject areas that are more subjective. Remember that there are two types of data: qualitative and quantitative

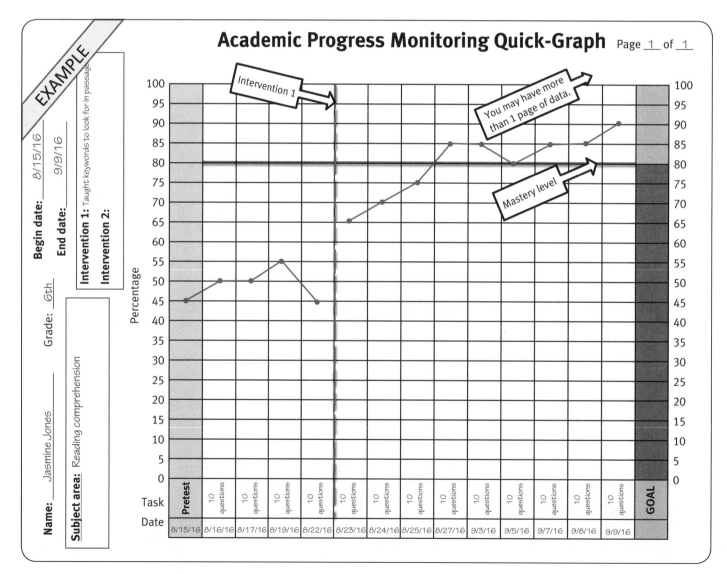

Figure 3.1. Academic Progress Monitoring Quick-Graph (Example).

(Mertler, 2016). Qualitative data are presented as narrative evaluations or descriptions of a product or end result (e.g., a written evaluation of an essay). Qualitative data are not typically presented in a numerical format and are not as easily quantifiable. Quantitative data, on the other hand, are based on a numerical format, are easily quantifiable, and are even easier to graph. A great marriage of these two data types is the rubric.

Consider the use of a rubric for a permanent product—a writing assignment. A permanent product is the concrete item that results from a behavior or from completing a task (e.g., a written essay). Long ago when I was in school, and 3 decades ago when I began teaching, written assignments were graded using the dreaded red pen. Corrections and comments were written all over the paper without thought to how seeing the graded paper covered in red ink would affect the confidence level of the student. Essays were usually qualitatively assessed. At the end of the paper were typically some comments and maybe a numerical grade that was subjectively given by the teacher.

When a writing assignment is graded in this way, the teacher cannot compare the student's first attempt to a later one because there is no clear way to measure progress on the individual elements of writing. How did spelling and grammar progress from one paper to the next? What about the inclusion of the main idea, conclusion, and supporting sentences? The only way to compare any of these areas is to analyze the comments from the teacher, which is time-consuming and difficult. Thus, the only source of comparison for progress monitoring purposes is the final numerical score or grade, which gives limited information.

Enter the rubric. As mentioned previously, a rubric is a great combination of qualitative and quantitative scoring. You can graph the results of a writing rubric so that each element of the writing process can be tracked for progress toward mastery. Figure 3.2 is an example of a Writing Rubric Quick-Graph completed for Ana.

Do you see how this rubric involves both qualitative and quantitative data? Ana received a pretest score of 8 out of 20, or 40%. On the posttest, she improved with a score of 16 out of 20, or 80%. Each area of progress in the writing samples—the introduction, body, conclusion, grammar, and mechanics—can be compared against a predetermined mastery level to see in which areas Ana needs the most improvement. You can attach the Writing Rubric Quick-Graph to the permanent product, and it will not only serve as an analysis of the work sample but also provide data and a visual graph so that you can follow the progress in each of the areas assessed. The Writing Rubric Quick-Graph is easy, effective, and available in Section IV: Your Classroom Data Toolkit (see Form 2A), along with a more generic rubric, the Academic Rubric Quick-Graph, that can be customized for other academic subjects (see Form 3A). See also the About the Forms and Tools page at the beginning of this book for instructions on downloading printable copies of these forms.

Task Analysis

Task analysis is very important when measuring a student's progress on some types of tasks (Rowe & Test, 2013). Both academic skills (e.g., completing multistep math word problems, writing a research paper, using context clues to answer comprehension questions, using the scientific method to complete science experiments) and functional skills (i.e., practical, everyday skills needed for living and learning) typically involve several embedded steps or tasks. In order to show a complete picture of progress, you must task-analyze the main skill and collect data on mastery of each discrete step.

Consider the functional task of cleaning the kitchen and the data sheet used for analyzing John's performance in Figure 3.3. It is difficult to determine the progress John has made on his ability to clean the kitchen area. You can tell that John is not able to clean the kitchen, but what good does that do? Has he made any progress at all? Can he do some things in the kitchen? There is no way to tell. Though this data sheet tells us that John

Writing Rubric Quick-Graph

Page 1 of 1

EXAMPLE

Name: Ana Guitierrez

Pretest date: 9/5/16

Posttest date: 10/15/16

Pretest total points:

Posttest total points:

Topic or directions for assignment: Write one-page essay on topic of choice.

		0 — No response	1 — Minimal	2 — Adequate	3 — Strong	4 — Outstanding
Introduction		Did not submit or unable to score due to amount of errors.	No introduction at all or main idea is not clearly introduced.	Introduction is short, and main idea is vague.	Introduction sets up the main idea with adequate information.	Introduction clearly sets up the main idea and transitions to the supporting details.
	Pre	○	○	●	○	○
	Post	○	○	○	○	●
Body		Did not submit or unable to score due to amount of errors.	There are no supporting detail sentences, and the body is difficult to understand and does not stay on topic. Too short.	Some supporting details but not enough. Little expansion of information and too short.	Good supporting details that follow main idea through the topic with adequate amount of information.	Expansion of main idea is clear and consistent with ample amount of supporting details—easy to understand and follow.
	Pre	○	●	○	○	○
	Post	○	○	●	○	○
Conclusion		Did not submit or unable to score due to amount of errors.	No conclusion paragraph and ends abruptly without proper transition. Little or no connection to main idea or topic.	Conclusion paragraph ends appropriately but too short or only some connection to topic.	Conclusion paragraph transitions adequately and connects back to main idea.	Paragraph clearly transitions to the conclusion. Ends appropriately with ample review of topic/main idea.
	Pre	○	○	●	○	○
	Post	○	○	○	●	○
Grammar		Did not submit or unable to score due to amount of errors.	Several grammar and word usage errors.	Some grammar errors and 3–4 word usage errors.	Few grammar errors; and only 1 or 2 word usage errors.	No grammar errors, and word usage is correct.
	Pre	○	○	○	●	○
	Post	○	○	○	○	●
Mechanics		Did not submit or unable to score due to amount of errors.	Many spelling and punctuation errors; sentence fragments; incorrect use of capitalization.	Some spelling errors; most sentences have correct punctuation and are complete; some capitalization errors.	Few spelling errors; correct punctuation; complete sentences and few capitalization errors.	Correct spelling and punctuation; complete sentences; correct use of capitalization.
	Pre	○	●	○	○	○
	Post	○	○	○	●	○

Figure 3.2. Writing Rubric Quick-Graph (Example).

consistently failed to clean the kitchen, there is no indication of how he performed on individual steps of the task, so you cannot get a sense of his progress.

Figure 3.4 shows a completed Task Analysis Quick-Graph for John. It breaks down the act of cleaning the kitchen into small, individual tasks. This data sheet allows the observer to mark which level of assistance John required to accomplish each task, with Level 0 indicating that he made no attempt to complete the task and Level 4 indicating that he completed the task independently.

Unlike the previous rudimentary data collection sheet (see Figure 3.3), where the observer simply checked off yes or no to whether John cleaned the kitchen each day, the Task Analysis Quick-Graph (see Figure 3.4) shows the specifics of John's performance and exactly where he needs the most assistance. The Quick-Graph shows which areas need to be addressed and gives you an idea of which prompts to use to assist John in completing the task as well as how frequently he should be prompted (e.g., full verbal and physical

Date	Goal	Yes	No
1/16/16	Clean the kitchen.		×
1/20/16	Clean the kitchen.		×
1/25/16	Clean the kitchen.		×
1/27/16	Clean the kitchen.		×

Figure 3.3.   Basic kitchen cleaning data sheet for John.

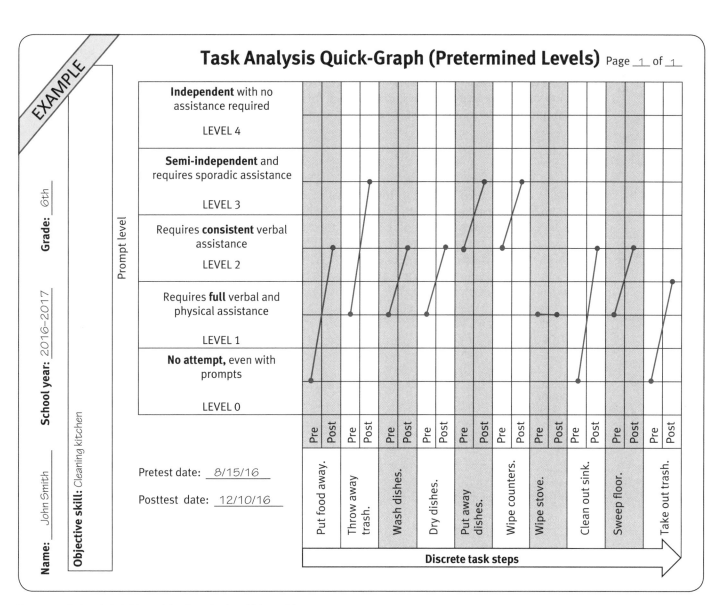

Figure 3.4.   Task Analysis Quick-Graph (Predetermined Levels) (Example).

assistance, consistent verbal assistance, more sporadic assistance). For instance, just by glancing at this form, you can see that John is not making as much progress in wiping the stove as he is in other areas of cleaning the kitchen. Though he is not yet independent in completing any of his kitchen-cleaning tasks, he is making progress in many areas.

The Task Analysis Quick-Graph is not only easy to use, but it also provides an easy-to-view graph that you can take to a meeting as a visual of the data. It is not a typical prompt-level data sheet using visual, verbal, partial physical, full physical, and other types of prompts, but it yields similar types of data that are collected for the same purpose—to encourage and work toward a student's independent performance of a task or skill. Blank photocopiable versions of the Task Analysis Quick-Graph (with and without predetermined prompt levels), along with detailed instructions for use, are provided in Section IV: Your Classroom Data Toolkit (see Forms 4A and 5A). See also the About the Forms and Tools page at the beginning of this book for instructions on downloading printable copies of the forms.

If you have common tasks that many students complete, break the tasks down into steps and then save the steps for reference with multiple students. Use a table in a word-processing document to break down the task, then save the template. You can print and reuse it with multiple students because task analyses are general and can be used over and over. For example, an English teacher may want to analyze the task of writing a research paper and break the larger, more complex task into simple steps. This task analysis could be saved and filed so that it could be used year after year.

Yes/No Data

Sometimes you just want to know if a student has exhibited a skill or not, and straightforward yes/no data can be helpful in these cases. You can collect yes/no data in a variety of settings and for a number of tasks, including social skills and other basic functional skills. Figure 3.5 provides an example of a teacher tracking each student's ability to rote count from 1 to 20 during circle time by simply circling Y or N for each date.

Simple yes/no data collection is a good way to assess whether skills have been generalized to different, more natural environments because it provides a simple method of checking for the presence of the skill in a variety of settings. Collecting this kind of data is also a good way to assess whether the student is independent in completing the skill; yes/no data are typically used for situations that measure independent mastery of the skill without the use of prompts. Consider using this method of data collection for group

Circle time	Dates									
Is able to rote count 1–20?	1/7/16	1/8/16	1/9/16							
Sammy	Y / **(N)**	Y / **(N)**	**(Y)** / N	Y / N	Y / N	Y / N	Y / N	Y / N	Y / N	Y / N
Ahmed	Y / **(N)**	Y / **(N)**	**(Y)** / N	Y / N	Y / N	Y / N	Y / N	Y / N	Y / N	Y / N
Abbey	Y / **(N)**	**(Y)** / N	**(Y)** / N	Y / N	Y / N	Y / N	Y / N	Y / N	Y / N	Y / N
Tanisha	**(Y)** / N	**(Y)** / N	**(Y)** / N	Y / N	Y / N	Y / N	Y / N	Y / N	Y / N	Y / N

Figure 3.5.   Simple yes/no data collection.

instruction in the morning, using a form with all of the students listed. During group or circle time, ask each student the assessment question. Can the students answer correctly or perform the skill? This type of straightforward assessment is similar to collecting cold probe data, which is discussed in detail in Chapter 6.

Using the Yes/No Quick-Graph, you can create a simple graph to display yes/no data. You can quickly note how many yes/no responses your students have given in order to determine which students are able to do the task. Figure 3.6 is a completed example of a Yes/No Quick-Graph that provides a snapshot of yes/no data for one particular student, Jasmine. The teacher collected data on the functional skill of being able to recite and share personal information (e.g., address, birthday, full name, phone number, parents' names) by circling Y or N for whether Jasmine could complete each of these tasks on a daily basis over a period of 10 days. The yes/no responses are shaded in the bar graph area on the

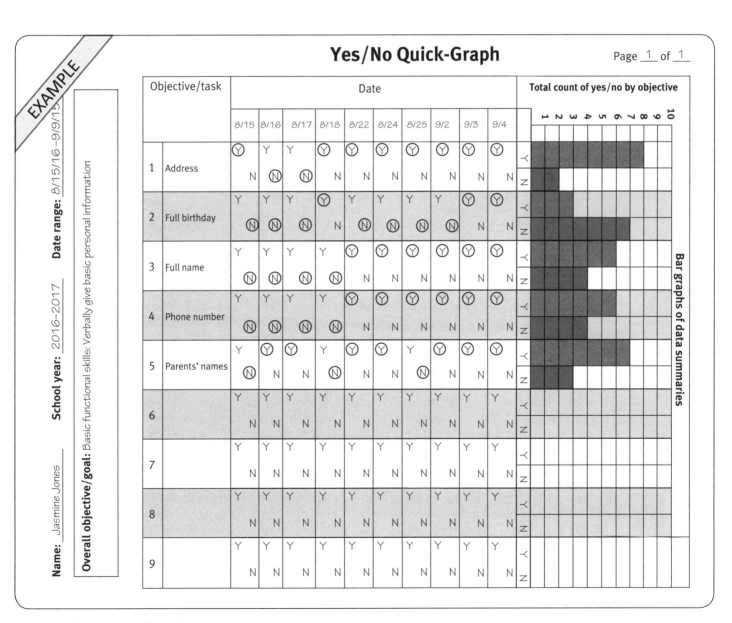

Figure 3.6. Yes/No Quick-Graph (Example).

right side of the form to provide a visual bar graph summarizing the data. A blank photo-copiable Yes/No Quick-Graph (see Form 6A) and full instructions for use are available in Section IV: Your Classroom Data Toolkit. See also the About the Forms and Tools page at the beginning of this book for instructions on downloading a printable copy.

Prompt-Level Data

A prompt is a way of assisting or encouraging a student to give a certain response. Prompt hierarchies set the foundation for teaching in this area. A prompt hierarchy is a list of prompts that moves from either *least invasive to most invasive* or from *most invasive to least invasive*. For example, a more invasive prompt may require the teacher to use a full physical prompt or hand-over-hand assistance with the student in order for him or her to respond. If a student struggles to write his or her name, a full physical prompt would involve the teacher placing hands over the student's hands in order to assist the student with writing the letters of his or her name. A least invasive prompt may be just a gentle verbal reminder of what to do. If a student is struggling with the steps for completing a division problem, the teacher can say a mnemonic to prompt the student's memory of the steps to complete.

Educators typically choose prompts that are indicated by the student's academic data. They also determine whether it is appropriate to use a least-to-most or most-to-least prompting procedure. A least-to-most procedure typically is used when the students have demonstrated the ability to learn skills rather quickly (Smith, Ayres, Mechling, Alexander, Mataras, & Shepley, 2013). This type of prompt procedure may involve the student learning from the errors he or she makes while performing a task, so it may not be appropriate in every situation (e.g., learning to cross the street).

The most-to-least procedure is used when the learning style or level of the student is unclear or when making errors negatively affects the student's ability to learn. A most-to-least prompt procedure is used in the errorless teaching strategy. This is a teaching strategy that sets up the environment so that the student always responds with a correct response, thereby having no opportunity to make errors. Errorless teaching also employs a time-delay prompting procedure, in which the time between the directive and prompt slowly increases. The most-to-least hierarchy of prompts is depicted in Figure 3.7.

When data are collected using prompt levels, the type of prompt is recorded, and the student shows progress by moving up or down the hierarchy. The teacher records data on those prompts that are most effective in encouraging an accurate response by the student. The goal is always to move toward independence.

Section IV: Your Classroom Data Toolkit provides two Prompt Levels Quick-Graphs that can be modified to fit your environment. Form 7A includes predetermined prompt levels; see Form 8A for a blank prompt levels version. (Refer to the About the Forms and Tools page at the beginning of this book for instructions on downloading printable copies of both forms.)

Figure 3.8 for an example of a completed Prompt Levels Quick-Graph for Jasmine. The figure shows the kinds of prompts used to support Jasmine in correctly performing the functional skills of washing and drying hands and combing hair; it graphs how the level of prompting needed for a successful response changed over time. For washing hands, for instance, the daily bar graphs indicate that Jasmine initially either did not respond at all or required a full physical prompt. Over time, she needed less intensive prompts and was eventually able to wash her hands independently.

There are two ways the Prompt Levels Quick Graph can be completed. One is to shade in the boxes to form a bar graph (as was done for washing and drying hands), and the other is to place dots and connect them to form a line graph (as was done for combing hair). Either way works.

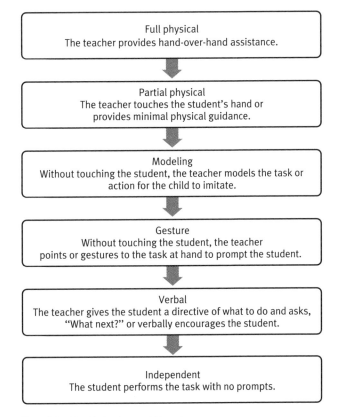

Figure 3.7.   Most-to-least prompt hierarchy.

Prompt-level data can be used for DTT sessions or for any type of teaching that requires the measurement of prompt levels. Remember that DTT is the procedure of using a task analysis to break down a skill into smaller chunks or steps. Each discrete step is then taught to mastery (based on data) before the next step is taught. This procedure continues until the student learns the skill in its entirety.

Figure 3.9 depicts a Discrete Trial Quick-Graph for another student, Olga, on the over-all goal of identifying shapes. The skill of identifying shapes has been broken down into the individual targets of identifying a square, circle, triangle, rectangle, and star. Data col-lected during these discrete trial sessions measure the level of prompting needed for each task. Using this information, the teacher could track when Olga met the specific criteria for mastery. A preassessment was completed prior to beginning data collection in order to determine if Olga had mastery of any shapes. This preassessment provided information about the level of prompt to use at the beginning of instruction.

In Figure 3.9, the criterion for mastery is three consecutive independent responses identifying the correct shape. Each dashed horizontal line indicates the baseline data col-lected on Olga's performance before the discrete trial was conducted. To use this type of form for data collection, begin by placing a dot in the Baseline box by the level of prompt indicated on the preassessment. This teacher used only four prompt levels. You can choose the prompt levels to use in your instruction sessions.

Looking at the baseline information in Figure 3.9, you can see that Olga was bet-ter able to identify the square, needing only a partial physical prompt. The triangle and rectangle had no response from Olga, meaning the teacher had difficulty getting her to respond, even with a full physical hand-over-hand prompt. With a full physical prompt, Olga was compliant and able to identify the circle and the star. This is a great starting

Prompt Levels Quick-Graph
(Predetermined Prompt Levels)

Page _1_ of _1_

EXAMPLE

Prompt level key

	Independent with no prompts
V	Verbal
G	Gesture
FP	Full physical
0	No response, even with Prompting

Name: Jasmine Jones

Date range: 8/15/16–9/9/16

Subject area or overall task: Basic functional skills

Objective	Prompt level	8/15/16	8/16/16	8/17/16	8/18/16	8/19/16	8/24/16	8/25/16	8/26/16	8/27/16	8/30/16	9/3/16	9/4/16	9/5/16	9/8/16	9/9/16
Dates																
Wash hands	I															
	V															
	G															
	FP															
	0															
Dry hands	I															
	V															
	G															
	FP															
	0															
Comb hair	I															
	V															
	G															
	FP															
	0															
	I															
	V															
	G															
	FP															
	0															

Figure 3.8. Prompt Levels Quick-Graph (Predetermined Prompt Levels) (Example).

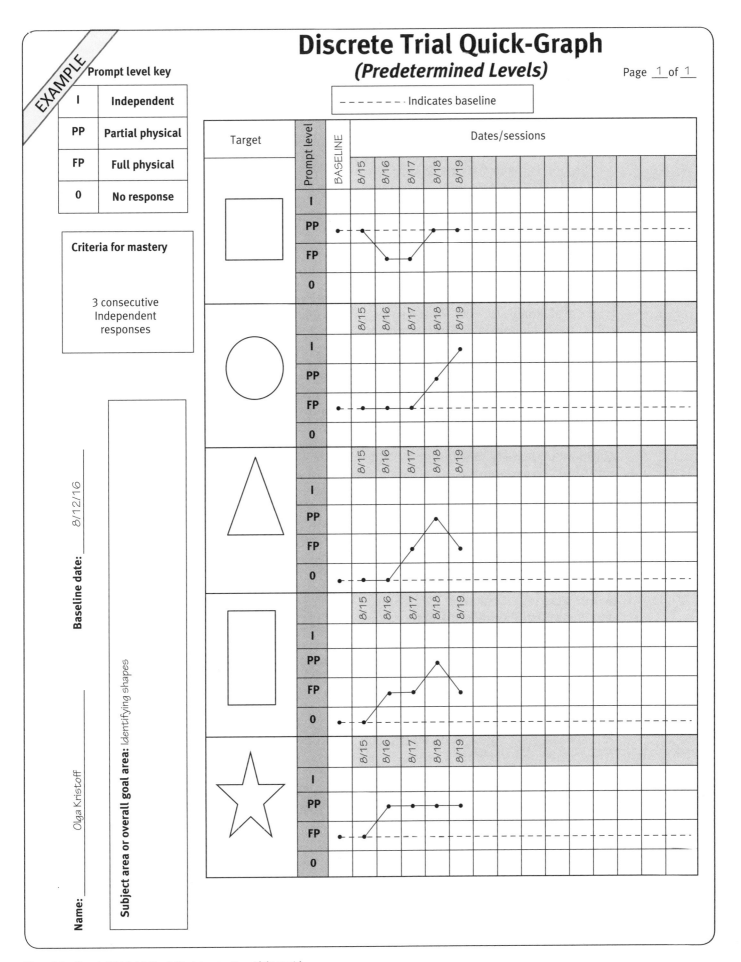

Figure 3.9. Discrete Trial Quick-Graph (Predetermined Levels) (Example).

point! Now, with instruction sessions, the teacher can plot Olga's level of independence in identifying shapes over time and can periodically compare Olga's current performance to the baseline in order to monitor her progress toward mastery of goals.

Section IV: Your Classroom Data Toolkit provides two blank photocopiable Discrete Trial Quick-Graphs for your use. Whereas Form 9A includes predetermined prompt levels, Form 10A is a blank prompt levels version. (Refer to the About the Forms and Tools page at the beginning of this book for instructions on downloading printable copies of both forms.)

REVIEW OF THE FACTS AND A PEEK AHEAD

In this chapter, you learned about a variety of academic data that you may need to collect when evaluating students' progress and performance. There are several methods for collecting academic data. Although many school systems who have adopted RTI/MTSS monitor academic progress through larger, countywide, Internet-based data programs, you may need to measure a student's academic skills through informal observation and data collection. In this case, you can use simple progress monitoring data forms to graph progress and measure the student's responses to interventions and specialized instructional strategies. Other times, you may want to know whether students have successfully generalized skills to a variety of natural settings. In these cases, simple yes/no data, in which you record whether the student is able to accurately perform a skill or answer a question in a variety of settings without prompting, can be effective. For more complicated tasks or assignments, an accurate measure of the student's progress might require breaking the task down into small steps via task analysis to see specifically where the student needs the most support and assistance.

It is also important to measure how independently a student is performing in the classroom, which can be achieved by collecting prompt-level data that reveals the level of assistance or cues provided to the student to elicit a desired response. Some methods of teaching new skills, particularly DTT, rely heavily on prompt-level data. The goal for mastery is typically independent performance of all discrete steps included in the larger skill or task. Your chosen methods for measuring progress in the classroom should depend on the needs of the student and the type of data necessary for answering the presenting issue or question.

In Chapter 4, you will learn more about collecting behavioral data to address challenging behaviors in the classroom setting.

QUICK QUIZ

1. Task analysis is a preliminary step in DTT.
   a. True
   b. False

2. This term describes a structured set of written guidelines that ensures consistent evaluation of a student's performance.
   a. CBA
   b. Rubric
   c. Prompts

3. This type of prompt hierarchy is typically used when errors seem to negatively affect a student's ability to learn.
   a. Most to least
   b. Least to most
   c. Neither a or b

4. This is the simplest form of data collection that allows you to document whether a student can independently perform a task.
   a. Qualitative data
   b. Prompt-level data
   c. Yes/no data

5. This term is another word for a cue that is used to encourage a desired response from a student.
   a. Guideline
   b. Prompt
   c. Hint

CHAPTER 4

Behavioral Data

 MISSION: To learn to record and graph behavioral data and how to determine the type of behavioral data required to address challenging behavior in the classroom

QUESTIONS TO INVESTIGATE

- What are the types of behavioral data, and how do I determine which data to collect?

DEFINITIONS OF TERMS AND ABBREVIATIONS

Duration data   Data that reflect the length or amount of time that a behavior occurs.

Frequency data   Data that provide information about the number of times a behavior occurs during a certain time period.

Intensity data   Data that reflect the degree of severity of a behavior.

Interval recording   Data that reflect whether a behavior occurs within a predetermined interval of time.

Latency data   Data that reflect the amount of time between the antecedent and the occurrence of a behavior (e.g., time between a teacher's direction and the student's compliance with the directive).

Scatterplot data   Data that assist in determining the time of day a behavior occurs.

There are many reasons you can collect data about student behavior:

- To support the writing of a BIP
- To gather data for an FBA
- To quantify a student's behavioral issues for a parent
- To quantify behavioral information to a psychologist for an evaluation
- To determine appropriate behavioral interventions for a student in the RTI/MTSS process
- To gather behavioral progress data for a student's IEP goals or objectives

To address challenging behavior in the classroom, it is especially important to be systematic about the type of data collected. There are many ways to take behavioral data, but different situations call for different methods and kinds of information. The Eyewitness Account discusses this challenge.

 Eyewitness Account

> As a school psychologist, I spend a great deal of time in the classroom working with teachers. This year, I have had to focus on a classroom with several students with behavioral challenges. The teacher is currently finding it very hard to manage her classroom. Though she collects copious amounts of data on the frequency of her students' behaviors, she is struggling to determine which interventions will meet the needs of the students and decrease the challenging behaviors. All she knows is that challenging behavior is occurring many, many times throughout the day.
>
> I stressed to the teacher that she will need to be specific and strategic in the type of behavioral data collected for each student and that she will need to analyze the data she collects regularly. Only this will help us decide on appropriate, individualized interventions.
>
> I will not be able to take the data due to other obligations, so data collection will be up to the classroom staff. How can I support the teacher in determining which type of data to collect and in collecting and analyzing the relevant behavioral data? Is there a way to encourage her so that she feels less overwhelmed?
>
> —*Dr. Lynn Suarez,*
> *School Psychologist*

Behavioral data are vital to the implementation of appropriate interventions, but it is very important to be precise and systematic about the kinds of data taken. You have to have an initial question you want answered about the behavior and then select the type of data needed to answer that question. This chapter introduces you to several types of behavioral data, with guidelines on how to determine which type of data to collect. If you are struggling to support your students with challenging behavior, the easy-to-use forms and tools provided will help you be more strategic in collecting and analyzing data that will actually make a difference.

WHAT ARE THE TYPES OF BEHAVIORAL DATA, AND HOW DO I DETERMINE WHICH DATA TO COLLECT?

This chapter focuses on four main types of behavioral data that can be collected in the classroom: frequency, duration, intensity, and scatterplot. Each of these types of data is useful in a variety of scenarios involving students. In order to decide on the specific type of data you need to collect, you first need to determine the specific issue and target behavior (see Chapter 2). Remember to always work with the end result in mind: What do you hope to learn from the data? See Figure 4.1 for guidance on deciding which kind of behavioral data to collect. (A full-page photocopiable version of Figure 4.1 is available in Appendix A; see also the About the Forms and Tools page at the beginning of this book for instructions on downloading a printable copy.)

In addition to these four main types of behavioral data, other kinds of behavioral data are also touched on at the end of the chapter, including data that help uncover the function of a behavior. The following sections discuss each type of behavioral data in detail, beginning with a classroom scenario that walks you through the thought process of determining the kind of data you need.

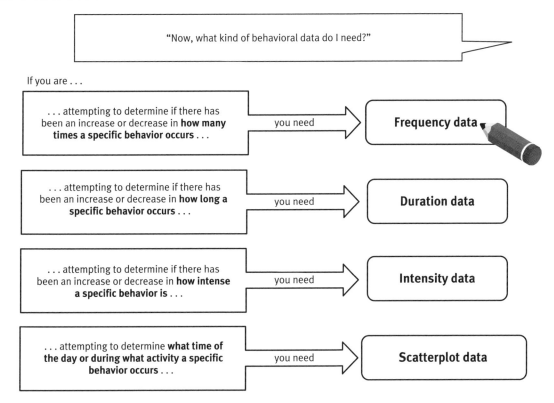

Figure 4.1. Guidance on which kind of behavior data to collect.

Frequency Data

Consider the following scenario:

Sanjay has attention-deficit/hyperactivity disorder. He is bright but interrupts the class by talking out every couple of minutes during the class period. The teacher has begun using a new intervention to influence Sanjay's behavior. After using the intervention for 2 weeks, the teacher cannot determine if there has been any progress. Sanjay's parents are coming in for a conference next week, and the teacher would like to share data on how Sanjay is doing, but the teacher is not sure where to begin in collecting data on this behavior. She realizes that it would have been better if preintervention data had been kept for comparison purposes. She is also unsure whether to determine the amount of off-task time in the classroom or the number of times that Sanjay talks out.

Sanjay is struggling in the classroom, and so is his teacher. In order to assess whether Sanjay's talking out has improved after the intervention, the teacher should have determined a baseline of functioning. Going forward, the teacher will need to quantify Sanjay's behavior so that progress can be measured. Based on Sanjay's behavior, carefully consider the four main types of behavioral data to determine the appropriate data to collect. Do you need

- *Duration data?* Not unless you are a glutton for punishment and want to time each and every instance of talking out. The main problem is not the duration of Sanjay's talking but, rather, how often the talking occurs and how many times the class is interrupted.

- *Intensity data?* You might want to measure the intensity of the behavior when Sanjay's talking seems loud and overbearing, but this data will not be overly useful in revealing whether the intervention has worked and would just describe the nature or degree of the interruption.

- *Scatterplot data?* If you did not know when the behavior occurred, then it may be helpful to take this type of data in order to determine exactly what was going on during the day—but in this situation, you already know that Sanjay talks out every couple of minutes, so this type of data would not be revealing.

- *Frequency data?* Here's your answer! Because Sanjay has a pattern of talking out in class every few minutes, the teacher's goal would be to decrease the number of these interruptions, so it makes sense to take data on the frequency of Sanjay's behavior. You want to find out if there has been an increase or decrease in how many times Sanjay talks in class in order to determine if the intervention put into place has resulted in any improvement.

Recording and Graphing Frequency Data

The classroom scenario with Sanjay is a good example of when frequency data might be important to collect. Once you have determined that collecting data on the frequency of a student's behavior is warranted, consider using one of the three Frequency Quick-Graphs as a means of both recording and providing a graphic summary of your data. Figures 4.2, 4.3, and 4.4a-b provide examples of these data sheets that have been completed for a student named Tyler.

When given a directive, Tyler is noncompliant, which may involve throwing himself on the floor, throwing objects, screaming, hitting others, hitting his head, and biting himself and others. Figures 4.2 and 4.3 are data sheets that provide two ways of tallying the frequency of this behavior in the classroom, and they both provide an easy way to count behaviors. (See Forms 1B and 2B in Section IV: Your Classroom Data Toolkit for blank photocopiable versions; see also the About the Forms and Tools page at the beginning of this book for instructions on downloading printable copies of the forms.)

The only difference between the first two data sheets is the location of the numbers for counting. By putting a slash mark in the box corresponding with each numbered row (see Figure 4.2) or directly on the number (see Figure 4.3), the teacher is able to easily tally the number of times each day that Tyler displays noncompliance with physical aggression. A vertical line can also be drawn on the graph to compare baseline and intervention data, as shown in Figure 4.2. Although these two forms allow you to tally up to 25 behaviors, Frequency Quick-Graph 3 gives you the option of collecting data on higher frequency behaviors, allowing you to tally up to 50 instances of the behavior. (See Form 3B in Section IV: Your Classroom Data Toolkit for a blank photocopiable version; see also the About the Forms and Tools page at the beginning of this book for instructions on downloading a printable copy.)

At times, it may be important to take several types of behavioral data simultaneously to get a complete picture of what is going on with the student. Figure 4.4a-b provides an example of Frequency/Intensity Quick-Graph 1 completed for Tyler; the teacher collected data on both the frequency and the intensity of Tyler's behavior. (See Form 4Ba-b in Section IV: Your Classroom Data Toolkit for a blank photocopiable version of this form. Form 5Ba-b is a similar form that can be used to record frequency and intensity data for high-frequency behaviors. See also the About the Forms and Tools page at the beginning of this book for instructions on downloading printable copies of these forms.)

Frequency/Intensity Quick-Graph 1 provides you with a way of collecting data in two different areas. If a behavior occurs frequently but at different intensity levels, it may be important to gather information about both factors. Instead of using two different data collection forms (frequency and intensity), why not collect and graph both types of data at the same time?

Look at Tyler's Frequency/Intensity Quick-Graph. Not only is each instance of his behavior tallied, but the slash marks are color-coded to indicate intensity. Remember that

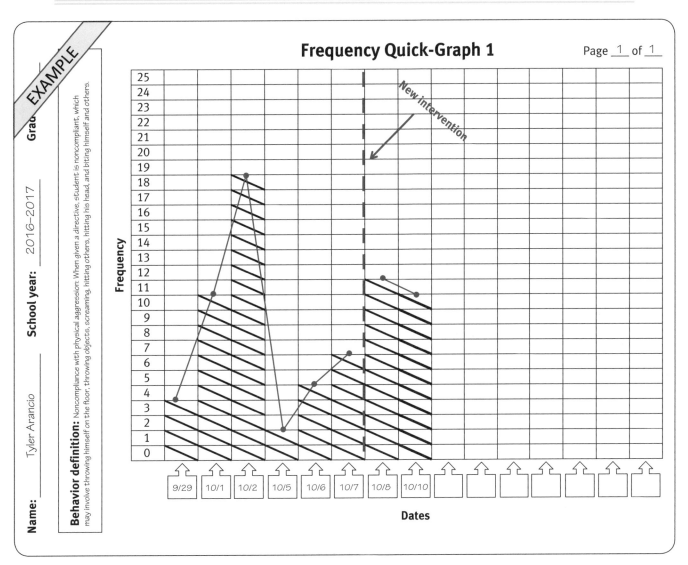

Figure 4.2. Frequency Quick-Graph 1 (Example).

different people see behavior intensity at different levels. A Level 3 behavior for you may be a Level 1 for someone else. A behavior at the beginning of the day, when you are rested and patient, may be coded at Level 1, but by the end of the day, when you are exhausted, might be coded at a Level 3! In order for the data to be valid, the intensity levels must be clearly and behaviorally defined.

Figure 4.4a-b provides a key defining what mild, moderate, and intense behaviors look like for Tyler. This key could be printed on the back of the data sheet or on a separate paper. If you look at the data recorded in Figure 4.4a-b, you will notice that most of Tyler's behaviors occur at a mild level, which is defined as "noncompliance with no physical aggression." When given a directive, Tyler is usually noncompliant by just sitting and refusing to do what was asked. You likely would not have known this information if you only took a frequency count. The Frequency/Intensity Quick-Graph therefore provides a more comprehensive picture of what Tyler's behavior in the classroom entails and tells how many instances of intense, severe behavior are actually occurring.

Frequency Quick-Graph 2

Name: Tyler Arancio

School year: 2016–2017 **Grade:** ____

Behavior definition: Noncompliance with physical aggression: When given a directive, student is noncompliant, which may involve throwing himself on the floor, throwing objects, screaming, hitting others, hitting his head, and biting himself and others.

Frequency

25	25	25	25	25	25	25	25	25	25	25	25	25	25	25
24	24	24	24	24	24	24	24	24	24	24	24	24	24	24
23	23	23	23	23	23	23	23	23	23	23	23	23	23	23
22	22	22	22	22	22	22	22	22	22	22	22	22	22	22
21	21	21	21	21	21	21	21	21	21	21	21	21	21	21
20	20	20	20	20	20	20	20	20	20	20	20	20	20	20
19	19	19	19	19	19	19	19	19	19	19	19	19	19	19
18	18	18	18	18	18	18	18	18	18	18	18	18	18	18
17	17	17	17	17	17	17	17	17	17	17	17	17	17	17
16	16	16	16	16	16	16	16	16	16	16	16	16	16	16
15	15	15	15	15	15	15	15	15	15	15	15	15	15	15
14	14	14	14	14	14	14	14	14	14	14	14	14	14	14
13	13	13	13	13	13	13	13	13	13	13	13	13	13	13
12	12	12	12	12	12	12	12	12	12	12	12	12	12	12
11	11	11	11	11	11	11	11	11	11	11	11	11	11	11
10	10	10	10	10	10	10	10	10	10	10	10	10	10	10
9	9	9	9	9	9	9	9	9	9	9	9	9	9	9
8	8	8	8	8	8	8	8	8	8	8	8	8	8	8
7	7	7	7	7	7	7	7	7	7	7	7	7	7	7
6	6	6	6	6	6	6	6	6	6	6	6	6	6	6
5	5	5	5	5	5	5	5	5	5	5	5	5	5	5
4	4	4	4	4	4	4	4	4	4	4	4	4	4	4
3	3	3	3	3	3	3	3	3	3	3	3	3	3	3
2	2	2	2	2	2	2	2	2	2	2	2	2	2	2
1	1	1	1	1	1	1	1	1	1	1	1	1	1	1

Dates: 10/12, 10/13, 10/14, 10/17, 10/18, 10/19, 10/20

Dates

Figure 4.3. Frequency Quick-Graph 2 (Example).

Calculating Frequency Rates

There will be times when you will need to calculate a rate in order to get more details about your frequency data. First, note that there is a difference between frequency and rate. Frequency is the count or total number of behaviors that occur in a period of time. Rate is a ratio. This is typically described as a certain number of behaviors per minute, hour, or day. The unit of time selected depends on the behavior.

Consider the following example of how sharing the rate of a behavior can be more helpful and informative than simply sharing a frequency count. Imagine that a teacher explains the following to a parent: "Blanca is having some difficulty with calling out in class, and it not only distracts her but also distracts those around her. The frequency data show that she has talked out in class about 223 times in the last week." The parent might be overwhelmed or confused by the number, thinking, "Two hundred twenty-three times—is that bad, and how bad is it?"

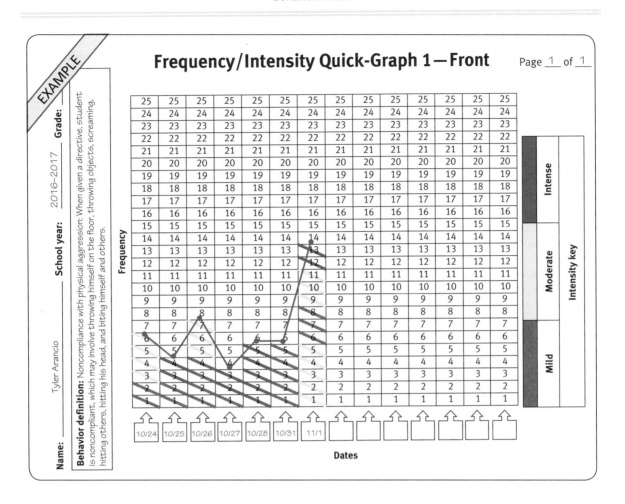

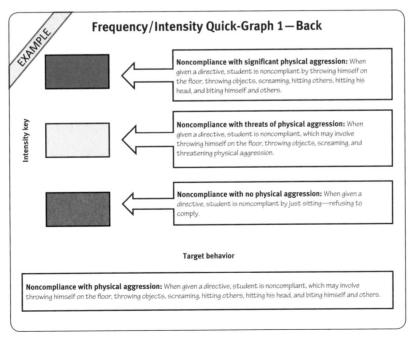

Figure 4.4a–b. Frequency/Intensity Quick-Graph 1 (Front and Back) (Example).

Frequency data are helpful, but with this particular behavior, it may be easier to grasp the issue if the teacher explained it like this: "Blanca is having some difficulty with calling out in class, and it not only distracts her but also distracts those around her. We collected data, and the rate at which she calls out in class is about one time every 2 minutes. Do you see how, at that rate, her behavior is distracting?" In this case, the data are much better explained and are presented in a more practical, user-friendly way.

There is still another reason that you would want to calculate a frequency rate. Consider this example:

Sarah is having a difficult time with her behavior in some of her classes. She calls out in class, which causes a disruption for both herself and her peers. Each of her teachers began to take frequency data, but when they began comparing the numbers, they noticed that the observation period lengths were different. How could they make an accurate comparison if the observations were different lengths of time?

If the periods of time during which you have collected frequency data are different, you cannot make direct comparisons of the frequency data. It is like comparing apples to oranges. This is a situation where calculating a frequency rate can be helpful. Here is the formula for calculating frequency rates:

$$\frac{\text{Number of behaviors}}{\text{Total unit of time (minutes/hours/days)}}$$

For example, if a student calls out in class 27 times in a 55-minute class period and you need a per-minute rate, then record both numbers:

$$\frac{27}{55}$$

Dividing the number of times the student called out by the number of minutes in the class period, you can determine that the student is calling out about 0.5 (or 1/2) times every minute of the class period, or the student is calling out about one time every 2 minutes. Because it is not realistic or pragmatic to describe 1/2 of a behavior, just double the number to get about one time every 2 minutes. This helps translate your calculation into an observable, measurable rate of behavior that makes sense and is simple to explain in a meeting. According to your needs, you can also use hours or even days as the standard unit of measure. For example, the ratio may need to be described as "The student is noncompliant at a rate of 4 times per day" or "15 times per week."

This book includes a Frequency Rate Data Sheet for recording and calculating daily frequency rate, as well as a companion form, the Frequency Rate Graph, for graphing frequency rate over time. (See Form 6B for the data sheet and Form 7B for the graph in Section IV: Your Classroom Data Toolkit for blank photocopiable versions; see also the About the Forms and Tools page at the beginning of this book for instructions on downloading printable copies of the forms). Figure 4.5 is an example of a completed Frequency Rate Data Sheet, and Figure 4.6 is an example of a completed Frequency Rate Graph. Section IV provides instructions for using the Frequency Rate Data Sheet.

Consider how these tools could be used to collect data for Morgan, another student who calls out in class. Looking at the example in Figure 4.5, you will see that frequency data were collected for Morgan during seven different observation periods, but note that the length of time was different for each observation. For an observer looking just at the total frequency counts for each period, it would seem that the frequency between 11:00

Frequency Rate Data Sheet   Page <u>1</u> of <u>5</u>

EXAMPLE

Name: Morgan Custodio   **School year:** 2016–2017   **Grade:**

Behavior definition: Talking out in class

Times intervals

	Frequency (F) data	TOTAL by time interval	TOTAL F count / TOTAL minutes	Rate per minute
2:00–3:00	llllllllllllll	16	16 / 60	.27
1:15–2:00	lllll	5	5 / 45	.11
12:30–1:15	llllllll	8	8 / 45	.17
11:00–12:30	lllllllllllllll	17	17 / 90	.19
10:00–11:00	lllll	5	5 / 60	.08
9:15–10:00	lllll	5	5 / 45	.11
8:00–9:15	llllllllll	11	11 / 75	.15

Date: 10-3-16

Number of behaviors / Total minutes = Rate of behavior per interval of time

Figure 4.5. Frequency Rate Data Sheet (Example).

and 12:30 was the highest, with a raw score of 17, but keep in mind that this was also the longest observation time—a 90-minute interval. It would be inaccurate to say that this time period is when the behavior is most significant without making a more precise comparison of the data for different periods. The frequency rate actually shows that the behavior was more significant between 2:00 and 3:00, which had the highest rate of talking out in class. Rate data can be very important in helping you to make accurate comparisons among your frequency data, particularly when data are collected during different lengths of time.

As a companion to the Frequency Rate Data Sheet, consider using the Frequency Rate Graph to provide a visual of frequency rate over time. Be sure to determine the scale you want to graph. In Figure 4.6, rate per minute is used, with the rate divided out by 0.02. This works well because the teacher can place a dot in the middle of the lines to indicate an odd number rate. Looking at Figure 4.6, you can see that the data are quite scattered for rate per minute of Morgan's calling out in class; the rate varies, but there are spikes of increase over time. See Section IV: Your Classroom Data Toolkit for full instructions on how to fill out the Frequency Rate Graph.

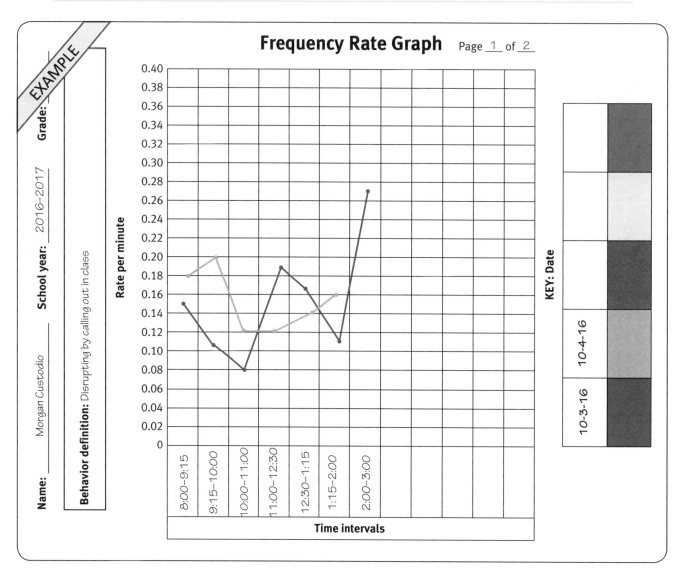

Figure 4.6. Frequency Rate Graph (Example).

Duration Data

Consider the process for determining which type of behavioral data to collect in the next classroom scenario:

Sayuri is a child with intellectual disability. She has significant behaviors that are affecting her ability to progress in school. Sayuri is flopping onto the floor and refusing to get up. She is a larger child and is difficult to handle when she flops in the hallway and refuses to comply with directions. The teacher has begun to implement a new intervention, but she does not feel that it is working. The other staff members, however, believe that it is making a difference. The only data that are currently being collected are frequency data, which show no change in the number of episodes.

The teacher began observing Sayuri's behavior more closely, and she believes that her episodes are taking less time. If the student is spending less time engaged in the behavior, this could certainly indicate progress! The teacher is considering taking data in a different way to determine if this is correct.

Sayuri certainly has significant behaviors that are affecting her ability to function and progress in the classroom. Data have to be collected, so follow the same questioning process as in the first scenario. Do you need

- *Frequency data?* This type of data is already being collected but is not as helpful as originally thought. Frequency data are not indicating progress. You can certainly count the number of times that Sayuri flops on the floor, but it seems that the same number of behaviors are occurring. So, this type of data may not answer your question as to whether the intervention is helping or provide you with a thorough view of what is happening.

- *Intensity data?* Again, this type of data may be helpful and appropriate but not as the primary type of data because it does not tell the entire story, only how intense the behavior is. Even though her behavior is still intense, Sayuri may be making progress.

- *Scatterplot data?* Maybe. This may be the first type of data that you would have collected. It would certainly help to determine when and where Sayuri flops to the floor, but this is still not solving the main issue. The focus question is "Is the intervention that has been implemented making a difference?"

- *Duration data?* Yes! In this scenario, this type of data should be your primary focus. Observations have shown that the intervention being used with Sayuri may be lessening the total time that she remains flopped on the floor. It does not matter if she is still flopping down 10 times a day. If the total amount of off-task time was 60 minutes and this time has decreased to 35 minutes with the intervention in place, then Sayuri has made progress. Collecting duration data is the way to go if you are attempting to determine whether there has been an increase or decrease in how long a specific behavior occurs.

Recording and Graphing Duration Data

This section introduces several types of duration data forms, including one that measures a combination of duration and intensity. Figure 4.7 shows Duration Data Quick-Graph 1 completed for Tyler, the student mentioned previously, whose behavior included noncompliance with physical aggression. (See Form 8B in Section IV: Your Classroom Data Toolkit for a blank photocopiable version of this form. Form 9B, Duration Data Quick-Graph 2, is a similar form that allows you to customize the sequence of minutes when measuring and graphing duration; see also the About the Forms and Tools page at the beginning of this book for instructions on downloading printable copies of the forms.) This time, you are calculating the length of time that his behavior occurred. This Quick-Graph not only allows you to measure the beginning to ending time of the behavioral event, but it also provides a way for automatic graphing of the data.

Notice that on 10/7/16 an intervention was implemented for Tyler, as indicated by the dotted horizontal line drawn on the graph between 10/6/16 and 10/7/16. For comparison purposes, baseline data points are not connected to the data points plotted after the intervention took place.

Figure 4.8a-b is an example of the Duration/Intensity Quick-Graph completed for Tyler. (See Form 10Ba-b in Section IV: Your Classroom Data Toolkit for a blank photocopiable version of this form; see also the About the Forms and Tools page at the beginning of this book for instructions on downloading a printable copy.) This data sheet allows you to collect both duration and intensity data simultaneously on the same form.

Notice that this data sheet has two sides and could be printed on the front and back of one page or on separate pages. It is important to include the second page so that everyone

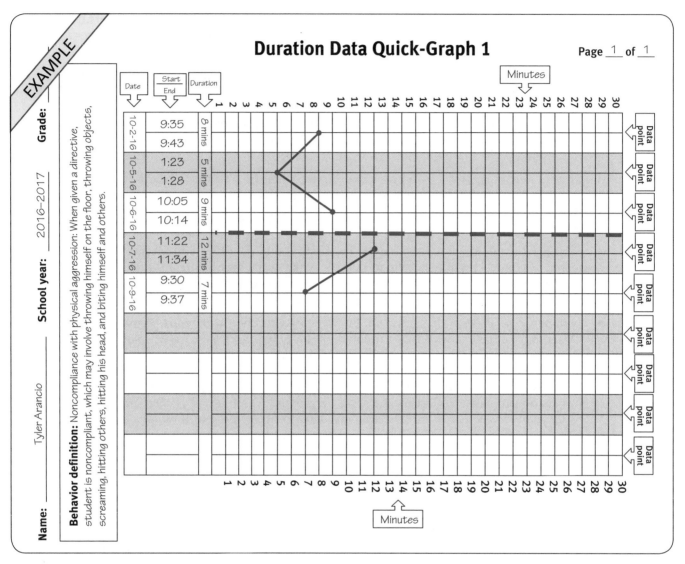

Figure 4.7.   Duration Data Quick-Graph 1 (Example). (Key: *mins*, minutes.)

has the Intensity Key. Remember that if the intensity levels of the behaviors are not specifically defined, then the validity of the data is questionable.

Placing dots and drawing lines to connect the data points can easily create a graph of the duration of the behavior, with the shaded, color-coded boxes indicating intensity level. (For the purposes of showing a line graph, suppose that no intervention had been implemented; as you know, when an intervention is implemented, preintervention data points should not be connected to postintervention data points.)

Calculating Duration Percentages

When dealing with duration data, there will be times when you will need to calculate a percentage of the day when a particular behavior occurs. To make it easy for you to do so, this section includes additional forms that are helpful in calculating duration percentages. The formula for calculating a duration percentage is

$$\frac{\text{Length of behavior}}{\text{Total time}} \times 100 = \%$$

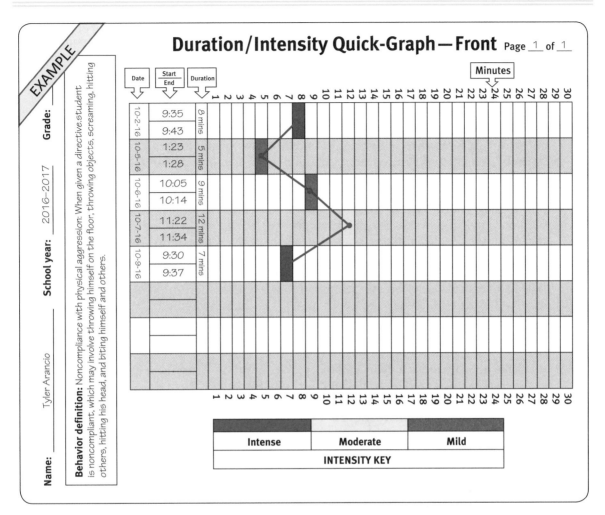

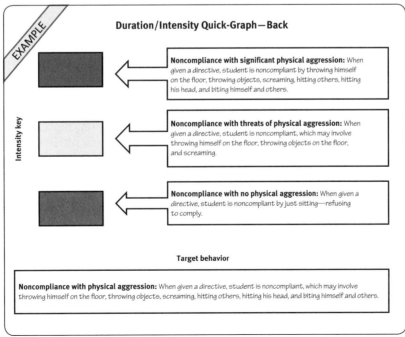

Figure 4.8a–b. Duration/Intensity Quick-Graph (Front and Back) (Example).

Consider this example. If a student has tantrums four times a day for a total of 54 minutes and the day is 7 hours long (or 420 minutes in length), then the formula will look like this:

$$\frac{54}{420} \times 100 = 12.8\% \quad \text{or} \quad 0.128 \times 100 = 12.8\%$$

According to this calculation, the student has tantrums approximately 13% of the entire day. It is easier to understand the data this way and also much easier to explain to a parent or team member. Without calculating the duration percentage, the teacher might simply say, "George has really struggled today with his tantrum behaviors. He has been involved in tantrum behaviors for about 54 minutes." (Note that the term *tantrum behaviors* has been specifically defined but simplified down to this term for ease of communicating with parents.) In this case, the parent might try to calculate in his or her head, "Now, how many minutes are in a full day, and is George's behavior taking up an unreasonable length of time?"

Using the duration percentage, the teacher could have explained the behavior like this instead: "George has really struggled today with his tantrum behaviors. He has been involved in tantrum behaviors for about 13% of the whole day." This puts the data into perspective a little more. This type of duration data may not be needed for every type of behavior, but you now have the knowledge and the tools to collect and analyze duration percentages, if and when you need them.

This book includes a blank photocopiable Duration Percentage Data Sheet (Form 11B in Section IV: Your Classroom Data Toolkit) for recording data and determining the duration percentage, as well as a Duration Percentage Data Graph (Form 12B), which creates a graph for summarizing the duration percentages. (See also the About the Forms and Tools page at the beginning of this book for instructions on downloading printable copies.) Section IV provides instructions for completing the Duration Percentage Data Sheet.

Figure 4.9 shows a Duration Percentage Data Sheet completed for Zofia, another student displaying aggressive behaviors in the classroom. The total time interval or observation period for each day was from 8:00 a.m. to 3:00 p.m., or 420 minutes long. The observer recorded the duration of each instance of physical aggression and, at the end of the day, added up the total minutes the student engaged in the behavior. The observer divided this number by 420 to yield a duration percentage. You will see that Zofia was involved in aggressive behavior for the highest percentage of the day on 10/4, with duration percentage calculated at 10%. This brings a little more detail to the analysis of duration data, so the teacher might describe the behavior as occurring 10% of the entire day.

Figure 4.10 is an example of a Duration Percentage Data Graph, a companion to the Duration Percentage Data Sheet. This graph provides a visual representation of duration percentages over time. This visual is created by forming a simple line graph that connects data points indicating the duration percentage calculated for each day. Full instructions for completing this graph are provided in Section IV: Your Classroom Data Toolkit.

Intensity Data

Consider the next classroom scenario and how the education team decided which data to collect:

Amanda is a child with an emotional and behavioral disorder who demonstrates explosive behaviors that are difficult to predict. Amanda's IEP meeting is next month, and the team feels that she is making progress with the implementation of the new intervention, but the data

Duration Percentage Data Sheet

EXAMPLE

Name: _Zofia Kozlowski_   **School year:** _2016–2017_   **Grade:**

Behavior definition: Noncompliance with physical aggression: When given a directive, student is noncompliant, which may involve throwing objects, yelling, and punching or kicking others.

Date and total time		10/3		10/4		10/5					
		8:00–3:00		8:00–3:00		8:00–3:00					
Start	9:00		6 mins	8:30	12 mins	9:15	4 mins				
End	9:06			8:42		9:19					
	11:30	11 mins		10:30	12 mins	11:25	6 mins				
	11:41			10:42		11:31					
	2:00	5 mins		12:00	10 mins	1:12	8 mins				
	2:05			12:10		1:20					
				1:30	8 mins						
				1:38							

Total duration / Total time

$\frac{22}{420} \times 100$	$\frac{42}{420} \times 100$	$\frac{18}{420} \times 100$	$\times 100$	$\times 100$
5%	10%	4%		

↑ Percentage

Figure 4.9. Duration Percentage Data Sheet (Example). (Key: *mins*, minutes.)

show that she continues to have the same number of explosive outbursts. The staff took not only frequency data but also duration data, and both sets of data show no change. A few weeks before the IEP meeting, someone suggested that the intensity of the behaviors appears to be lessening.

Is it possible for two different types of data to show no change, even though progress was made? As Amanda's story indicates, absolutely! That is the reason why the data collection process should be fluid. Changes to the data collection process may be needed as you analyze the data. (For a more thorough discussion of data analysis, see Chapter 7.) Look at the team's thought process in determining which type of data needed to be collected. Does the team need

- *Duration data?* The team determined that this type of data was appropriate. However, duration data alone was not revealing any changes in Amanda's behavior, even though the team felt that progress had been made. Upon analysis of the duration data, the team determined that they needed to collect more information.

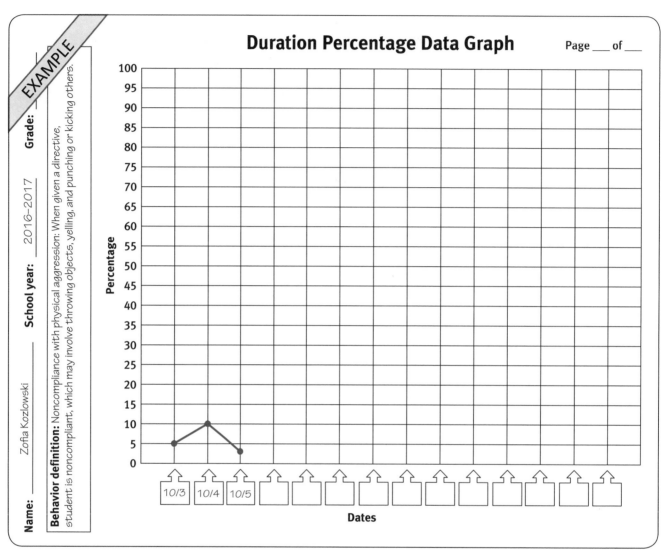

Figure 4.10. Duration Percentage Data Graph (Example).

- *Scatterplot data?* The staff is already collecting two types of data (duration and frequency) and did not feel that scatterplot data were appropriate to use in this situation and at this time. Remember that scatterplot data help reveal the time of day a behavior occurs or during which activities it occurs. The team did not collect this type of data because it would likely not answer the target question: Is the intervention working for Amanda?

- *Frequency data?* Though the team is already collecting frequency data, the data appear stagnant. The behavior is continuing to occur at the same rate, even though it appears as if progress is being made. This type of data was helpful, revealing, and appropriate to collect, but the data collection process needs to be modified so that the team can collect further evidence demonstrating progress.

- *Intensity data?* Both frequency and duration data have been collected. The behavior appears to be at a standstill in terms of the data but seems to be getting better in real life. The team hypothesized that Amanda's behavior was becoming less intense, so they decided that collecting intensity data was the way to go.

The team defined each level of intensity and rated each episode that occurred. The team was correct; the intensity had decreased. The data revealed that Amanda's behavior is getting less intense but is occurring at the same rate and for the same amount of time. There is progress, so the intervention is working. Next, Amanda's team plans to work on reducing the duration (i.e., decreasing the amount to time she is involved in the behavior) and frequency (i.e., decreasing the number of behavioral episodes).

Recording and Graphing Intensity Data

So far, this chapter has introduced you to several combination data sheets that are meant to collect data on the behavior's intensity alongside other types of behavioral data (e.g., frequency and duration). In this section, you will find an example of a Quick-Graph dedicated to measuring and graphing intensity. Figure 4.11 is an Intensity Quick-Graph showing behavioral data for Tyler, the student described earlier in this chapter who has been displaying noncompliance and aggression. (See Form 13Ba-b in Section IV: Your Classroom Data Toolkit for a blank photocopiable version; see also the About the Forms and Tools page at the beginning of this book for instructions on downloading a printable copy.) The Intensity Quick-Graph is a one-page form that allows you to track the intensity of more than 25 behavioral events on one sheet. The bottom axis has a place to put the date or time. (The intensity of behavioral events can be tracked across several days, or multiple events can be tracked over the course of 1 day.) The intensity levels of the behaviors are defined on the left axis, and the data points are connected by lines, which will form a graph of the final data. The shading on the graph serves as visual support for increasing intensity levels, with darker shading indicating greater intensity.

Calculating Intensity Level Percentages

In some instances, you will need to calculate an intensity level percentage. The formula is

$$\frac{\text{Number of behaviors at a certain level}}{\text{Total number of behaviors}} \times 100 = \%$$

Consider Amanda's example. If Amanda has a total of 16 behaviors in a week and 6 of those behaviors are at an intensity level of 4 (highest level), then the formula should look like this:

$$\frac{6}{16} \times 100 = \% \quad \text{or} \quad 3.75 \times 100 = 37.5\%$$

So, based on this calculation, 37.5% of Amanda's behaviors were at the severest, or highest, intensity level.

After implementing an intervention, the teacher was able to report the following to Amanda's parents: "Mr. and Mrs. Knight, as you know, we have been collecting data on the intensity level of Amanda's behaviors. We know that you are concerned, as are we, and we have put some interventions in place. Even though Amanda continues to have a great deal of behavior struggles, we see progress. It looks as if she is having the same number of behavioral outbursts, but we feel that the intensity level is decreasing. In order to show that, we calculated the percentage of time that Amanda spent exhibiting the most severe level of behavior. It appears that last week, 37.5% of the behavioral outbursts that she had were at the most intense level. But look at this week—of the behaviors she exhibited, only 18% of them were at the highest level of intensity! That is progress!"

Progress is not always evident at first glance—as in Amanda's case, where she was displaying the same number of behaviors. Intensity level percentages are one way to show

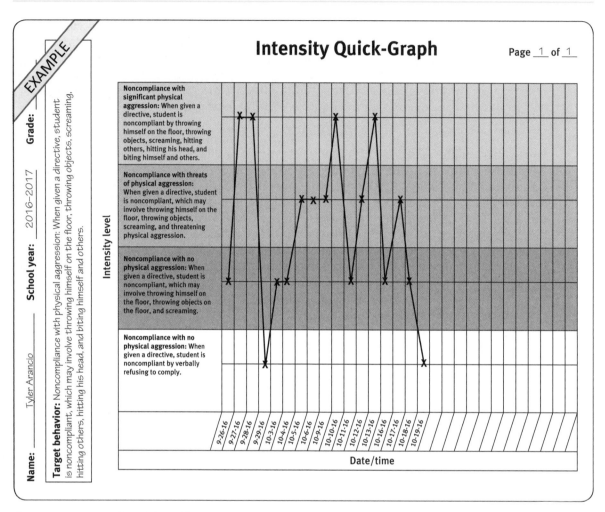

Figure 4.11.   Intensity Quick-Graph (Example).

more subtle progress. The Intensity Level Percentage Data Sheet and the Intensity Level Percentage Graph are useful tools to help you calculate, track, and graph intensity level percentages. (See Forms 14Ba-b and 15Ba-b in Section IV: Your Classroom Data Toolkit for blank photocopiable versions; see also the About the Forms and Tools page at the beginning of this book for instructions on downloading printable copies of the forms.) The Intensity Level Percentage Data Sheet is used to calculate the percentage of intensity for a behavior, and the Intensity Level Percentage Graph allows you to graph these calculations. Section IV provides steps for completing the Intensity Level Percentage Data Sheet and the Level Percentage Graph.

Figure 4.12a-b provides an example of a completed Intensity Level Percentage Data Sheet. Once the intensity level percentages have been calculated and recorded on the Intensity Level Percentage Data Sheet, they can be plotted on the Intensity Level Percentage Graph (see Figure 4.13a-b). Note that in Figure 4.13a-b, the percentages for each intensity level of a student's behavior are plotted over time, and the data points are connected to create a line graph. Each line graph is color-coded to indicate the four intensity levels.

In this example, notice how the blue line (indicating the lowest intensity level) rises and then spikes, showing that the intensity of the behavior is decreasing, with a higher percentage of behaviors at the least intense level (i.e., noncompliance with no physical aggression). Meanwhile, the red, yellow, and green lines show a significant dip in the percentages of higher intensity behaviors. Something might be having a positive effect—perhaps the interventions or something else that is going on in the classroom, at home, or with the student. The teacher should investigate!

Scatterplot Data

Consider the final classroom scenario on collecting behavioral data:

Jay is a student with learning and behavioral needs. He struggles to follow directions and maintain attention. Over the last few weeks, his behavior has been regressing. His daily point sheets show that he is struggling with getting to class on time and complying with teacher directives. Jay's point sheets are the only data being kept, and it is difficult to determine the reason for his recent behavior. Mr. Melfy, Jay's teacher, wants to start gathering data to determine when and why the behavior is occurring.

So far, the team knows that Jay is struggling to comply with directions. He is a student who is not exhibiting significant behaviors, but the behavior—particularly his lateness for class—is affecting his grades. Consider each type of behavioral data, and think through which type the team should collect. Does the team need

- *Duration data?* Other than measuring how late Jay is to class, duration data would not be applicable. This information would not be helpful in revealing the reason for the behavior or in supporting Jay to be on time.

- *Frequency data?* Possibly knowing how many times Jay is late would help in some way, but will these data push the team forward in the development of an intervention? Will the data help the team to determine the reason behind the behavior? Probably not.

- *Intensity data?* It would be hard to measure how "intense" Jay's lateness is. Collecting this type of data does not make sense for the behavior in question.

- *Scatterplot data?* Absolutely! This type of data will assist in answering the question, "Why is the behavior occurring, and what can be done about it?" There will be a wealth of information gained by determining when the behavior occurs.

In Jay's case, Mr. Melfy decided to start gathering scatterplot data to determine the time period during which Jay's behaviors were occurring. The data showed that the behaviors were not occurring all day but only after the class break, when he had to use his locker. Through investigation, the team determined that Jay did not know his locker combination and had to wait for someone to help him. By the time he arrived to class, he was not only late but angry, frustrated, and quick tempered. He was also too embarrassed to ask for help. Case solved! The team was able to privately help Jay learn his locker combination and thereby alleviate the behavior. This simple solution made a big difference in Jay's day.

Recording and Graphing Scatterplot Data

The scatterplot is the easiest data form to analyze and probably the most important initial data that you will gather. Figure 4.14 provides an example of a Time Interval Scatterplot Quick-Graph filled out for Tyler. (See Form 16B in Section IV: Your Classroom Data Toolkit for a blank photocopiable version; see also the About the Forms and Tools page at the beginning of this book for instructions on downloading a printable copy.) The bottom axis includes dates, and the left axis displays increments of time during the school day. Xs were placed in the squares next to the times when Tyler's aggression occurred each day. No graphing is needed for this form because analyzing the data simply involves determining the time period in which the most behaviors occur. As shown in Figure 4.14, Tyler's behavior episodes tend to occur most between 11:00 and 11:20 a.m.

Intensity Level Percentage Data Sheet—Front

Page ___ of ___

EXAMPLE

Name: _____ Isobel Diaz

School year: 2016–2017

Grade: _____

Target definition: Noncompliance with physical aggression: When given a directive, student is noncompliant, which may involve throwing herself on the floor, throwing objects, screaming, hitting others, hitting her head, and biting herself and others.

Intensity levels →

DATE	10/3/16				10/4/16				10/6/16				10/7/16				10/7/16			
	1	2	3	4	1	2	3	4	1	2	3	4	1	2	3	4	1	2	3	4
Behavior incidents	✓	✓		✓		✓	✓	✓	✓	✓	✓		✓	✓	✓	✓	✓			
	✓	✓				✓	✓		✓				✓	✓			✓			
		✓							✓					✓			✓			
Total	2	3	0	1	0	2	2	1	3	1	1	0	2	3	1	1	3	0	0	0
/ Sum of behaviors	6				5				5				7				3			
×100 = %	33	50	0	16	0	40	40	20 / 60	20	20	0 / 28		42	14	14		0	0	0	

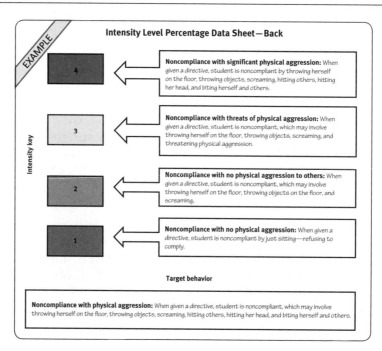

Intensity Level Percentage Data Sheet—Back

EXAMPLE

Intensity key

4 — **Noncompliance with significant physical aggression:** When given a directive, student is noncompliant by throwing herself on the floor, throwing objects, screaming, hitting others, hitting her head, and biting herself and others.

3 — **Noncompliance with threats of physical aggression:** When given a directive, student is noncompliant, which may involve throwing herself on the floor, throwing objects, screaming, and threatening physical aggression.

2 — **Noncompliance with no physical aggression to others:** When given a directive, student is noncompliant, which may involve throwing herself on the floor, throwing objects on the floor, and screaming.

1 — **Noncompliance with no physical aggression:** When given a directive, student is noncompliant by just sitting—refusing to comply.

Target behavior

Noncompliance with physical aggression: When given a directive, student is noncompliant, which may involve throwing herself on the floor, throwing objects, screaming, hitting others, hitting her head, and biting herself and others.

Figure 4.12a–b. Intensity Level Percentage Data Sheet (Front and Back) (Example).

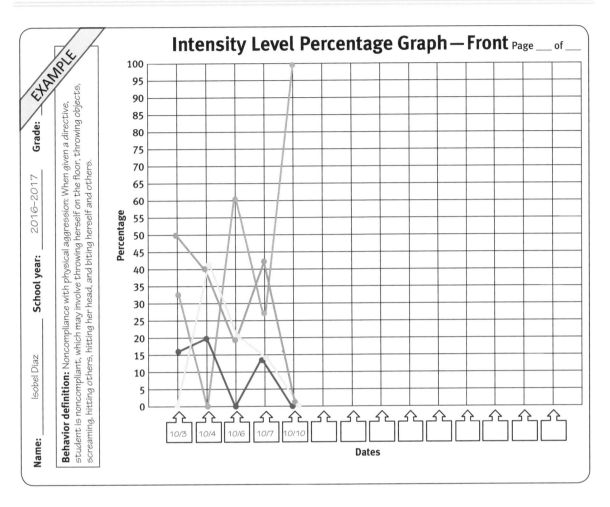

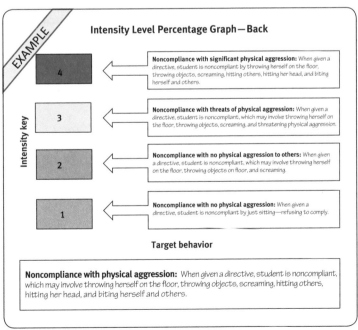

Figure 4.13a–b. Intensity Level Percentage Graph (Front and Back) (Example).

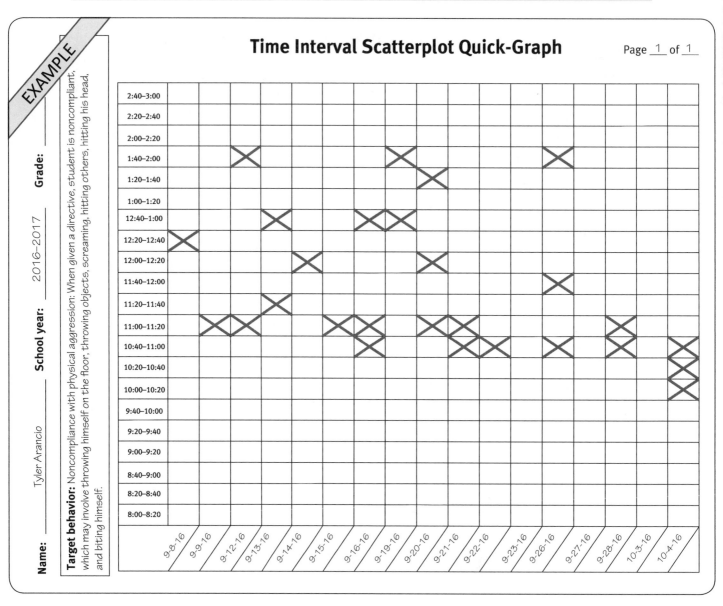

Figure 4.14. Time Interval Scatterplot Quick-Graph (Example).

Figure 4.15a-b shows a similar scatterplot form, the Time Interval/Intensity Scatterplot Quick-Graph, completed for Tyler. Note that it also shows intensity data. (For a blank photocopiable version, see Form 17Ba-b in Section IV: Your Classroom Data Toolkit; see also the About the Forms and Tools page at the beginning of this book for instructions on downloading a printable copy). Like the other combination data forms you have encountered in this chapter, this form is two pages, with an Intensity Key included. This time, there are five color-coded intensity levels available, with clear and specific definitions of what Tyler's behavior looks like at each level. The intensity level is indicated by shading the box next to the time interval in the corresponding color.

Calculating Scatterplot Percentages

It is very easy to inspect and analyze scatterplot data using a simple visual analysis, but if at any time you are required to quantify the data, you will need to have a simple method

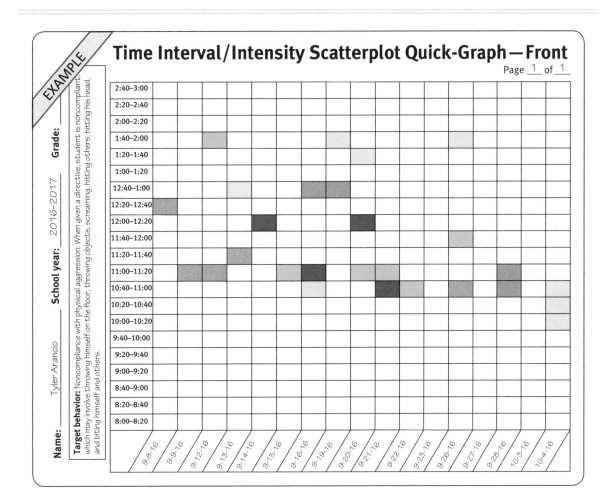

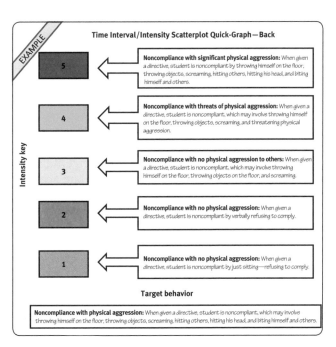

Figure 4.15a–b. Time Interval/Intensity Scatterplot Quick-Graph (Front and Back) (Example).

to do so. One way to quantify scatterplot data is to calculate the overall percentage of time that a student exhibits the target behavior. The formula is as follows:

$$\frac{\text{Number of intervals of time with behavior}}{\text{Total segments or intervals of time}} \times 100 = \%$$

Consider this example.

Hayley was having a significant number of behavioral issues. For data-collection purposes, her teacher divided the 7-hour day into 20-minute intervals, which worked out to 21 segments of time during which she might take data. Hayley did not follow directions for 8 of the 21 total time intervals in the day, so the percentage of the time intervals with this behavior was

$$\frac{8}{21} \times 100 = 38\%$$

The teacher quantified and explained Hayley's behavior to the principal: "Principal Hayden, Hayley seems to be having behavioral issues over a significant amount of the school day. I know that the last time I brought this problem up to you, you said that you needed to know what a significant amount of time meant and that you also wanted the data to support my concerns. I showed you the scatterplot that clearly shows that she is struggling at midday. You mentioned that you need numbers, like a percentage, so that you can document the issue, and I understand. So, look at this.

"I divided the day into 20-minute intervals and recorded data for each interval. Running this calculation, it seems that Hayley is not following directions during 8 of the 20-minute time intervals daily—or 38% of the intervals. This means that for 38% of the intervals of time that stretch over the entire school day, she did not follow directions at least once during that interval. These numerical data show that the behavior is significant."

This is a great example of how quantifying scatterplot data can help to clarify and enhance the data. This book offers two data forms for calculating scatterplot percentages: the Scatterplot Percentage Data Sheet and the Scatterplot Percentage Graph. Forms 18B and 19B in Section IV: Your Classroom Data Toolkit are blank photocopiable versions of these materials (see the About the Forms and Tools page at the beginning of this book for instructions on downloading printable copies). Section IV provides the steps for completing both forms.

The Scatterplot Percentage Data Sheet allows you to record and calculate the percentage of time intervals during the day when at least one incidence of challenging behavior occurred. Figure 4.16 is a completed Scatterplot Percentage Data Sheet that provides a visual of how to record data on the form and calculate scatterplot percentages for an example student. Figure 4.17 is a completed example of the Scatterplot Percentage Graph, the companion to the Scatterplot Percentage Data Sheet that tracks scatterplot percentages over time via a simple line graph. As noted, see Section IV: Your Classroom Data Toolkit for full instructions for completing this graph.

Additional Types of Behavioral Data

Besides frequency, duration, intensity, and scatterplot data, there are a few other types of data that can be collected when assessing behavior. This book does not include data collection forms for all of these types of behavioral data, but it is important that you understand their function and purpose.

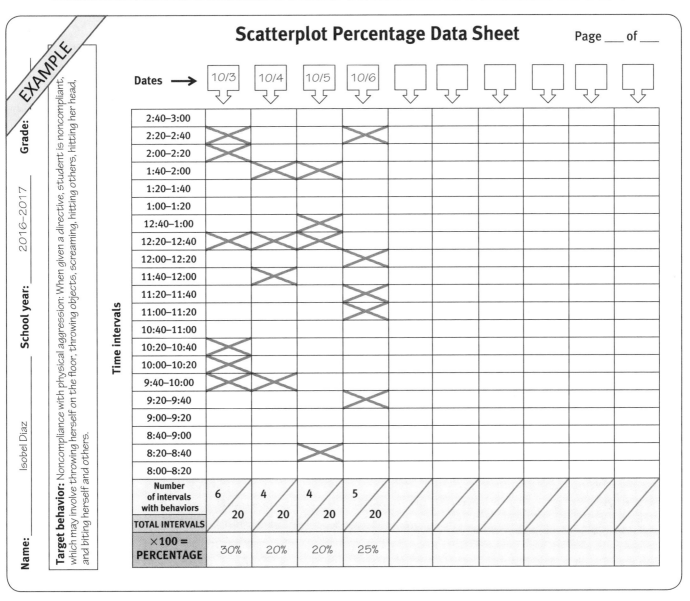

Figure 4.16. Scatterplot Percentage Data Sheet (Example).

Latency Data

Latency data measure the time period between a directive being given and compliance. This is an important type of data and can be very useful in the classroom. Suppose you want to determine if a student is making progress in following directions. The student is complying, but there seems to be a lag time before he or she responds. In this case, you would want to collect latency data. To do so, you would measure the time between the teacher giving the direction and the student actually beginning the task. The goal would be to shorten the latency time.

Interval Data Sampling

Interval data sampling involves estimating the duration of the behavior, but the recorder does not have to continually observe the student. There are a few types of interval

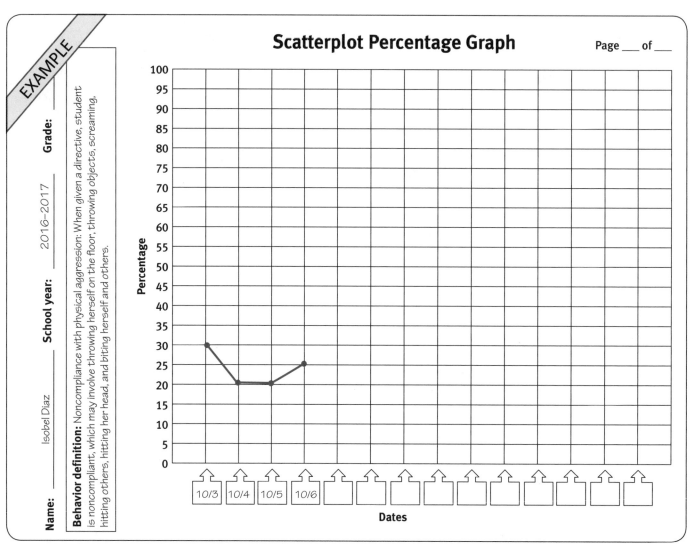

Figure 4.17.   Scatterplot Percentage Graph (Example).

recording forms, but the basic premise is to determine if a behavior occurs during a preselected period of time:

- *Whole interval:* The observer marks yes or no to indicate whether the behavior lasts for one whole, preselected interval of time.

- *Partial interval:* The observer marks yes or no to indicate whether the behavior occurred at least one time during the preselected time interval.

- *Momentary time sampling:* The observer monitors for the presence of the behavior at specific, predesignated points in time, marking yes or no to indicate whether the behavior occurred at that selected moment. This is at a very precise time mark and is very tedious.

ABC Data

Collecting ABC (antecedent, behavior, consequence) data is a process used to help determine the function of a behavior so that appropriate interventions can be implemented.

Antecedents are events that occur just prior to a specific behavior and may be contributing to or serving as a trigger for the behavior. Every behavior has consequences that immediately follow and may serve to reinforce or maintain the behavior. The ABC Data Sheet and Quick-Graph offers a structure for you to record and graph your observations of challenging behavior. (See Form 20Ba-b in Section IV: Your Classroom Data Toolkit for a blank photocopiable version; see also the About the Forms and Tools page at the beginning of this book for instructions on downloading a printable copy.) The analysis of the data gathered on this form will help you determine potential functions of the behavior, or reasons why the behavior is occurring. This will help the team better understand the events and circumstances that contribute to the behavior, which, in turn, will lead the team in the development of more appropriate interventions that target the function of the behavior.

The ABC Data Sheet and Quick-Graph is a detailed, two-page form that allows you to record the events that took place prior to the occurrence of the behavior (i.e., antecedents), describe the behavior in specific terms, record any data that have been collected on the behavior, and describe the consequence of the behavior (i.e., what happened in response). This form allows you to select among several common functions for challenging behaviors: to gain access, to gain attention, to communicate a want or need, to escape a challenging demand or task, or to regulate sensory input. Sometimes, a behavior may be caused by sickness or pain. The form also lists an "other" option to specify any other possible functions.

Figure 4.18a-b is an example of an ABC Data Sheet and Quick-Graph completed for a student named Tuan, who frequently yells at teachers and peers when frustrated. As an example, the first behavioral incident indicates that Tuan yelled at his teacher when asked to make the transition from drawing to reading time. He demanded to continue drawing and expressed anger and frustration over being denied access to a preferred activity. Based on that information, school staff hypothesized gaining access was the behavior's function. Tuan wanted access to the task of drawing; he wanted his drawing materials and did not want to do the reading task. In contrast, when Tuan yelled at a group of students in the lunch line, the team hypothesized that the function of his behavior was based on sensory stimulation. He was overwhelmed by the crowded, noisy cafeteria, and the antecedent to his behavior was high sensory input.

The first page of the ABC Data Sheet and Quick-Graph allows the team to observe and record several incidents of challenging behavior. The context (environment or setting), antecedent (what happens immediately before the behavior), behavior, behavioral data (frequency, duration, and intensity), consequence (what happens immediately after the behavior), and possible function can all be documented on this page. By recording these observations about the behavior, the team is able to get a detailed look at how the environment is affecting the behavior and gain insight into why the behavior might be occurring.

You might print and reuse several of the first pages in order to document many behavioral incidents over time. (In this case, only a snapshot of the total data collected for Tuan is shown.) It would be very difficult to determine the function of a behavior if you only observed the student for one incident and made assumptions from that limited data. Extend the period of ABC observation in order to collect ample data.

The second part of the form helps you determine the function of the behavior by providing you with a Quick-Graph. On this page, frequency counts are kept on the proposed function of each behavioral incident. In Tuan's case, after several more behavioral incidents were documented, the Quick-Graph was completed to help pinpoint some of the functions of his challenging behaviors. For example, an initial review of Tuan's Quick-Graph indicates that as many as four instances of challenging behaviors occurred when he was denied access to something (antecedent). Based on observation, the team determined that the hypothesized function of the behavior was to gain access to items and checked off the "access" function on the graph.

ABC Data Sheet

Name Tuan Thanh   **School Year:** 2016–2017   **Grade:** 4th

You may have more than one data sheet – good way to number.

8/10/16–8/23/16

Incident	Context (Give info about the following:)		Antecedent (What went on before the behavior occurred?)	Behavior (What did student do?)	Data — Intensity	Data — Duration	Data — Frequency Count	Consequence (What did staff do?)	Possible Function (Why did it happen?)	
1	Date	8/15/16	☒ Denied Access	Student yelled out at teacher, saying he did not want to read the book but wanted to continue drawing.	☐ Low ☒ Medium ☐ High	☐ <1 min ☒ 1–5 min ☐ 5–10 min ☐ 10–30 min	=	Teacher redirected student back to task. Loss of points on point card, and teacher reminded Tuan to get on task, saying that he could draw during the break. Reminded twice.	X	Access
	Time	9:00 a.m.	☐ Transition							Attention
	Setting	Classroom	☐ Directive							Communication
	Activity	Reading book	☐ New Task							Escape
	People	Teacher	☐ Told No							Sensory
	Group size	15 students	☐ Waiting							Sickness/Pain
	Subject	Reading	☐ Unstructured Time ☐ High Sensory Input ☐ Low Sensory Input ☐ No attention							Other
2	Date	8/16/16	☒ Denied Access	Student yelled out again at peer – wanted to sit in certain chair but other student got chair first. Tuan stated he always sat in that chair. Students were asked to work in small groups on math assignment.	☐ Low ☐ Medium ☒ High	☐ <1 min ☐ 1–5 min ☒ 5–10 min ☐ 10–30 min	–	Teacher reminded Tuan to lower voice and ask appropriately. Reminded about point loss if behavior continued. Redirected to other chair, and Tuan complied.	X	Access
	Time	10:35 a.m.	☐ Transition							Attention
	Setting	Classroom/small group	☐ Directive							Communication
	Activity	Small group	☐ New Task							Escape
	People	Teacher	☐ Told No							Sensory
	Group size	5 students	☐ Waiting							Sickness/Pain
	Subject	Math	☐ Unstructured Time ☐ High Sensory Input ☐ Low Sensory Input ☐ No attention							Other
3	Date	8/16/16	☒ High Sensory Input	Student yelled at students in line who were standing right beside his place at table. He put hands over his ears and slammed head down on table.	☐ Low ☒ Medium ☐ High	☐ <1 min ☒ 1–5 min ☐ 5–10 min ☐ 10–30 min	=	Teacher guided student to the chair at end of the table out of crowd of students and away from traffic flow. Tuan complied after 2 verbal redirections.		Access
	Time	11:45 a.m.	☐ Transition							Attention
	Setting	Lunchroom	☐ Denied Access							Communication
	Activity	Lunch	☐ Directive							Escape
	People	Students/adults	☐ New Task						X	Sensory
	Group size	100 students	☐ Told No							Sickness/Pain
	Subject	Lunch	☐ Waiting ☐ Unstructured Time ☐ Low Sensory Input ☐ No attention							Other

Figure 4.18a–b. ABC Data Sheet and Quick-Graph (Example).

ABC Data Quick-Graph

EXAMPLE

Access

6	6	6	6	6	6	6	6	6	6	6	6
5	5	5	5	5	5	5	5	5	5	5	5
4	4⁄	4	4	4	4	4	4	4	4	4	4
3	3⁄	3	3	3	3	3	3	3	3	3	3
2	2⁄	2	2	2	2	2	2	2	2	2	2
1	1⁄	1	1	1	1	1	1	1	1	1	1

Attention

6	6	6	6	6	6	6	6	6	6	6	6
5	5	5	5	5	5	5	5	5	5	5	5
4	4	4	4	4	4	4	4	4	4	4	4
3	3	3	3	3	3	3	3	3	3	3	3
2	2	2	2	2	2	2	2	2	2⁄	2	2
1	1⁄	1	1	1	1	1	1	1	1⁄	1	1

Communication

6	6	6	6	6	6	6	6	6	6	6	6
5	5	5	5	5	5	5	5	5	5	5	5
4	4	4	4	4	4	4	4	4	4	4	4
3	3	3	3	3	3	3	3	3	3	3	3
2	2	2⁄	2	2	2	2	2	2	2	2	2
1	1	1	1	1	1	1	1	1	1	1	1

Escape

6	6	6	6	6	6	6	6	6	6	6	6
5	5	5	5	5	5	5	5	5	5	5	5
4	4	4	4	4	4	4	4	4	4	4	4
3	3	3	3⁄	3	3	3	3	3	3	3	3
2	2	2	2⁄	2	2	2	2	2	2	2	2
1	1	1	1⁄	1	1	1	1	1	1	1	1

Sensory

6	6	6	6	6	6	6	6	6	6	6	6
5	5	5	5	5	5	5	5	5	5	5	5
4	4	4	4	4	4⁄	4	4	4	4	4	4
3	3	3	3	3⁄	3	3⁄	3	3	3	3	3
2	2	2	2	2⁄	2	2⁄	2	2	2	2	2
1	1	1	1	1⁄	1	1⁄	1	1	1	1	1

Sickness/Pain

6	6	6	6	6	6	6	6	6	6	6	6
5	5	5	5	5	5	5	5	5	5	5	5
4	4	4	4	4	4	4	4	4	4	4	4
3	3	3	3	3	3	3	3	3	3	3	3
2	2	2	2	2	2	2	2	2	2	2	2
1	1	1	1	1	1	1	1	1	1	1	1

Other:

6	6	6	6	6	6	6	6	6	6	6	6
5	5	5	5	5	5	5	5	5	5	5	5
4	4	4	4	4	4	4	4	4	4	4	4
3	3	3	3	3	3	3	3	3	3	3	3
2	2	2	2	2	2	2	2	2	2	2	2
1	1	1	1	1	1	1	1	1	1	1	1

| Transition | Denied Access | Directive | New Task | Told "No" | Waiting | Unstructured Time | High Sensory Input | Low Sensory Input | No Attention | | |

Other:

6	6	6	6	6	6	6	6	6	6	6	6
5	5	5	5	5	5	5	5	5	5	5	5
4	4	4	4	4	4	4	4	4	4	4	4
3	3	3	3	3	3	3	3	3	3	3	3
2	2	2	2	2	2	2	2	2	2	2	2
1	1	1	1	1	1	1	1	1	1	1	1

| Transition | Denied Access | Directive | New Task | Told "No" | Waiting | Unstructured Time | High Sensory Input | Low Sensory Input | No Attention | | |

Name: Tuan Thanh   **School year:** 2016–2017   **Date range:** 8/10/16–8/23/16

Target behavior: Verbal aggression

Figure 4.18a–b. (continued)

REVIEW OF THE FACTS AND A PEEK AHEAD

Collecting behavioral data is an essential part of addressing challenging behavior in any classroom or learning environment. This chapter focused on four primary types of data to collect in order to provide appropriate interventions for challenging behaviors: frequency data (how many times a specific behavior occurs), duration data (how long a specific behavior occurs), intensity data (how intense a specific behavior is), and scatterplot data (during what time of day or in what activities a specific behavior occurs). Knowing the basics about how to record and graph these types of behavioral data will provide you with an important foundation in how to monitor improvements in behavior and students' response to intervention. Other forms of behavioral data can also be useful as well, particularly ABC data, which helps the team hypothesize the function of a behavior. This can be very helpful in the process of conducting an FBA and developing a BIP. By quantifying and providing a visual analysis of your students' challenging behaviors, you can better communicate with parents and education team members to make informed decisions about how to support students to succeed socially, emotionally, and academically. Chapter 5 will introduce you to IEP data.

QUICK QUIZ

1. Which type of data do you use for determining the time during the day when a behavior occurs?
    a. Frequency
    b. Scatterplot
    c. Intensity

2. It is possible to take two types of data at the same time (e.g., duration and intensity)?
    a. Yes
    b. No

3. In an interval recording, a behavior will be documented as occurring or not occurring during a certain time period.
    a. True
    b. False

4. When collecting data, the use of color can make analysis a much simpler process.
    a. True
    b. False

5. Which type of data reflects the period of time between a teacher giving a direction and a student complying with the direction?
    a. Intensity data
    b. Frequency data
    c. Latency data

CHAPTER 5

IEP Data

 MISSION: To learn to organize, collect, and graph IEP data and measure progress toward goals and objectives

QUESTIONS TO INVESTIGATE

- What are some easy ways to organize data collection for IEP goals and objectives?

DEFINITIONS OF TERMS AND ABBREVIATIONS

IEP goals Annual statements developed by the IEP team that describe what the student will achieve or learn with supports. Goals, which can be academic, behavioral, or functional, are designed to meet the student's needs that result from his or her disability so that the child can be involved in and make progress in the general education curriculum (Individuals with Disabilities Education Improvement Act [IDEA] of 2004, PL 108-446, § 300.320[a][2][i][A] and [B]). Goals should be measurable, include benchmarks for mastery, and specify the time frame for monitoring progress (i.e., 1 year).

IEP objectives Specific, discrete steps to achieving an IEP goal. Although IDEA 2004 only requires that short-term objectives be written for children with alternate assessments, many states have continued the practice of including both goals and short-term objectives in IEP goals (Winterman & Rosas, 2014).

When working with students with IEPs, it is essential to collect good data in order to write measurable IEP goals and objectives for the year, measure progress toward those goals and objectives, and monitor how the student responds to interventions and supports. Data inform the development of the IEP document, alerting the team if goals for the student need to be revised or if more supports are needed to maximize the student's participation and success in the learning environment. Yet, if educators do not have an organized system or plan for collecting and presenting IEP data, this can be a daunting task. Consider the challenges faced by a new teacher in the Eyewitness Account.

Eyewitness Account

I can remember being very nervous about the first IEP meeting of my new teaching job. I was knowledgeable about the IEP process and had ideas about new goals that should be drafted for the student but was not really sure how prepared I should be in terms of going through data on current goals. I knew that this data would drive the decisions that would be made about the current IEP. I had interned in several settings and saw many teachers facilitate IEP meetings, all in different ways; each person had his or her own agenda and way of going through the process. I had data but really did not have a plan for walking through this data with the IEP team. Preparing for this first meeting was very stressful.

—Mr. Feldman,
Special Education Teacher

Mr. Feldman is certainly on the right path. He has data and wants to apply what he has learned from the IEP meetings he attended to create his own style for facilitating meetings, but he realizes that it is difficult to find a way to easily and thoroughly present IEP data and use the data to guide the meeting. This chapter provides forms, tools, and tips for maneuvering the IEP process, organizing data, and presenting data during IEP meetings, which can be complicated and cumbersome tasks for new and veteran teachers alike.

WHAT ARE SOME EASY WAYS TO ORGANIZE DATA COLLECTION FOR IEP GOALS AND OBJECTIVES?

Imagine an educator speaking about a student's progress to parents during an IEP meeting. Which educator are you?

Scenario 1: Mr. and Mrs. Mulhern, I would like to talk about Regina's IEP goals. If you look at Goal 1, you see that the mastery level for basic math facts was set at 75%, and I would guess that she began the year at about . . . maybe 50%? During the first 3 weeks, she seemed to make progress. She was learning her math facts and did pretty well on most of the work. But she did fail a test. Did you get that test I sent home? Overall, though, I think Regina's doing well. I really love her; she's such a sweet girl. We did take lots of data, but I think I must have left those data sheets in the room. I have nearly 100 of them, and they are pretty hard to carry. So, we probably should just keep the math goal on Regina's IEP because I don't think she's quite mastered it yet. What do you think? Maybe if you could help her with her homework and her studying, we could get rid of that goal during our next IEP meeting.

Scenario 2: Mr. and Mrs. Mulhern, I would like to talk about the data that we have been collecting on Regina's four IEP goals. If you look at Goal 1, shown in red, you will see that the mastery level for basic math facts was set at 75%, and her baseline data showed that she began at the 45% mastery level. During the first 3 weeks, she stayed at a pretty consistent level, but you can see that around January 19 she began to rapidly make gains. Regina really began to grasp her math concepts, and she ended up achieving the mastery level that we set for her by the first week of February. That is remarkable! Here are analyzed work samples that are shown by the data points on this graph. Do you see the upward trend shown on this graph? I put copies of the data and graphs in a folder of IEP handouts to take home.

Hopefully you find yourself in Scenario 2. There are so many things wrong with Scenario 1. Here are just a few:

- The teacher did not bring the data sheets to the meeting.

- The teacher did not summarize, analyze, and graph the data.

- The teacher had to guess at the baseline level.

- The teacher said, "She's such a sweet girl." The student may be, but in this case, the comment rings insincere, and the teacher is covering up for not being prepared.

- The teacher said, "She seemed to make progress." All it would take to call this statement into question is for the parent to ask, "How do you know?"

- The teacher put the responsibility (or blame) back on the parents by saying, "If you could help her with homework."

In Scenario 2, there were so many things done right, such as the following:

- The teacher summarized and graphed the data.

- The teacher calculated baseline levels and compared them to the mastery level.

- The teacher showed and explained the trendline.

- The teacher brought analyzed work samples and matched them to the data points.

- The teacher provided the parents with a copy of the data and graphs.

Scenario 2 is the best way to collect and share data! However, in order to collect the data on IEP goals, you must first write goals that are measurable. There are so many times that teachers spend hours and hours writing the perfect IEP goal only to forget about how they are going to measure progress toward the goal in the classroom. This chapter first explains how to write a measurable IEP goal or objective and then discusses ways to organize a system for collecting data on these goals and objectives. Finally, the chapter explains how to organize other important information related to the IEP.

How to Write a Measurable IEP Goal

Writing a measurable IEP goal is a big task, but good data collection hinges on this important step. If you write the goals correctly, then the data collection method should naturally follow, and the data you gather should in turn inform decisions related to the IEP as you monitor the student's progress. The process of writing a measureable IEP goal can be broken down into discrete steps; the acronym GOAL makes the steps easy to remember (see Figure 5.1). This acronym is provided on the Writing IEP Goals bookmark in Appendix A. (See also the About the Forms and Tools page at the beginning of this book for instructions on downloading a printable copy.) The bookmark can be printed on cardstock and taken to IEP meetings to make sure that all goals are written correctly.

Look at the acronym in Figure 5.1: GOAL. The *G* stands for "given." When writing a goal, best practice is to begin with the word *given* so that the condition is set or the parameters around which you plan to measure progress are defined. *O* stands for "observable." In order for you to collect data, the behavior or action must be observable. *A* stands for "A target is set." You have to set a target for exactly what the student will do: how much, how often, and at what level. *L* stands for "limit time." There has to be a time limit. When do you project that the goal will be mastered? If you address all the components contained in the acronym, then you will have a well-written goal. (This material also is provided on the Writing IEP Goals bookmark in Appendix A; see also the About the Forms and Tools page at the beginning of this book for instructions on downloading a printable copy.)

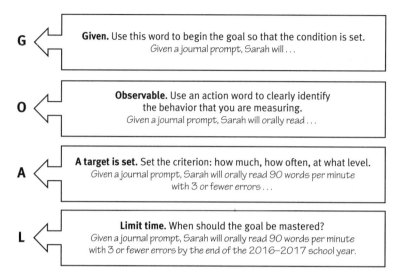

Figure 5.1. GOAL: Breaking down an IEP goal.

In order to accurately design a data collection system to measure your students' progress on their IEP goals, you must first correctly write the target or criteria for the goals. There are typically three types of criteria used to measure goals: rate, time, and percentage. Figure 5.2 provides examples and definitions of each of these criteria. (This material also is provided on the Setting Criteria bookmark in Appendix A; see also the About the Forms and Tools page at the beginning of this book for instructions on downloading a printable copy.)

Goals are custom-written to match the student's current functioning. Consider each goal before determining whether rate, time, or percentage is the best way to measure mastery. When rate is used as a criterion, the skill or behavior has to be repeated a certain number of times for mastery (e.g., correctly completing 4 out of 5 assignments). The student may have accomplished a skill or task once, but this typically does not mean that the student has mastered it. Rather, repeated success on trials indicates mastery.

Time parameters are also important considerations for determining mastery. For example, say that a student takes 180 minutes to correctly read four sentences in an oral reading passage. In hopes of helping the student improve his or her reading speed, you might set a goal that the student will correctly read four sentences in 5 minutes.

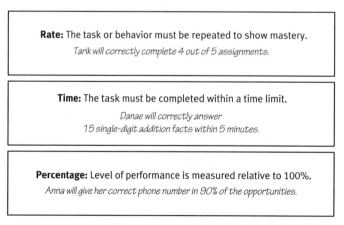

Figure 5.2. Setting criteria: Definitions and examples of criteria for rate, time, and percentage.

The last criterion commonly used to measure progress toward IEP goals is percentage (out of 100%). Depending on the student's specific IEP goals, this percentage criterion may be written as an average of correct responses or as a percentage of successful opportunities.

How to Organize a System for Measuring IEP Goals and Objectives

This section introduces helpful data collection sheets that center on the IEP process. These forms help you create an organized system for measuring IEP goals and objectives.

The first form is the IEP Goal Data Sheet, which can be used to record progress for any type of IEP goal and can be completed on a weekly basis. (A blank photocopiable version of this form is included as Form 1C in Section IV: Your Classroom Data Toolkit; see also the About the Forms and Tools page at the beginning of this book for instructions on downloading a printable copy.) The IEP Goal Data Sheet provides space for you to list each goal, indicate the method of measurement being used, and track the student's progress on his or her IEP goals for each day of the week. You then record weekly total progress and compare it to the criteria for mastery.

Figure 5.3 is an example of a completed IEP Goal Data Sheet for a student named June. Two of June's IEP goals measure progress using percentages. Her second IEP goal

IEP Goal Data Sheet   Page 1 of 1

EXAMPLE IEP date: 3/16

School year: 2016–2017

Name: June White

#	Goals/objectives	Method of measurement	Dates					Week total / Mastery
			8/29/16	8/30/16	8/31/16	9/1/16	9/2/16	
1	Given a list of sight words, June will orally read 20 third-grade sight words with a 90% accuracy for 4 out of 5 consecutive data collection days by 5-2-17.	%	60% Accuracy	—	90% Accuracy	100% Accuracy	90% Accuracy	3/4 days / 90% 4/5
2	Given writing prompts, June will write three 5-word sentences with correct grammar and punctuation 4 out of 5 times a week over 3 consecutive weeks by 5-2-17.	Rate	III Sentences	III Sentences	IIII Sentences	I Sentences	II Sentences	3/5 days / 4/5 days
3	Given daily math problems, June will correctly complete 50 single-digit addition problems, achieving an 80% weekly average for 3 consecutive weeks by 5-2-17.	%	60% Accuracy	60% Accuracy	90% Accuracy	80% Accuracy	90% Accuracy	76% / 80%
4	Given independent work, June will work independently for 10 minutes with less than 2 verbal prompts 4 out of 5 consecutive days by 5/2/17.	Prompt	IIIII Verbal prompt	—	IIII Verbal prompt	II Verbal prompt	IIIII Verbal prompt	0/4 days / 4/5 days

Figure 5.3. IEP Goal Data Sheet (Example).

uses a frequency count: June completes a certain number of sentences for a specific number of days. Her last IEP goal uses the number of prompts she is given to track her progress toward working independently for 10 minutes. Figure 5.3 shows that during this week, June did not reach mastery level for any of her IEP goals. The goals should be mastered by the end of the IEP year, May 2, 2017.

The IEP Goal Data Sheet is useful because you can customize it to document the method of data collection required by the IEP goal. It also reminds you which type of measurement you need to document (e.g., rate, time, percentage).

The second form is the IEP Goal Mastery Quick-Graph, which helps you create a visual representation of progress on IEP goals and objectives. (A blank version of this form is included as Form 2C in Section IV: Your Classroom Data Toolkit; see also the About the Forms and Tools page at the beginning of this book for instructions on downloading a printable copy.) Figure 5.4 shows June's weekly progress on each of her IEP goals via shading. The education team simply shades the box for Yes or No at the end of the week to indicate whether June met the mastery level for each goal.

The IEP Goal Mastery Quick-Graph provides a good visual to use in meetings to document ongoing progress on each goal. It also allows you to see if an IEP goal has been mastered if the goal is based on time. For instance, this form will graphically show progress if the student meets a specific goal for 2 consecutive weeks or 4 out of 5 consecutive days.

How to Organize Other IEP-Related Information

More is required to adhere to your students' IEPs and support their success in school than just measuring their progress on goals and objectives. Your responsibilities also include organizing the students' academic day, ensuring that all students' academic needs are met, and monitoring your teaching methods. This section introduces two helpful forms related to these responsibilities.

The first form is the Academic Needs Checklist, which helps you organize your students' IEP information according to the supports, services, and environments they need to meet their goals. (A blank photocopiable version of this form is included as Form 3C in Section IV: Your Classroom Data Toolkit; see also the About the Forms and Tools page at the beginning of this book for instructions on downloading a printable copy.) Are your students with special education needs served in general education? Are they cotaught, or will they be taught in pull-out settings? Are special materials needed for any subjects during the school day?

It can be hard to keep up with all the variables involved in carrying out IEPs, but this checklist is a helpful organizational tool. First, list your caseload of students and the subject areas you teach, the subject areas required by grade, or the subject areas referenced in the IEP goals. Next, check off the environment where the students should be taught, and list any specific teaching materials needed. Specific materials that would be beneficial to one student may be discussed in the IEP meeting, but it is difficult to remember this information when you get back to the classroom. This form helps you organize these details because it places all IEP-related information for your entire caseload in one spot.

Figure 5.5 shows the first page of Mr. Lin's four-page Academic Needs Checklist. Mr. Lin used this form to organize the needs of his caseload of 12 students with IEPs. Notice that two of his students are taught in a variety of ways depending on the subject—in a regular class, with coteaching, and even in a small group. After completing the form, Mr. Lin notices that implementing a small-group writing activity would be a way to cover at least two of his students' needs related to writing.

Another helpful tool is the Teaching Programs form. (A blank photocopiable version of this form is included as Form 4C in Section IV: Your Classroom Data Toolkit; see also the About the Forms and Tools page at the beginning of this book for instructions on downloading a printable copy.) This form provides a helpful way to keep track of the teaching

IEP Goal Mastery Quick-Graph

EXAMPLE

IEP date: 5/3/16

Grade: 4th

School year: 2016–2017

Name: June White

#	Goals/objectives	Mastered	Dates (Week ending)									
			9-9-16	9-16-16	9-23-16	9-30-16						
1	Given a list of sight words, June will orally read 20 third-grade sight words with a 90% accuracy for 4 out of 5 consecutive data collection days by 5/2/17.	Yes				■						
		No	■	■								
2	Given writing prompts, June will write three 5-word sentences with correct grammar and punctuation 4 out of 5 times a week over 3 consecutive weeks by 5/2/17.	Yes										
		No	■	■	■	■						
3	Given daily math problems, June will correctly complete 50 single-digit addition problems with an 80% weekly average for 3 consecutive weeks by 5/2/17.	Yes										
		No	■	■	■	■						
4	Given independent work to complete, June will work independently for 10 minutes with less than 2 verbal prompts across 4 out of 5 consecutive days by 5/2/17.	Yes			■							
		No	■	■								
		Yes										
		No										

Figure 5.4. IEP Goal Mastery Quick-Graph (Example).

Academic Needs Checklist

EXAMPLE

Teacher: _____ Mr. Lin _____   School year: _____ 2016–2017 _____

Student	Subject	Specific materials	Grouping					
				Coteaching	With speech teacher in classroom		Small group	Individual
Jeremy	Math		X					
	Reading		X					
	Social studies			X				
	Science			X				
	Writing	"Learning Box – Writing"					X	
	Spelling			X				
	Speech				X			
Jordan	Math			X				
	Reading		X					
	Social studies			X				
	Science		X					
	Writing	"Learning box – Writing"					X	
	Spelling		X					
	Speech		4					X

Figure 5.5.   Academic Needs Checklist (Example).

methods used with your students. You might be wondering how teaching methods relate to data collection. To answer this question, not only is it important for you to collect data on your teaching methods to determine their effectiveness, but it is also important to monitor and ensure that the teaching methods and strategies used in the classroom are consistent.

Think about it this way: If you are using DTT sessions to work on a certain set of IEP goals or if you are working with a student in a one-to-one setting on IEP goals, it is important that the student is taught using the same methods by all staff members. Consider the example shown in Table 5.1. On Monday, the teacher works with a student in an individual center on word recognition. On Tuesday, the paraprofessional works with the same student on the same skill. Both educators gather data.

In each of these lessons, the student made an error on the word *horse*, but the error correction procedure (or the way in which errors were handled) was not consistent. This

Table 5.1.   Example of inconsistent teaching methods used during data collection

Monday—Teacher	Tuesday—Paraprofessional
Teacher: "Read this word."	Paraprofessional: "Tell me what this word says."
Student: "Tree"	Student: "Tree"
Teacher: "Good job!"	Paraprofessional: "Okay."
Teacher: "Read this word."	Paraprofessional: "What about this one?"
Student: "House"	Student: "House"
Teacher pauses a minute.	Paraprofessional: "No, that word is not *house*. Look at that word and tell me what it says."
Teacher: "Read this word."	
Teacher prompts student by sounding out each letter.	Student: "Houses?"
Teacher and Student: "Horse"	Paraprofessional: "No, the word is *horse*. Let's go to the next one."
Teacher: "Read this word."	
Student: "Horse"	
Teacher: "Good job!"	

Teaching Programs

EXAMPLE

Materials
Second-grade flash cards
Data sheet

Student name: _Sarita Patel_

School year: _2016–2017_ **Subject area:** _Reading_

Grouping (circle): *individual* (*small group*) *large group*   **IEP goal (circle)** (Yes) No

⭐ **IEP GOAL:** Given a list of grade-level sight words, Sarita will identify 15 of 20 grade-level sight words by orally reading words with 90% accuracy on 4 out of 5 days by 5-2-17 or the end of the IEP year.

Method

Teacher directive

Show the flash card and say, "What word?"

For correct response

Say, "Good reading" or "Good job." Continue to the next card with the same directive.

For no response or incorrect response

Ignore the incorrect response. Put the flash card on the table for a second, then show it again and repeat the

verbal direction above. This time, immediately prompt by sounding out the word. After the student says the word,

then say, "What word?" Say the word with the student.

Turn the card over and show it again, repeating the directions "What word?" Repeat the step above as needed.

Additional information

Take data on the IEP Goal Data Sheet.

⭐ **Were data taken? (Circle.)** (YES) NO

Figure 5.6. Teaching Programs (Example).

may have been from lack of training on the part of the paraprofessional. In this case, the student may be confused, and the data may not be as reliable as it should have been. Creating teaching protocols and placing them in a book to be used with the student will assist all staff with consistency, maintain the integrity of the teaching methods used, and remind all staff of the teaching methods and materials that will help students achieve their IEP goals.

Figure 5.6 is an example of a completed Teaching Programs form for a student named Sarita related to her reading IEP goal. The form indicates the teaching materials needed for working on his goal, the grouping for the lesson, and the exact teaching procedures and protocols for helping Sarita improve her reading. This includes the teacher directive, what to do in case of an error, and the procedure to use for a correct response. It also indicates that data will be kept on this task. This alleviates questions as to how to teach Sarita in a one-to-one setting. It also helps to lessen the chance of inconsistencies in the data. Filling out these forms may be a little time-consuming at first, but they will save you time in training other staff on exactly how to teach certain skills and will increase the integrity of both teaching and data collection.

As you complete these forms for your students, you can create a Teaching Programs book for individual students, for centers, for subjects, or for entire caseloads of students. A photocopiable cover page for this book is included in Appendix A: Building Your Data Collection Notebook: Handouts, Embellishments, and Extras; see also the About the Forms and Tools page at the beginning of this book for instructions on downloading a printable copy.

REVIEW OF THE FACTS AND A PEEK AHEAD

The IEP process depends on collecting solid and consistent classroom data that show your students' progress toward their goals and objectives and their response to individualized supports. In order for the education team to gauge student progress, the IEP document must include clear and measurable educational goals (remember the GOAL acronym!) with specific criteria for mastery and how the goals will be measured (i.e., rate, time, or percentage). Next, the teacher needs to organize a system for measuring each student's progress toward IEP goals and objectives. Helpful tools such as the IEP Goal Data Sheet and the IEP Goal Mastery Quick-Graph help teachers monitor whether students are meeting their goals and track their mastery on a regular basis. Equally important, teachers should come up with a system for meeting each student's individual needs as specified in the IEP, making sure to track particular learning materials, supports, or classroom arrangements necessary to promote success. Finally, to ensure that IEP data are accurate and reliable, educators should have a means of ensuring that teaching methods and procedures used with students are consistent—for example, compiling a Teaching Programs book to share with other education team members who will be providing instruction to the student and helping him or her work toward mastering the IEP goals.

Now that you have learned about the three core types of classroom data (academic, behavioral, and IEP), you are ready to learn about the process for setting up a comprehensive data collection system in your classroom.

QUICK QUIZ

1. IDEA 2004 requires that both short-term objectives and long-term goals be written for every IEP.
   a. True
   b. False

2. Which of the following is important to include in an IEP meeting discussion?
   a. Analyzed work samples brought and matched to the student data
   b. Baseline levels calculated and compared to the mastery level of each goal
   c. a and b
   d. None of the above

3. When rate is used as a criterion, the skill or behavior has to be repeated a certain number of times for mastery (e.g., correctly completing 4 out of 5 assignments).
   a. True
   b. False

4. The acronym GOAL provides the reader with an easy way to remember the important aspects of writing IEP goals. The following are included in the acronym:
   a. "Given" (this word is used to set the condition)
   b. Observable (an action word helps identify the behavior)
   c. A target is set (the criterion for mastery is provided)
   d. All of the above

CHAPTER 6

Establishing Your Data Collection System

 MISSION: To establish an efficient and organized classroom data collection system

QUESTIONS TO INVESTIGATE

- What are some ideas for using technology to collect data?
- What are some ideas for organizing the data collection process in the classroom?

DEFINITIONS OF TERMS AND ABBREVIATIONS

Cold probes The collection of data from the first trial of a task. These occur after a period of time with no reinforcement for appropriate responses and no practice of the skill.

Raw data Data that have not yet been compiled, graphed, or analyzed.

Self-graphing data sheets Data collection forms that will create a graph at the same time that the raw data are being collected so that immediate and continual analysis can take place.

Work sample analysis A way of scoring an academic work sample against predetermined criteria so that an analysis of progress toward mastery can be made.

Chapter 6 focuses on ways to create and implement an organized and efficient classroom data collection system. When implementing any task within a classroom, especially one that involves a great deal of paperwork, it is helpful to establish a clear-cut process or routine that will make the task more manageable. Data collection is one of those classroom tasks that can become overwhelming if a process is not put into place. This chapter will provide you with ideas of ways to use technology in the classroom, options of how to set aside time for data collection, examples of forms that will help you collect data regularly and efficiently (i.e., cold probe, round robin), and general ways to organize the classroom environment for success.

Sometimes these skills are not specifically discussed in teacher preparation courses, and newly trained teachers starting their first job may forget about setting this aspect of classroom management as a priority. I was one of those teachers—thinking I was prepped and ready to tackle my first teaching assignment but forgetting one important task.

Eyewitness Account

I was a new teacher just out of college and was beyond excited to have my first job teaching in a middle school special education pull-out/resource classroom for students with learning disabilities. I took a great deal of time getting my room ready and preparing for my incoming students. When I went to my first team meeting with the other special education teachers, they were discussing how they planned to collect data in their classrooms for the upcoming year. One of the teachers really wanted to design an easier way to collect data on the student's IEP goals and objectives. Another talked about a couple of behavioral data sheets that she would like to try in order to monitor student progress in the area of behavior and time on task. Others were discussing how they would build in a data collection time during the week in order to monitor academic progress.

Hearing this, I went cold, realizing that I had forgotten something. I had my room beautifully arranged, lesson plans written, and the new school year organized, but I hadn't thought about data. I realized that I needed to design a data collection system for my classroom, and I was at a loss for where to begin.

WHAT ARE SOME IDEAS FOR USING TECHNOLOGY TO COLLECT DATA?

In 1983, when I first began teaching, computers in the classroom were unheard of. In fact, even home computers were few and far between. I collected some data in the classroom on my students with special needs, but probably very little, and it was the paper-and-pencil kind. Now, with computers and all types of mobile devices, it seems as if technology rules. There have been huge advancements in the world of educational data collection. Teachers have numerous technological options for data collection as long as they have access to that technology and the know-how to use it. Yet, even with these advancements, there are still pros and cons regarding the use of technology in data collection. Some of these pros and cons are listed in Table 6.1.

As shown in Table 6.1, there is a strong case for the use of technology, but there is also a strong case for sticking with paper-and-pencil collection methods. Yes, technology is easy to use if you know how. Yes, technology can assist you in creating wonderful graphs. Technology is mobile, and it allows you to digitally send the data to others and attach data to another document. If the user is knowledgeable about the data collection program, then data sheets can be modified to fit the specific needs of the classroom.

However, there are also some drawbacks to technology as well. Some of the spread-sheet-type programs used with data collection are very complicated to set up and use.

Table 6.1.   The pros and cons of using technology in data collection

Pros	Cons
Technology can be easy to use.	Technology is expensive to get started.
Teachers can create all types of graphs.	Some programs have a steep learning curve.
Data can be sent electronically.	Technology is not always accessible.
Technology can be mobile.	Unless technology is mobile, it can be cumbersome to use in the classroom.
If the user is knowledgeable in the program, the data tools can be modified.	Teachers are subject to having technology that works.

Technology can also be expensive. Classrooms in some public school systems do not have the funding for technology. There may be stipulations on the use of technology that classrooms do have, and the technology may be for student use only. Teachers may have only a laptop, which is not mobile enough to use for data collection. What if paraprofessionals also collect data but the teacher's laptop is password protected? That situation can make for an ethical dilemma. It is also very time-consuming to collect data using paper-and-pencil methods and then to input the same information into a spreadsheet program. It seems like double the work!

Even the most up-to-date and state-of-the-art technology can come with challenges. As the principal of a special education program, I tried to implement the most cutting-edge data collection technologies in order to increase the efficiency of the classrooms and ease the stress of the teachers. In doing so, I was also the one who received feedback on whether the ideas actually worked and, in some instances, took the brunt of the critical feedback. In terms of the data collection program, here are a few of the actual comments I encountered from my staff over the period of about 2 months:

- "We need a data collection person or an extra planning period during the day to plug all the raw data from our data sheets into our Excel program so that it can be analyzed, graphed, and printed. We do not have time to do this, and we are tired of working at night from home."

- "We have a serious issue with the Excel program in five of our classrooms. The trend-line is showing up as a big blob on the side of the graph, and I have an IEP meeting tomorrow morning. All I have is the raw data, which cannot be analyzed. Help!"

- "Can we please schedule an all-day training on the use of the data collection program in Excel? I can't figure it out, even with the manual."

- "My computer just made a horrible screaming noise and then crashed. I lost everything, including all student data. I haven't backed up my data since September, and I threw away the paper copies of my raw data because I did not think I needed them anymore. What now?"

Yes, these were real-life issues, and yes, I had to come up with real-life solutions! These issues show just a few of the questions and challenges that technology can raise in terms of data collection. This experience is, by no means, a warning against technology—remember that there are many pros as well as cons—but it serves as a glimpse into the many factors that need to be considered with technology use. Regardless of whether you choose to use technology or paper-and-pencil data sheets, here are my biggest tips for using technology in classroom data collection:

1. Do NOT throw paper copies of raw data away. It does not matter how many digital copies you have. You should always keep the original data sheets as backup.

2. If you have funds available for and access to tablet technology, there are several great apps for data collection available. When choosing a program or app, there are a few things you need to remember:

   a. Begin with the end in mind. Figure out what you need first and then find the program or app that meets that need.

   b. Do not pay a high price and be impressed by bells and whistles. If the application or program is too complicated, you will not have time to use half of what is available. Sometimes simple is best.

   c. If available, get a free trial version. It is like test-driving a car. Do not buy it until you try it.

d. Carve out enough time to research data collection programs and apps. There are too many apps available to purchase the first one you see. That app is probably the one with the largest marketing budget, but it may not be the most useful.

e. Determine if the application can be personalized or modified to meet your needs.

f. Find out if you can print from the app and have the data look the way you need them to look. You need to be able to do so—unless you plan on including the whole technological device in the student's file, which is obviously not feasible!

3. Teach other adults in the classroom (if you have the luxury of having other adults in the classroom) to use the program.

4. Data collection using your smartphone is certainly an option. There are several apps available for taking baseline data during an observation, but remember you are responsible for managing data confidentially on a personal device. That can be challenging.

5. Make backups of the data. When you make digital backups, open them to make certain that the data were actually saved.

6. When using a new technology, implement it gradually. Use a new data collection program for a few months with one student to work out the kinks. You may find that the technology works great, but you may find that it does not fit your needs.

7. Did I say to keep paper copies of the raw data? This bears repeating.

Now that you've gone through the pros and cons of technology use, let me offer my opinion on the best kind of data collection system. Regardless of whether you incorporate technology, using self-graphing data sheets such as the ones in this book works best for data collection. These types of data forms

- Are easy to understand

- Are portable

- Require a very small learning curve in terms of recording and analyzing data

- Make it very easy to understand and explain data analysis to others

- Can be filed in an individual student's folder

- Do not require funding to purchase expensive technology

- Will not become obsolete when technology changes or updates

- Can be used by multiple people at the same time

- Can be provided to general education teachers, who may not be trained in complicated data collection systems

- Can be used in the home, in private therapeutic settings, or even on the playground

So, my verdict is in. Though technology is helpful and certainly might be an option in your classroom or setting, paper-and-pencil data collection rules!

WHAT ARE SOME IDEAS FOR ORGANIZING THE DATA COLLECTION PROCESS IN THE CLASSROOM?

How do you actually organize your time for collecting data in the classroom? Because every educational environment is different, there is no one, hard-and-fast answer to this critical question, but this section provides a few ideas to help you creatively design a personal data collection process that is effective and efficient for you. You will learn about organizing your data collection process in terms of both time and materials.

Time Management of the Data Collection Process

There are a few ways you can organize time for data collection in your classroom. However, it is important to note that when you are collecting data on behavior, unless you are collecting interval data, you will collect data when the behavior occurs. Behavior is, by nature, sporadic and cannot be scheduled. If you have completed a scatterplot, then you may know the time of day the behaviors are occurring, but unless you are going to predesignate time intervals for data collection, then you cannot schedule times to collect behavioral data. However, there are several ways to manage your time when collecting other types of data. The following techniques can be helpful:

1. Data collection days

2. Stations

3. Round robin data collection

4. Cold probes

Data Collection Days

It is important as you monitor student progress to have some type of data collection schedule. This schedule could stipulate that data collection occur monthly or weekly. Progress monitoring has been described by Stecker, Fuchs, and Fuchs (2008) as "a system of brief assessments that are given frequently, at least monthly, to determine whether students are progressing through the curriculum in desired fashion and are likely to meet long-term goals" (p. 11). Even though monthly data collection to document student progress may be adequate, there is research to support the use of more frequent weekly or biweekly sessions (Fuchs & Fuchs, 2006). Data that are collected on a more frequent basis can bring awareness of difficult-to-manage issues that may arise suddenly.

In order to manage data collection in the classroom for RTI/MTSS progress monitoring or monitoring progress on IEP goals, you may want to set up specific days for collecting data. This is a good way to manage your time and hold you accountable for data collection. When I was a teacher in the classroom, my schedule would get so busy that if an activity was not written into the lesson plan, it did not happen. Data collection would get pushed down the priority list. When an administrator walks through your classroom, you need to be following a schedule, and for data collection to happen, it needs to be on that schedule.

Try scheduling consistent days for data collection. You could vary the days of the week that are selected in order to get a good cross section of time (e.g., do not repeatedly take data on the same days of the week, every week). For instance, your data collection days could be Monday and Wednesday of the first week of the month and Tuesday and Thursday of the second week of the month. Or you could choose to keep the data collection days consistent so that every other Tuesday you collect reading data for the group or you collect data on IEP goals every Wednesday. Choose the option that works best for your setting and for your schedule.

Consider the following example:

Every Monday and Wednesday morning, Ms. Garrison collects academic data on every student. She arranges the schedule so that she can spend time with each student and makes sure that she has data sheets and materials handy to make the time management easier. In addition to meeting with each student individually, Ms. Garrison also collects math fluency data for the group, assessing students with timed math drill sheets. Building data collection into her schedule forces Ms. Garrison to be consistent so that she will have ample data to make decisions about student interventions.

Ms. Garrison has a good plan in place for collecting both group and individual student data. She is disciplined in managing her time so that she can spend a few minutes with each student in order to gather individual data on math skills. She chooses data collection days and times that work for her classroom. Ms. Garrison knows that if data collection is documented as part of the weekly schedule, then she will be more regimented in the process, and the entire process will be easier to manage.

Stations

Do you have workstations or centers in your classroom? Try placing data sheets on clipboards in these centers so that you have easy access to them. When managing time for data collection using stations, teachers can arrange a "station time" or "center time" during the day. The students will move from station to station, one of which is one-to-one time with the teacher for data collection purposes. Consider the following example:

Ms. Panto has set up her elementary school classroom in stations. A few days a week, she has the students travel from station to station during reading class. The stations include individual worksheets, a computer game in reading, silently reading a novel, and working with the teacher. During the individual time with the teacher, Ms. Panto pulls data sheets with IEP goals for the students with IEPs to assess their progress on reading goals. This way, all students are involved in an academic task while she is collecting data.

Good job, Ms. Panto! Stations are great ways to organize the data collection process.

Round Robin Data Collection

If students are moving about the classroom, such as from one station or one activity to another, a round robin method of data collection may work well. This approach is particularly effective if there is another adult in the classroom besides the teacher, but that is not required. Round robin data collection can be set up so that each of the stations in the classroom involves a method of data collection. Consider the following classroom scenario:

Mr. Helmsy has 12 students and one paraprofessional in his special education classroom. All of the students' IEPs include goals and objectives in a variety of areas. Mr. Helmsy has found that a round robin approach to data collection is an easier way for him to make sure that data collection is completed at least two times per week. He has arranged the schedule so that every other day is a data collection day. His schedule is written so that he alternates Week A (Monday, Wednesday, Friday data collection) and Week B (Tuesday, Thursday data collection). This way, he collects data on each day of the week within a 2-week period of time.
Mr. Helmsy sets up several areas for data collection in his classroom:

- *The computer reading program,* which collects progress monitoring data on reading comprehension
- *One-to-one time with the paraprofessional,* who collects data on reading fluency for one student
- *Small-group time with the teacher,* who collects data on two students in a small group (The students complete individual worksheets on drilled tasks [e.g., worksheet assessing knowledge of multiplication or addition facts]. As the task is completed, the teacher records the student's score as data to monitor progress.)

- *Workboxes,* which are tasks that can be quickly checked by a staff member who records a simple yes or no to the question, "Was the student able to adequately complete the workbox task?" (*Note:* It's helpful to determine in advance how many "yes" responses are needed for a given workbox to demonstrate mastery of a skill; after mastery has been exhibited by reaching this predetermined number of "yes" responses, the student may need to move to a different workbox task.)

Each station collects data in a different way.

The round robin approach can be a little cumbersome to set up at first, but after it is organized, it works well and will supply an ample amount of data. There are many ways to implement round robin data collection. The important thing is that each student has individual time with a staff member so that data can be collected on the goals that require one-to-one time.

Figure 6.1 is an example of a completed Round Robin Organization Chart for a class of 12 students. (See Form 1D in Section IV: Your Classroom Data Toolkit for a blank photocopiable version. Form 2D provides a similar chart for use with customizable stations; see also the About the Forms and Tools page at the beginning of this book for instructions on downloading printable copies of the forms.)

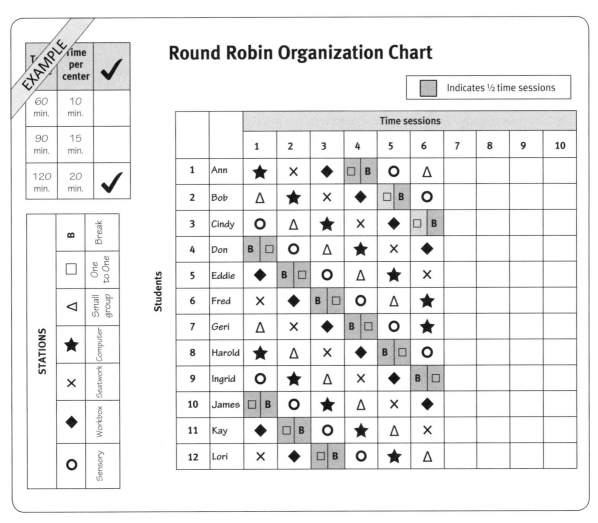

Figure 6.1. Round Robin Organization Chart (Example).

Instructions for using the Round Robin Organization Chart (Customizable Stations) are as follows:

1. Fill in the coding for the number of centers or stations you want. You could use shapes (as shown in Figure 6.1), colors, letters, or numbers. Be creative! You could even use tiny stickers that would help you organize stations for younger students.

2. Determine the total length of center time. Divide this number by the number of centers to get the amount of time per center. Fill this information in the box at the top left.

3. List the student names in the second column, next to the numerals.

4. Divide the students into the centers using the predetermined code.

5. If you want to divide a session in half, indicate that.

6. Give the students bookmark strips (see Form 3D: Round Robin Center Bookmarks, discussed later) so they can independently navigate the centers.

The Round Robin Organization Chart is certainly not required if you choose to use this type of classroom activity, but it will help organize both you and the students. It may seem cumbersome at first, but once it's set, the same schedule could be used with several different activities.

As noted, Figure 6.1 uses symbols and shapes to represent each station, center, or activity. You may decide to color-code the stations instead of using shapes. The Round Robin Organization Chart displays the order of stations or centers to visit for each student in the class and designates how long each student will be engaged with each activity. In Figure 6.1, the box in the top left corner indicates that station time is 2 hours, or 120 minutes, long. With each of the 12 students in the class rotating through six different stations, that averages out to be 20 minutes for each station. Notice that one session is split into two parts, giving each student one-to-one time with the teacher as well as a short break from activities, such as a bathroom or water break. This allows each student in the classroom to receive some one-to-one time with the teacher for data collection and individual assistance. (Note that this form includes more columns than stations to allow students to rotate through some stations a second time, depending on the number of stations you use and the time allotted for each activity.)

Once you have designed your round robin approach, you can get students actively involved in the process by giving them a bookmark or index card that lists the order of centers or stations they will visit. You might use colors, pictures, or fun shapes for the students that provide a map of where they will go during station time. If you have students who have more significant communication needs, try using picture symbols. Make sure to label the stations with the picture symbols to assist with independent navigation of the space.

Figure 6.2 shows the template that one teacher used to cut and create bookmarks for his students. The bookmarks indicated the order in which students should rotate through the round robin centers using the shapes from Figure 6.1. A blank photocopiable template for creating your own Round Robin Center Bookmarks is provided as Form 3D in Section IV: Your Classroom Data Toolkit; see also the About the Forms and Tools page at the beginning of this book for instructions on downloading a printable copy. Just fill out the template, and print it on cardstock. Then, cut the template at the places indicated, and hand a bookmark to each student prior to the station or center time. Make sure to label each of your round robin centers.

Another way to motivate the students is to give them stickers or stamps at each station. At the end of station time, they can trade their completed bookmarks for a dip in a treasure chest! Another cool way to engage the students would be to complete the bookmarks as passports around the world, with each station serving as a different country. After students receive their stamps from each country, they turn in their passports for a "vacation" (also known as a preferred activity break)!

Round Robin Center Bookmarks

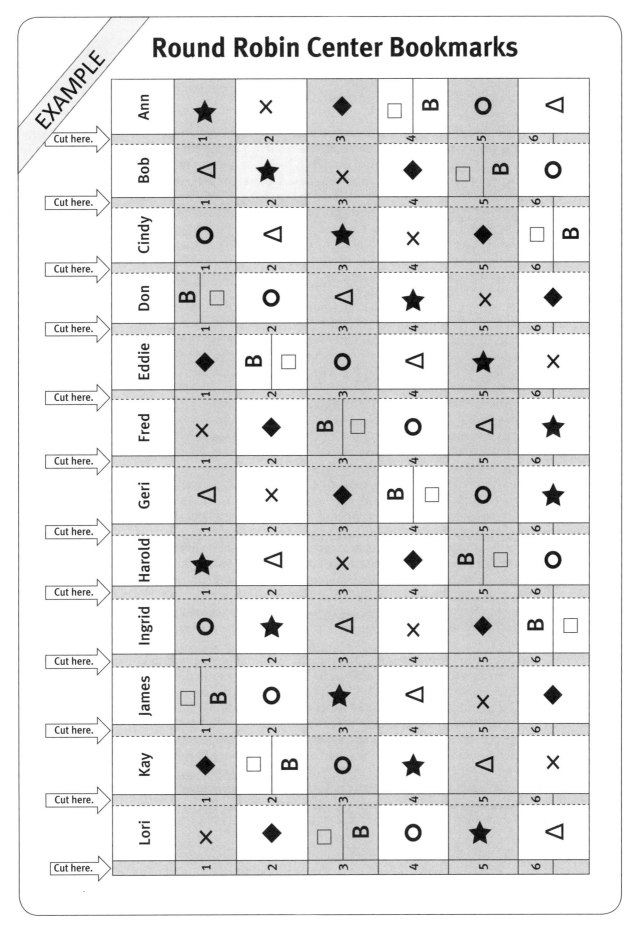

Figure 6.2. Round Robin Center Bookmarks (Example).

Cold Probes

Cold probe data is, in essence, data that indicate whether a student has mastered a task and is free from competing variables such as practice or reinforcement. This type of data is collected during the first trial of a task in order to get the most accurate sense of the student's performance level. By collecting data the first time the student performs the task, teachers get more precise data on whether the student has truly mastered the skill because the student has not had any practice time or received reinforcement for a specific response.

Think about it this way: A teacher takes data on basic sight words in reading. The student has been practicing the sight words for about 10 minutes as a group activity. The teacher pulls the student from the group during an individual data collection time and collects data on whether the student can orally read the group of flash cards. Do you think the student has had an advantage?

Now, consider this scenario: The same teacher has a list of the sight words on a data collection form. As the students enter the classroom in the morning, before the first teaching session (reading), the teacher calls each student to her desk. Using the flash cards, she assesses each student's ability to read the sight words. No teaching is involved—just assessing the ability to remember the words. Do you think this is a better measure of the students' ability to read the words?

Do you see how doing cold probe data collection may be a more precise way of collecting data on a student's true mastery of a skill? There are several ways teachers can conduct cold probes in a classroom. Consider how one teacher, Ms. Weeks, worked cold probe data collection into her busy classroom schedule:

Ms. Weeks is considered the data expert on her special education team. She is very organized with her paperwork and is consistent with her data collection procedures. She begins every morning with collecting cold probe data. Ms. Weeks has each student's goals listed on a cold probe goal sheet, and all are held on a clipboard. She has a colored dot at the top of each student's sheets to make for easy filing within her color-coded paperwork system. In the mornings, prior to beginning academic tasks, Ms. Weeks sets up a journal activity. While the class is journaling, she has each student come to her desk and quickly runs down the student's goals. This cold probe data collection only takes a few minutes each day. It is completed prior to beginning the review of skills and without including a teaching session or reinforcement for correct responses or skill practice. This shows Ms. Weeks if the students have truly mastered and retained the skill she is assessing.

Taking cold probe data is similar to taking yes/no data (see Chapter 3) because it simply involves indicating a yes/no answer to the question of whether a student has mastered the skill, as shown in Figure 6.3. Cold probe data can be collected for any subject area and can be used to assess a range of functional and academic skills. Figure 6.3 shows that Gabby demonstrated the ability to verbally rote count from 1 to 25.

This book provides several data sheets that would be helpful in the collection of cold probe data. There are a couple of ways to organize your cold probe data process. One way to organize cold probe data forms is to have one data sheet for similar goals. For example, you may have all of your classroom circle time goals on one sheet. Every student would be listed on that one sheet, and as you do circle time, you would run down the list, assessing each child on each goal. The downside to this method of cold probe data collection is that

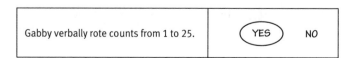

Figure 6.3. Simple cold probe data form.

for confidentiality reasons, you will not be able to file the sheets in individual student files because multiple student names are included on one sheet. To avoid having to transfer each student's data to a separate form, you might consider using a clipboard for circle time that holds a separate data sheet for each student's data. This way, the data sheets can be filed in individual student files.

This chapter introduces four Cold Probe Data Sheets. (Blank photocopiable versions are available as Forms 4D–7D in Section IV: Your Classroom Data Toolkit; see also the About the Forms and Tools page at the beginning of this book for instructions on downloading printable copies.) Cold Probe Data Sheet 1 is used to collect data on an individual student, and the other three data sheets are used for groups of students. Cold Probe Data Sheets 2 and 3 are daily sheets, and Cold Probe Data Sheet 4 can be used for up to 3 days of data collection. These four forms are structured and formatted in a slightly different way to give you options for collecting data.

Figure 6.4 is an example of Cold Probe Data Sheet 1 (Individual Student) completed for a first-grade student named Consuela. This form collects data on one student

EXAMPLE

Name: Consuela Cortez   School year: 2016–2017   Beginning date: 8/15/16

Subject area: Basic functional skills: Verbally give basic personal information

Criteria for mastery: 3 consecutive Y responses

Cold Probe Data Sheet 1 (Individual Student)   Page 1 of 1

Objective/task		8/15	8/16	8/17	8/18	8/22	8/24	8/25	9/2	9/3	9/4	9/5	9/9	9/13	Date mastered
1	Address	Y/N	Y/N	Y/N	Ⓨ/N	Ⓨ/N	Y/Ⓝ	Ⓨ/N	Ⓨ/N	Ⓨ/N	Y/N	Y/N	Y/N	Y/N	9/3/16
2	Full birthday	Y/Ⓝ	Y/Ⓝ	Ⓨ/N	Y/Ⓝ	Y/Ⓝ	Y/N	Y/N	Y/N	Y/N	Y/N	Y/N	Y/N	Y/N	9/2/16
3	Full name	Y/Ⓝ	Y/Ⓝ	Ⓨ/N	Y/Ⓝ	Y/Ⓝ	Ⓨ/N	Y/Ⓝ	Y/Ⓝ	Y/Ⓝ	Ⓨ/N	Y/Ⓝ	Ⓨ/N	Y/Ⓝ	
4	Phone number	Y/Ⓝ	Y/Ⓝ	Ⓨ/N	Y/Ⓝ	Y/Ⓝ	Y/Ⓝ	Ⓨ/N	Ⓨ/N	Y/Ⓝ	Y/Ⓝ	Y/N	Y/N	Y/N	9/13/16
5		Y/N	Y/N	Y/N	Y/N	Y/N	Y/N	Y/N	Y/N	Y/N	Y/N	Y/N	Y/N	Y/N	
6		Y/N	Y/N	Y/N	Y/N	Y/N	Y/N	Y/N	Y/N	Y/N	Y/N	Y/N	Y/N	Y/N	
7		Y/N	Y/N	Y/N	Y/N	Y/N	Y/N	Y/N	Y/N	Y/N	Y/N	Y/N	Y/N	Y/N	
8		Y/N	Y/N	Y/N	Y/N	Y/N	Y/N	Y/N	Y/N	Y/N	Y/N	Y/N	Y/N	Y/N	
9		Y/N	Y/N	Y/N	Y/N	Y/N	Y/N	Y/N	Y/N	Y/N	Y/N	Y/N	Y/N	Y/N	

Figure 6.4. Cold Probe Data Sheet 1 (Individual Student) (Example).

per sheet and provides space to write the subject area along with objectives or tasks. In this case, the subject area is basic functional skills. Consuela was initially assessed using the Brigance Inventory for Early Development III (Brigance & French, 2013). Within the Core Assessments—Academic/Cognitive domain, Consuela's inability to demonstrate knowledge of basic personal information was documented. This information included knowledge of first name, last name, age, and address. Because Consuela was unable to demonstrate mastery of these skills, the IEP committee used this information to develop her IEP goals. They also included the ability to verbally give her phone number as an additional objective because this skill would enhance her safety in the community. The individual objectives on her IEP include her knowledge of her address, full birthday, full name, and phone number.

There are two other students with similar IEP objectives in the classroom, so when assessing these functional skills for her students with IEPs, Consuela's teacher prints out a separate sheet for each student, places the sheets on the clipboard, and takes cold probe data on the skills in the morning before beginning academic subjects. For Consuela, mastery of this functional skill is documented on her IEP as "3 consecutive correct responses," captured by "3 consecutive Y responses" on the Cold Probe Data Sheet. As Figure 6.4 demonstrates, Consuela has achieved a mastery level on three of her objectives, as indicated by the horizontal line drawn through the three Ys for stating her address, full birthday, and phone number.

Figures 6.5, 6.6, and 6.7 are examples of completed classroomwide Cold Probe Data Sheets, another option in cold probe data collection. Cold Probe Data Sheets 2 and 3 are meant to be used daily. Cold Probe Data Sheet 2 (Daily—Multiple Students) (see Figure 6.5) lists students vertically, with each objective listed horizontally across the top of the form. Notice in Figure 6.5 how the teacher listed Annie, Billy, Consuela, and Dequan as the students, and listed the objectives being assessed across the top. The teacher simply circled Y or N based on whether each student was able to answer basic personal information questions. Notice that the mastery level for each student is "3 consecutive Y responses" marked on the form. Because this is a daily sheet, the teacher will have to compare different pages in order to note mastery level for an individual student on an individual goal. This form would probably not be suitable for IEP documentation but rather for follow-up monitoring of the class's continued mastery of skills and practice of the skills throughout the year.

Cold Probe Data Sheet 3 (Daily—Multiple Students) (see Figure 6.6) is very similar to Cold Probe Data Sheet 2 but is organized so that students are listed horizontally across the top and the goals are listed vertically on the left hand side of the form.

Finally, Cold Probe Data Sheet 4 (3 Days—Multiple Students) (see Figure 6.7) is used to collect cold probe data on multiple skills for multiple students for up to 3 days of data collection. If you take cold probe data 3 days per week, this form is convenient and could be used for the entire week. Another nice feature of this form is that there is space to document the number of "consecutive YES carry over" from the previous data form. In Figure 6.7, there are several students who met the mastery level of three consecutive Y responses, but their data spanned two separate sheets, a detail to keep in mind. In general, it is important to keep track of student progress and compare current and prior data sheets to see if mastery has been met. For example, if you choose to use a daily Cold Probe Data Sheet, you will need to keep track of prior sheets to track whether your students have met the mastery level for the skill (e.g., demonstrated the number of correct consecutive responses over time).

Management of Data Collection Materials and Paperwork

There are several ways to organize the paperwork involved in data collection. Regardless of your method, your organization system needs to be simple, neat and organized, easy

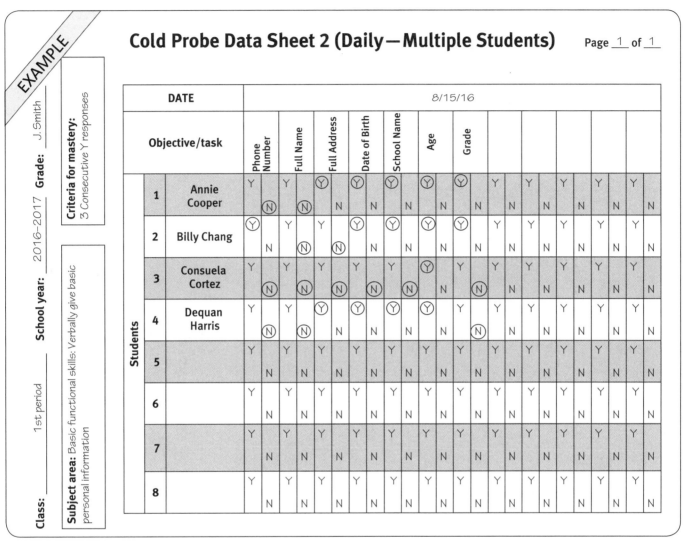

Cold Probe Data Sheet 2 (Daily—Multiple Students)   Page 1 of 1

EXAMPLE

Class: _____ 1st period   School year: 2016–2017   Grade: J. Smith

Criteria for mastery: 3 Consecutive Y responses

Subject area: Basic functional skills: Verbally give basic personal information

DATE		8/15/16												
Students / Objective/task		Phone Number	Full Name	Full Address	Date of Birth	School Name	Age	Grade						
1	Annie Cooper	Y / **Ⓝ**	Y / **Ⓝ**	**Ⓨ** / N	**Ⓨ** / N	**Ⓨ** / N	**Ⓨ** / N	**Ⓨ** / N	Y / N	Y / N	Y / N	Y / N	Y / N	N
2	Billy Chang	**Ⓨ** / N	Y / **Ⓝ**	Y / **Ⓝ**	**Ⓨ** / N	**Ⓨ** / N	**Ⓨ** / N	**Ⓨ** / N	Y / N	Y / N	Y / N	Y / N	Y / N	N
3	Consuela Cortez	Y / **Ⓝ**	Y / **Ⓝ**	Y / **Ⓝ**	Y / **Ⓝ**	Y / **Ⓝ**	**Ⓨ** / N	Y / **Ⓝ**	Y / N	Y / N	Y / N	Y / N	Y / N	N
4	Dequan Harris	Y / **Ⓝ**	Y / **Ⓝ**	**Ⓨ** / N	**Ⓨ** / N	**Ⓨ** / N	**Ⓨ** / N	Y / **Ⓝ**	Y / N	Y / N	Y / N	Y / N	Y / N	N
5		Y / N	Y / N	Y / N	Y / N	Y / N	Y / N	Y / N	Y / N	Y / N	Y / N	Y / N	Y / N	N
6		Y / N	Y / N	Y / N	Y / N	Y / N	Y / N	Y / N	Y / N	Y / N	Y / N	Y / N	Y / N	N
7		Y / N	Y / N	Y / N	Y / N	Y / N	Y / N	Y / N	Y / N	Y / N	Y / N	Y / N	Y / N	N
8		Y / N	Y / N	Y / N	Y / N	Y / N	Y / N	Y / N	Y / N	Y / N	Y / N	Y / N	Y / N	N

Figure 6.5. Cold Probe Data Sheet 2 (Daily—Multiple Students) (Example). In this version, the students are listed vertically.

to access, and easy to keep up with on a daily basis. This chapter discusses the following ways of managing the materials and paperwork involved in data collection:

1. Data crates
2. Data notebooks
3. Clipboards
4. Inexpensive and innovative storage ideas

Data Crates

Plastic crates with hanging file folders are great for holding all types of paperwork. You might have one crate per student that contains folders and materials that are required by the student's IEP goals or objectives. As the data sheets are completed, you can place them in the crates so that they can be filed. You might also file your data by subject or area.

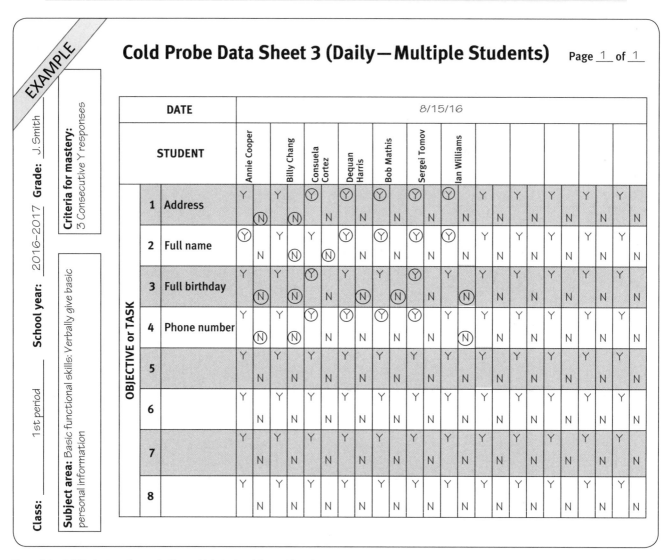

EXAMPLE

Class: _____   **School year:** _2016–2017_   **Grade:** _J. Smith_

Subject area: Basic functional skills: _Basic functional information_

Criteria for mastery: _3 Consecutive Y responses_

1st period

Cold Probe Data Sheet 3 (Daily—Multiple Students)   Page _1_ of _1_

DATE			8/15/16												
STUDENT		Annie Cooper	Billy Chang	Consuela Cortez	Dequan Harris	Bob Mathis	Sergei Tomov	Ian Williams							

OBJECTIVE or TASK

		Annie Cooper	Billy Chang	Consuela Cortez	Dequan Harris	Bob Mathis	Sergei Tomov	Ian Williams							
1	Address	Y / Ⓝ	Y / Ⓝ	Ⓨ / N	Ⓨ / N	Ⓨ / N	Ⓨ / N	Ⓨ / N	Y / N	Y / N	Y / N	Y / N	Y / N
2	Full name	Ⓨ / N	Y / N	Y / Ⓝ	Ⓨ / Ⓝ	Ⓨ / N	Ⓨ / N	Ⓨ / N	Y / N	Y / N	Y / N	Y / N	Y / N
3	Full birthday	Y / Ⓝ	Y / Ⓝ	Ⓨ / N	Y / Ⓝ	Y / Ⓝ	Ⓨ / N	Y / Ⓝ	Y / N	Y / N	Y / N	Y / N	Y / N
4	Phone number	Y / Ⓝ	Y / Ⓝ	Ⓨ / N	Ⓨ / N	Ⓨ / N	Ⓨ / N	Y / Ⓝ	Y / N	Y / N	Y / N	Y / N	Y / N
5		Y / N	Y / N	Y / N	Y / N	Y / N	Y / N	Y / N	Y / N	Y / N	Y / N	Y / N	Y / N
6		Y / N	Y / N	Y / N	Y / N	Y / N	Y / N	Y / N	Y / N	Y / N	Y / N	Y / N	Y / N
7		Y / N	Y / N	Y / N	Y / N	Y / N	Y / N	Y / N	Y / N	Y / N	Y / N	Y / N	Y / N
8		Y / N	Y / N	Y / N	Y / N	Y / N	Y / N	Y / N	Y / N	Y / N	Y / N	Y / N	Y / N

Figure 6.6.   Cold Probe Data Sheet 3 (Daily—Multiple Students) (Example). In this version, students are listed horizontally.

Data Notebooks

Consider creating data notebooks for each of your students and housing them in a data-keeping area of the room with your other data materials. Be sure the notebooks and other materials are secure for confidentiality purposes. If each of the data forms you complete for a student is filed immediately, you will be organized and able to carry the information with you to any of your IEP or RTI meetings. Appendix A includes a data collection notebook cover page that you can use for your student data notebooks.

Besides your graphs and data sheets, it is also important to keep analyzed work samples in your students' data notebooks. These are permanent products and documentation of student progress. Consider the following scenario, which demonstrates how important the analysis of work samples is to the student's data:

Mr. Lee, a second-grade teacher, was asked for some work samples from a student named Levon, who was struggling academically. The student was undergoing an academic evaluation to determine if he should be referred for eligibility for a special education program. The psychologist

EXAMPLE

Cold Probe Data Sheet 4 (3 Days—Multiple Students) Page 2 of 2

Class: 1st Period   School Year: 16–17   Data Taken by: J. Smith

Subject Area: Basic Functional Skills: Verbally give basic personal information

Criteria for Mastery: 3 consecutive Y responses

You may have more than 1 data sheet – good way to number

Student	Task/Objectives	# consec	Full Name 8/15	8/16	8/17	# consec	Phone Number 8/15	8/16	8/17	# consec	Date of Birth 8/15	8/16	8/17
1	Annie Cooper	2	(Y) / N	Y / N	Y / N	1	(Y) / N	(Y) / N	Y / N	1	(Y) / N	(Y) / N	Y / N
2	Billy Chang	2	(Y) / N	Y / N	Y / N	0	(Y) / N	Y / N	(Y) / (N)	0	(Y) / N	(Y) / N	Y / N
3	Consuela Cortez	1	Y / (N)	(Y) / N	(Y) / N	2	(Y) / N	Y / N	Y / N	1	Y / (N)	(Y) / N	Y / (N)
4	Dequan Harris	0	(Y) / N	(Y) / N	(Y) / N	0	Y / (N)	Y / (N)	Y / (N)	0	(Y) / N	Y / (N)	(Y) / N
5			Y / N	Y / N	Y / N		Y / N	Y / N	Y / N		Y / N	Y / N	Y / N
6			Y / N	Y / N	Y / N		Y / N	Y / N	Y / N		Y / N	Y / N	Y / N
7			Y / N	Y / N	Y / N		Y / N	Y / N	Y / N		Y / N	Y / N	Y / N
8			Y / N	Y / N	Y / N		Y / N	Y / N	Y / N		Y / N	Y / N	Y / N

Figure 6.7. Cold Probe Data Sheet 4 (3 Days—Multiple Students) (Example).

needed a few samples of the student's work in order to determine current functioning. Mr. Lee gathered a few samples and turned them in, along with a list of the student's current grades. In reviewing the samples, the psychologist was not able to determine exactly how the student was functioning in the classroom because the samples lacked information. Mr. Lee was confused because at least one of the samples had a grade on it. Wasn't that enough of an analysis?

To answer Mr. Lee's question, no! A grade on a paper is not an analysis of academic performance. Look at two of the work samples Mr. Lee submitted, shown in Figures 6.8 and Figure 6.9.

Figure 6.8 shows a math worksheet. It is great that the paper is scored for accuracy, but using a critical eye, you will notice that a few questions might come up when analyzing this work sample:

- What is the date of completion?

- Did Levon complete this assignment independently—without any help or prompts?

- Did Levon complete this assignment on the first try or tear up 14 papers before this one?

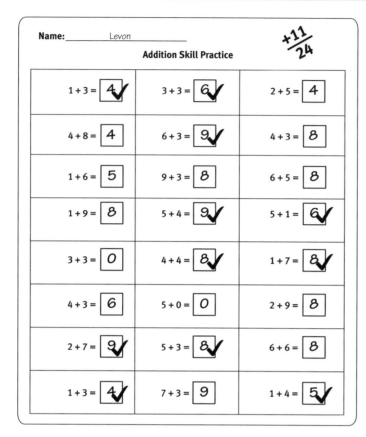

Figure 6.8. Levon's work sample for math.

Figure 6.9. Levon's work sample for spelling.

- Was this a homework assignment, where parents may have helped out?

- Was this assignment completed as a group with someone writing problems on the board and the class copying the answers?

- Were there manipulatives involved?

- Was the assignment timed, or did Levon take 1 hour and 35 minutes to complete the 24 problems?

- Was this an initial assignment in this area, or had Levon been working on this type of task for the last 2 weeks?

I could think of about 10 more questions to ask! Do you see how a grade is not an analysis? This permanent product is vital to determining current functioning in the classroom.

The work sample in Figure 6.9, the spelling test, lacks even more information.

1. There is no date. Was this test completed 3 months ago or last week?

2. There is no grade. I, for one, do not know if Numbers 5 and 9 are correct or not. It's not clear what words Levon was supposed to spell. Number 5 could be *hose* or *house* or even *horse*! Number 9 could have been *stare* or it could have been *star*! Who knows?

3. Was this test independently completed? Or was there hand-over-hand assistance? Verbal prompts?

4. Did the student take the test after studying these words for a week or a few months?

The point is clear: Analysis is important. Yet, analysis can be time consuming. If you do not analyze work samples immediately after the work is finished, you will not remember how the assignment was completed. But I have an answer to this dilemma!

A quick and easy way to analyze work samples or permanent products is to use Work Sample Analysis Stickers, which can be created using the template (Form 8D) and related instructions found in Section IV: Your Classroom Data Toolkit (see also the About the Forms and Tools page at the beginning of this book). The *Special Educator's Toolkit: Everything You Need to Organize, Manage, and Monitor Your Classroom* (Golden, 2012) discussed how student work samples are typically analyzed in two ways: the level of accuracy and the accommodations that were needed to complete the task. Simply indicating the percentage correct on the work sample does not reveal how the student carried out the task or the supports that were required to successfully complete the work.

Work Sample Analysis Stickers allow teachers to quickly record a number of helpful details about the work sample, including the level of prompting required to complete the work, whether multiple attempts or extended time were required, or whether the student had any behavioral issues. The teacher can also record the IEP goal or objective and the percentage correct.

Figure 6.10 shows Levon's math worksheet, this time analyzed with a Work Sample Analysis Sticker. Far more information can be gleaned from this permanent product. For example, Levon needed verbal prompts and extended time to complete the worksheet. You will also notice that this assignment is an IEP-driven task based on an IEP goal. Based on this information, the IEP team could refer back to the IEP goal to monitor progress. For Levon, the final mastery for his IEP goal was to independently complete the math worksheet in Figure 6.8 with no prompts. If, at the beginning of the year, Levon required a full physical (hand-over-hand) prompt to complete 11 of the problems, and now only verbal prompting is required, then you can certainly see that progress has been made—even with only a 46% accuracy level! Without this Work Sample Analysis Sticker, you would not have known this information.

Remember to print the Work Sample Analysis Stickers on mailing label paper so that you can easily write on them, pull them off, and stick them on the work sample. Instant analysis!

Clipboards

Clipboards are a staple in any classroom. You can house data sheets on the clipboards by student, by subject area, or by classroom. Keep the data confidential by placing colored paper on top, which also helps to color-code the clipboard (see Figure 6.11). If you are not the clipboard type, then use old-fashioned colored pocket folders (see Figure 6.12).

Inexpensive and Innovative Storage Ideas

Here are a few inexpensive, creative ideas for organizing paperwork:

- Save a couple (or more!) of heavy-duty boxes. Tape them together, and cover them with stiff felt and duct tape (see Figure 6.13). (These can be color-coded, also.) This makes a great place to hold papers or files, and it is very inexpensive! The felt on the outside allows the boxes to be used with Velcro for visuals.

- Recycle cereal boxes or any similar type of boxes by cutting as shown in Figure 6.14, painting them the color you need, and putting them on a shelf. You can label the bottom, front, or side.

- Do you sew or know someone who does? If so, there is an easy way to make paper or file holders that will hold up forever! Collect some vinyl placemats. Get as many as

Name: _____Levon_____

Addition Skill Practice

1 + 3 = **4** ✓	3 + 3 = **6** ✓	2 + 5 = **4**
4 + 8 = **4**	6 + 3 = **9** ✓	4 + 3 = **8**
1 + 6 = **5**	9 + 3 = **8**	6 + 5 = **8**
1 + 9 = **8**	5 + 4 = **9** ✓	5 + 1 = **6** ✓
3 + 3 = **0**	4 + 4 = **8** ✓	1 + 7 = **8** ✓
4 + 3 = **6**	5 + 0 = **0**	2 + 9 = **8**
2 + 7 = **9** ✓	5 + 3 = **8** ✓	6 + 6 = **8**
1 + 3 = **4** ✓	7 + 3 = **9**	1 + 4 = **5** ✓

WORK SAMPLE ANALYSIS		Date: March 9, 2016	
Prompt level	✓	**Additional analysis**	✓
Independent		Multiple attempts	
Verbal	✓	Extended time	✓
Gesture		Behavioral issues	
Modeling			
Partial physical		**IEP goal/objective**	✓
Full physical		**Percentage correct**	46%

Figure 6.10. Levon's work sample analysis. (Analysis included as sticker.)

Figure 6.11. Clipboards used for organizing a data collection system.

Figure 6.12. Pocket folders used for organizing a data collection system.

Figure 6.13. Heavy-duty boxes used for organizing a data collection system.

Figure 6.14. Cereal boxes used for organizing a data collection system.

Figure 6.15. Placemats used for organizing a data collection system.

you want, lay them on top of each other as shown in Figure 6.15, and sew up the sides and the bottom. Place a Velcro strip at the top to affix the file holder in the room as desired for storing data sheets.

REVIEW OF THE FACTS AND A PEEK AHEAD

Collecting data in the classroom is one task that is necessary if you want to create an environment that promotes academic and behavioral success. It can also be a tedious, stressful task if you do not have an organized plan in place to bring order to all the paperwork that will surely come with the task. There are so many simple yet very effective ways to bring order and organization to the process while collecting top-notch data that is easily analyzed. This chapter provided you with many tips for setting up a systematic way of scheduling, organizing, and managing the data collection process in the classroom. These tips included using self-graphing data sheets, data collection schedules, round robin and cold probe data collection methods, Work Sample Analysis Stickers, and data crates. From the tips, tricks, and information provided in this chapter, glean what is pertinent to your own setting, and implement the methods to create your own highly effective, low-stress data collection system.

QUICK QUIZ

1. This term is used to describe the collection of data from the first trial of a task.
   a. First trial data
   b. Cold probe
   c. Maintenance data

2. In order for work samples to be helpful, they should be analyzed.
   a. True
   b. False

3. Raw data are easier to analyze if graphed and put into a visual format.
   a. True
   b. False

4. Which of the following can be used as a method for the collection of data in the classroom?
   a. Cold probes
   b. Stations or centers
   c. Round robin data collection
   d. All of the above

5. What type of data sheet provides an easy way to quickly analyze raw data as you record it?
   a. Longitudinal data sheets
   b. X-axis data sheets
   c. Self-graphing data sheets

Data Analysis and Follow-Up

Data are not valuable unless they are put into an easy-to-understand visual format, analyzed, and used to inform educational decisions. This section of the book will teach you the skills you need to analyze data. First, it will explain how to visually graph your data, recognize patterns and trends, and interpret the data (Chapter 7). Once you are confident in interpreting your data, you will be better able to explain the data to parents or other education team members, with the goal of making decisions that will best help your students (Chapter 8).

CHAPTER 7

Analyzing Data

 MISSION: Understand how to analyze collected data

QUESTIONS TO INVESTIGATE

- What does it mean to analyze data?
- How do I analyze the data I have collected?

DEFINITIONS OF TERMS AND ABBREVIATIONS

Causal link   A link that is found to exist between the antecedent and the behavior (Cooper, Heron, & Heward, 2007).

Control group   A group or variable that remains constant and is not intervened with, so it can be used for comparison purposes.

Correlation   A connection or relationship.

Dependent variable   The variable that changes due to implementation of an intervention (e.g., reading scores are dependent variables because they will possibly change with the implementation of a different teaching method).

Independent variable   The variable that is manipulated or tested in a study (e.g., a teaching method or intervention is an independent variable because it is being tested for its success in changing reading scores).

Raw data   Data that have been collected but not yet put into a graphical format and analyzed.

Trendline   Line within a graphical depiction of data that indicates the course of the data. It can be increasing (moving up), decreasing (moving down), or zero (flat).

Variability   The spread of the data from data point to data point.

As you begin the journey into data analysis, think about this. Have you ever been involved in something or even in charge of doing something that you did not understand? It is like walking around in a dark room. You grope, stumble, and attempt to feel your way through what's ahead, unsure of what obstacles you'll bump into, what might trip you up, or where you are going. You try to pretend you have control of the situation, but you really do not.

This chapter shines some light on the process of data analysis by providing the tools, tips, and foundational knowledge you need to find your footing and feel more in control. The chapter concentrates on how to analyze the data that have been collected, how to create a graphical representation of the data, how to explain the data summary, and what to do next. By the end of the chapter, you will no longer feel in the dark when it comes to analyzing data!

Why is analyzing your data important? The following Eyewitness Account provides a firsthand perspective of what can happen when you don't know how to interpret, present, or summarize the data you collect in your classroom.

 Eyewitness Account

As an inclusion teacher at a local elementary school, I teach many students with IEPs who are faced with a variety of challenges. Each of the students is included on a full-day basis in a general education classroom. I am the inclusion coteacher in several classrooms and grade levels during the day, and I travel to meet the needs of my students. Each student's IEP requires data to be kept, and for the most part, I have a successful method of getting the data collected. What I struggle with is what to do next with all the mounds of data that I have on hand.

During the last IEP meeting for one of my students, the team asked me to summarize and analyze the data. In other words, what does the data really mean? I was unable to do so. I could only say that the data were collected, and they seemed to show progress. There were some very specific questions posed of me about the trendline and levels of functioning, and I was unable to answer any of them. I was uncomfortable and embarrassed. The IEP meeting was tabled, and it was decided that the meeting would reconvene when a more definitive analysis could be presented.

—Ms. Flores,
Elementary School Inclusion Teacher

This case is not unusual. In fact, I have been in IEP meetings just like this one, but legal representatives were involved. This is not an easy situation. Ms. Flores needs to be applauded for having data for her students, but in reality, data that are not analyzed are not useful and do not serve a purpose. Not analyzing your data is like collecting all of the pieces to a puzzle, turning them over on a board, and sitting there looking at them. What good is it to have the pieces if you cannot see the completed picture?

Remember the five steps for collecting data in the classroom: define target, select method, implement collection, analyze and graph, and make decisions (see Figure 1.1). You have finally made it to the last two steps! This chapter focuses on how to analyze and graph the data collected; Chapter 8 discusses how to make decisions through data analysis.

WHAT DOES IT MEAN TO ANALYZE DATA?

Have you ever been to an IEP meeting, or any type of meeting to discuss data, and not understood what was presented? Have you ever had to explain progress using the data you collected and felt as if you could not do it justice? Believe me, all teachers have been there.

Data are important in making decisions about the next steps to take in moving students forward, so teachers collect data. They prepare data forms, develop data collection procedures, provide training, and store the data. However, unless they use forms that automatically create a visual summary of the data, teachers will spend several hours pulling together the raw data so that a layperson can understand.

Remember the definition of *analysis* from Chapter 1: the examination and interpretation of data. When solving a case, a detective will find links or connections between the information that he or she collects. The process of analyzing academic or behavioral data is to look for trends, patterns, or relationships among the variables. You will compare the data values to each other to determine the variability of the data. You will also compare the data to a benchmark, which may be the baseline data taken prior to implementation of an intervention or some other standard. These processes are thoroughly explained in this chapter.

HOW DO I ANALYZE THE DATA I HAVE COLLECTED?

Remember that the act of data collection is best when worked backward—meaning that you begin with the end in mind. Think about the question or problem, and determine the strategy you need to put in place to answer that question or solve that problem. In order to bring structure and organization to the process of analyzing your data, think about the steps to data analysis as an acronym. The acronym *COVERT* goes with the detective theme because the act of collecting data, analyzing data, and intervening based on data is many times a covert operation; it does not interfere with the outcome.

1. *C*ollect the data.

2. *O*rganize the data.

3. *V*isually graph the data.

4. *E*xamine and compare the data to baseline and mastery standards.

5. *R*eview the data, looking for trends or patterns.

6. *T*est out interventions while continuing to collect data.

Step 1: Collect the Data

The first step is to actually collect the data. If you use the Quick-Graphs provided for you in Section IV: Your Classroom Data Toolkit, then you will have an instant way of visually analyzing the data in order to make decisions about how much data you need. There is no one rule for how many data points to collect, but typically the more data you have, the easier it is to determine patterns. As an example of how the number of data points affects analysis, look at Figure 7.1, which depicts a baseline graph with two data points.

Looking at the graph in Figure 7.1, can you project a pattern or trend? If so, can you determine if the data trend is increasing, decreasing, or remaining constant? It is pretty difficult to determine an answer with just two data points, isn't it? If you are leaning toward being thankful that your baseline data is now finished and you have determined that the trendline is increasing, think again. You do not have enough data.

Imagine that you were to add just one more data point to the graph. Figure 7.2, a baseline graph with three data points, indicates the many ways the trend might change. Do you see how just one more data point could go anywhere? You could have been right about the increasing trend, or maybe not. Perhaps that second data point was just a blip in the data.

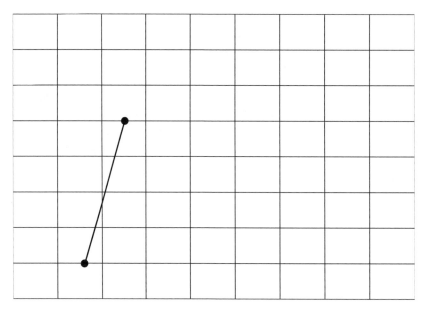

Figure 7.1. Baseline graph with two data points.

So, how many data points should you have in order to establish a baseline? Again, there is no definitive rule. You have to constantly look at the data to determine the answer. Just remember that you need enough data to establish a stable trend.

Step 2: Organize the Data

Have you ever watched a crime show where detectives or investigators go into a crime scene and gather evidence? They place the material in individual bags and use a coding system. It is extremely important to treat raw data with the same respect. Keep the data organized and in order.

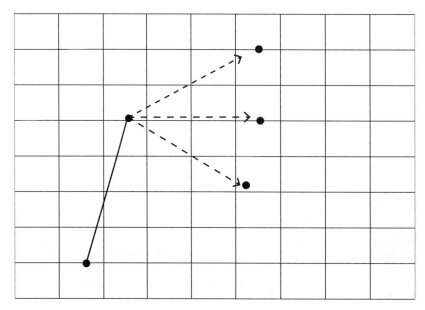

Figure 7.2. Baseline graph with three data points.

Organizing the data is simple when you use a data collection system as outlined in Chapter 6. You may choose to use crates to store your data forms after they are completed and pulled from the clipboards. Or you may choose to put your data in individual notebooks organized by student or in files. Regardless of the method, it will be much easier to organize your data if you already have an established system. If you do not, there is still hope!

I have gone into many classrooms and organized data chaos, so I know it is difficult. Here are my top three tips for data organization:

1. Gather the completed forms, and number each page using the "Page 1 of___" format (e.g., Page 1 of 5). This may seem simple, but it is important to know the total number of data sheets you have. Did you find 14 data sheets? Is that all you had? You may have forgotten about the other 30 sheets that are in a stack somewhere in the classroom closet! These missing data sheets could reveal very important information.

2. Make sure the data sheets are dated. When analyzing collected data, it is important to have an accurate timeline.

3. Put the sheets into a booklet or notebook so that you can flip through the pages as you analyze the data. Imagine trying to shuffle through 30 pages of data from a file folder. Putting data sheets in a notebook may sound like a waste of time, but it is much faster and more efficient to flip through pages and pages of data when they are neatly secured in a notebook rather than scattered or loose.

Step 3: Visually Graph the Data

Do not skip over this essential step! Graphing the raw data puts the information into a format that can be easily interpreted. Consider the analogy of baking a cake. Suppose you put all the ingredients on the counter, but you stop there. You never put them into a bowl and never mix them together to pour in a pan to bake. You just have the raw ingredients, which are unpalatable, if not inedible. Raw data that have not been graphed and analyzed are just as hard to digest and understand.

One of the ways I like to describe the graphical depiction of raw data is painting a picture of student progress. There are two basic types of graphs used with data collected in the classroom: bar graphs and line graphs. These graphs are used for different reasons.

Bar Graphs

Bar graphs are usually used when the data values are not connected to each other. A bar graph would be appropriate if you are using one data sheet for a classroom with several students or if you are collecting data for different goals or areas of assessment. The data values are separate entities, and there is no reason to see the connective progress between students or goals. Figure 7.3 uses a bar graph to present yes/no data for a student's mastery of sight words.

Do you need to know the connection between the yes/no responses or between the different sight words? Probably not. You just want to glance at this sheet and instantly see how many yes and no responses there are, instead of having to count them. Based on the simple bar graphs, you can see that for four out of five objectives, the yeses outnumber the nos. This student is mastering goals!

Line Graphs

Line graphs are typically used when the data are connected and you want to show changes to a behavior or skill over time. On a line graph, each data point is connected by a line, and the line is only broken when an intervention is implemented. When an intervention is implemented, a dotted or dashed vertical line is drawn to indicate when it began. The

EXAMPLE Objective/task: Recognition of third-grade Dolch sight words		Date											Total count of yes/no by objective										
		8/15	8/16	8/17	8/18	8/22	8/24	8/25	9/2	9/3	9/4		1	2	3	4	5	6	7	8	9	10
1	About	(Y)	Y	Y	(Y)	(Y)	(Y)	Y	(Y)	(Y)	(Y)	Y										
		N	(N)	(N)	N	N	N	(N)	N	N	N	N										
2	Better	Y	Y	Y	(Y)	Y	Y	Y	Y	(Y)	(Y)	Y										
		(N)	(N)	(N)	N	(N)	(N)	(N)	(N)	N	N	N										
3	Bring	Y	Y	Y	Y	(Y)	(Y)	(Y)	(Y)	(Y)	(Y)	Y										
		(N)	(N)	(N)	(N)	N	N	N	N	N	N	N										
4	Carry	Y	Y	Y	Y	(Y)	(Y)	(Y)	(Y)	(Y)	(Y)	Y										
		(N)	(N)	(N)	(N)	N	N	N	N	N	N	N										
5	Clean	Y	(Y)	(Y)	Y	(Y)	(Y)	Y	(Y)	(Y)	(Y)	Y										
		(N)	N	N	(N)	N	N	(N)	N	N	N	N										

Bar graphs of data summaries

Figure 7.3. Bar graph example.

new data are then connected to each other after that date. Line graphs create an easy-to-understand visual story of student progress and the impact the intervention is having on that progress. See Figure 7.4 for an example.

Notice the connection between the data points. The behavior for which the frequency data are being kept is "talking out or yelling out in class." The data points are connected to show the movement of behavior across days. The first three data points indicate a steady increase in the frequency of this behavior, with a small decline on Day 4. Days 5 and 6 show an additional increase in the frequency of the inappropriate behavior.

The teacher needed to put an intervention into place due to the significance of the behavior. The intervention began and was documented with a vertical dashed line. There is no connection between data points pre- and postintervention because a new variable was introduced. Data points after the intervention is implemented are connected.

This graph shows a sharp increase in the behavior right after the intervention was implemented, which is common with the implementation of a new variable. After this spike, the frequency began to decrease, showing that the intervention had a positive impact on the behavior. The behavior then continued to decrease.

You will determine which type of graph is better suited for the type of data you are collecting. Figure 7.5 illustrates a type of blank graph that can be used to collect data. You can add this photocopiable form to your data collection notebook to help you conduct student observations; see also the About the Forms and Tools page at the beginning of this book for instructions on downloading a printable copy. This template is useful for creating either line or bar graphs. If you use one of the Quick-Graphs provided for you in Section IV: Your Classroom Data Toolkit, your data will automatically be presented as a graph.

Step 4: Examine and Compare the Data to Baseline and Mastery Standards

Remember that analysis of data is not a one-time event. It is ongoing and begins at the first data point. In order to measure progress, you need to have a benchmark (Keller-Margulis, Mercer, & Shapiro, 2014). A benchmark establishes a ground zero. How do you know if you have made progress if you do not know where you started?

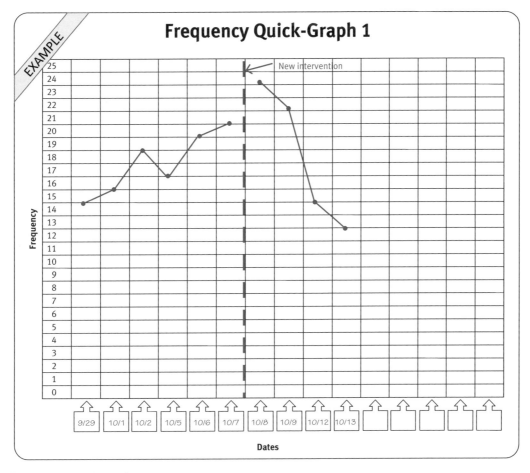

Figure 7.4. Line graph example.

To establish this benchmark, you might need to gather baseline data. Once you gather this baseline information, you may even determine that the issue was not as significant as you first thought, and you may decide not to proceed with the intervention. Or you may determine that the student needs further support, and you will be able to use your baseline as a helpful point of comparison to see if an intervention is working or progress is being made.

Depending on which type of data you collected, the benchmark can differ. There are five types of benchmarks:

1. Baseline data

2. Mastery level set by IEP team

3. A control

3. Standardized assessment mastery standards

4. Social level of mastery deemed appropriate for age level

5. Last documented functioning level in order to show progress

Baseline Data

If you choose baseline data to make your comparison, then you will collect data in preparation for implementing an initial intervention. After you implement the first intervention,

Line or Bar Graph of Data

Page ___ of ___

Name: _____

School year: _____

Grade: _____

_____ :

Figure 7.5. Line or Bar Graph of Data.

then you can begin to compare subsequent data to the baseline. It is like stepping onto the scale prior to going on a diet. Your diet is your intervention, and you first want to see where you are with your weight so you can track exactly how much progress you make after you change your eating habits.

Mastery Level Determined by the IEP Team

Sometimes the term *baseline* is given to the level at which a student is functioning on a particular IEP goal coming into an IEP meeting. The IEP team may ask about the student's baseline level for a goal in order to determine where to set the mastery level. If the student is coming into the IEP meeting functioning at 55% on a certain goal but the mastery level was previously set at 90%, the team may consider the 55% baseline and then choose to reduce the mastery level to one that is more accessible within a year. The 55% may be taken as the baseline, or the student's current functioning may be reassessed and then a comparison can be made to the mastery level indicated on the IEP.

Control

A control is a group or variable that remains constant and is not intervened with, so it can be used for comparison purposes (Gay, Mills, & Airasian, 2015). No intervention is given to the control group. If all other variables are accounted for, then a comparison to the control group will show the influence of the intervention.

A word about using a control group in education: Are you going to withhold something from a group of students or an individual student that you know may be beneficial in order to have a control group for comparison reasons? Of course not! Sometimes I would go into a classroom and observe the student in question while also observing a typical peer in order to make comparisons. I have also compared the student in question to the overall group by making statements such as, "Eddie has displayed 6 verbal callouts within the last 10 minutes as compared to the control student, who has displayed 0 within that time." Or, "Within the last 15 minutes, 2 out of 28 students have appeared to be off task, and Eddie is one of those 2 students." This is using a loosely defined control group for comparison purposes. Do you see how it creates a picture of what is going on in the classroom?

As an alternative, consider if all 28 of the control group students in the room were off-task during that time. Eddie's being off-task may not be due to his own issues but rather a case of poor classroom management.

Standardized Assessment Mastery Standards

Standard assessments come with built-in levels of mastery. If you are using these standardized assessments as tools to measure academic progress, you can easily make comparisons to a standard. The same holds true when comparing progress on functioning levels. The student has or has not increased his or her ability to do the particular task since the last assessment.

Social Level of Mastery Deemed Appropriate for Age Level

When collecting data in the area of social skills, you may want to measure a skill by what is deemed appropriate for the age level of the student. The most reliable way to determine what is appropriate for the age of the child is to compare to the typical developmental milestones. Developmental milestones are lists of behaviors or skills that should generally occur at certain age levels and can be found in places such as the Centers for Disease Control and Prevention (2016).

Prosocial skills can also be found on skill tracking systems such as The Assessment of Basic Language and Learning Skills–Revised (ABLLS-R) developed by Dr. James W. Partington (2006). This assessment tool contains lists of skills such as use of receptive language, labeling, syntax/grammar, play/leisure skills, and social interaction. It would certainly provide a list of positive social skills that are appropriate for development, such as sharing, returning greetings, or waiting for a break in conversation before interrupting. These are skills that you would want to see increase in students.

If the student's behavior is one that is socially unacceptable, then mastery is set as close to zero as possible. For instance, if the goal is to decrease the rate of self-injury or aggression toward another person, you would likely use zero as a mastery level for comparison purposes. Yes, you can certainly compare the rate of these types of behaviors to current functioning to show progress, but the behavior should be at zero. Even one incident of physical aggression is too many.

Last Documented Functioning Level in Order to Show Progress

This benchmark involves simply comparing the student's last documented level of functioning to how he or she is performing or functioning now. This way, you can see if any progress has been made since the student was last assessed.

Step 5: Review the Data, Looking for Trends or Patterns

You have summarized and graphed the data, so you now have a visual representation. You also have one of the following to determine progress: the baseline functioning coming into an IEP meeting, baseline data because you are implementing an intervention and want to make comparisons, a standard of expected mastery outlined by a standardized assessment or standard peer group, a standard of expected mastery as outlined by what is not acceptable (i.e., aggression), or how the student is currently doing in relation to his or her last documented functioning level (i.e., behavior).

Now, you are going to begin looking at trends, patterns, and relationships between variables. Looking back at the terms defined at the beginning of this chapter, you will notice that *correlation* does not mean *causation*. It indicates a relationship. Consider the following example:

Through examining the data, it appears that Nicole struggles with math assignments. All of the assignments are workbook tasks, and this is the only time during the day that Nicole uses a pencil; therefore, using a pencil is causing her math difficulty, so we suggest that she switch to using a pen in math class.

This is an obvious example of why it doesn't make sense to assume causation when looking at data. Yes, Nicole may be using her pencil during all of her workbook tasks, but clearly it is not logical to conclude that the pencil is the culprit in her math struggles. Still, the data could be used to try to prove that theory. This is an extreme example of how data can be misinterpreted, but it shows the fallacy of assuming causation rather than relationship when using data to interpret what is going on in the classroom.

Consider another example:

Through the analysis of Derrick's data, it appears that there is a relationship or correlation between Derrick's aggression and the lunchroom where the school serves food. There is a strong smell of food in that setting. Therefore, the committee concludes that the smell of food is causing his aggression, so Derrick should eat in the classroom with a mask over his nose.

This instance again illustrates how assuming causation isn't a sensible, practical, or effective way to interpret data and may even be contrary to the best interests of the student. You can perhaps determine a relationship between the lunchroom and Derrick's challenging behavior—but not causation. The point is that you should not analyze data to determine the cause of a problem but to determine appropriate interventions and investigate the impact they have on the behavior or issue.

Figure 7.6. Data-analysis checklist.

So, how should data be analyzed? There are formal, statistical ways to analyze data (O'Reilly, Dogra, & Ronzoni, 2013). You can run statistical formulas using computer-based programs in order to make comparisons between variables. It will provide you with a good amount of information, but if you are not a statistician, the results may be difficult to understand and explain. This book discusses simpler ways to analyze the data that involve common sense in addition to a few structured steps. Figure 7.6 summarizes this process in a concise visual checklist.

The steps to data analysis include determining levels, variability, patterns, and trends.

Levels

When looking at your graphed data, Step 1 is to determine the level of functioning. A visual example of how to do this is provided in Figure 7.7.

There are several ways to describe where the data points lie on the graph, but it is easiest to divide the graph into thirds and describe the levels as high, moderate, and low. Figure 7.7 shows the percentage of the school day that Alex exhibited noncompliant, physically aggressive behaviors. You can add the level to your analysis and explanation by determining at what level the data points lie. For instance, you might describe the data presented in Figure 7.7 like this: "The graphed baseline data for noncompliant, physically aggressive behavior shows that the percentage of the day Alex is exhibiting noncompliant behaviors appears to be at a low level."

Showing the level of the data tends to set the foundation for analysis. Now you know where Alex's behaviors lie compared to 100% of the time, and even though they are difficult behaviors to deal with, they may not be as bad as first thought.

Variability

Another part of your data analysis will be to determine variability. Variability refers to the spread of the data from data point to data point. Are the data consistent and stable or extremely variable? One of the most common ways to describe variability is range. The range is the difference between the largest and the smallest value of data points. For instance, look at the frequency data in Figure 7.8.

The variability of these data is considerable; the data look to be quite unstable, but there is a simple way to determine the range and provide statistical evidence to support that claim. First, list the data point values from the graph, like this:

6, 4, 7, 4, 5, 5, 13, 23, 12, 14, 3, 18, 6

Next, look at the values, and circle the largest and the smallest (see Figure 7.9).

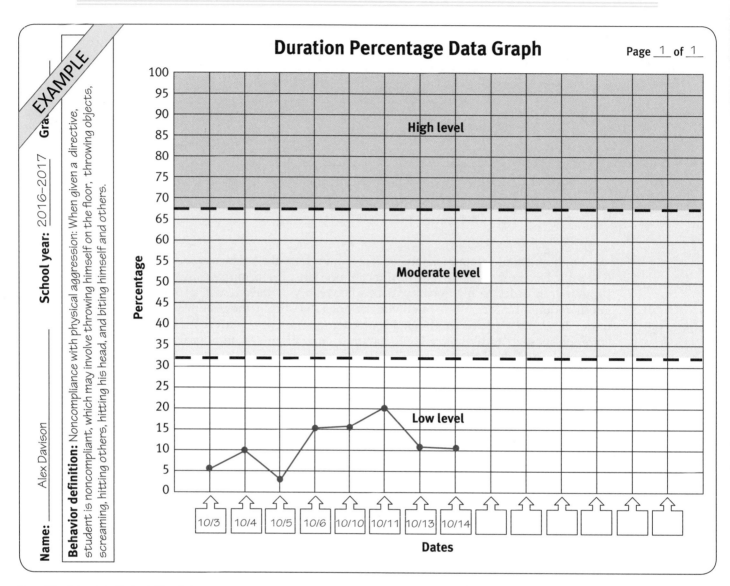

Name: Alex Davison

School year: 2016–2017

Behavior definition: Noncompliance with physical aggression: When given a directive, student is noncompliant, which may involve throwing himself on the floor, throwing objects, screaming, hitting others, hitting his head, and biting himself and others.

Figure 7.7. Determining the level of functioning.

These data points, or values, span the range from 3 to 23, so the range (the difference between them) is 20 points. To describe the range, you would say: "The graphed baseline data for noncompliant behavior shows the distribution of frequency data to be between 3 and 23 times a day, with a range of 20, which, visually analyzed, appears to be quite variable and not very consistent or stable."

This is certainly not a statistical description of the variance of data, but it is a layman's description of the data using the range as a measure of variance or variability. For an even more precise way to determine variability, consider the following steps.

1. Use the data points to find the mean (or average). For example, add 6, 4, 7, 4, 5, 5, 13, 23, 12, 14, 3, 18, and 6 together, and divide by the number of values, which is 13. This equals 9.2.

2. Divide the mean by 2. In this case, 9.2 divided by 2 equals 4.6.

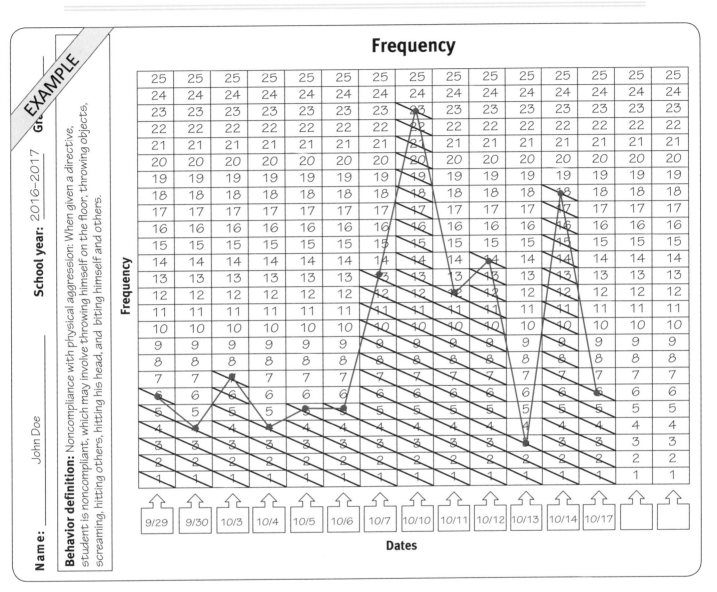

Figure 7.8. Variability example with frequency graph.

3. Add the number you calculated in Step 2 to the mean (calculated in Step 1). So, 9.2 plus 4.6 equals 13.8. This is going to signify the top boundary of what is going to be considered a stable range of data.

4. Subtract the number you calculated in Step 2 from the mean (calculated in Step 1). So, 9.2 minus 4.6 equals 4.6. This is going to signify the bottom boundary of what is going to be considered a stable range of data. In order to make this even easier to analyze and explain, round the numbers (13.8 rounds up to 14, and 4.6 rounds up to 5). So, the range of data that you would expect to indicate stability would be from 5 to 14.

6, 4, 7, 4, 5, 5, 13, ⓐ23,⃝ 12, 14, ⓐ3,⃝ 18, 6

Figure 7.9. Data point values.

You now have a precise range of data that indicates stability. You can statistically explain how the data are not stable and are quite variable using your formula and the visual. For comparison purposes, it may be good to extend the period for collection of baseline data until you have data that are as stable as possible.

Patterns and Trends

Looking for patterns and trends in data is also a form of visual analysis. The terms *data mining* or *data dredging* are sometimes used to describe the act of using huge amounts of data to fish for patterns without having an initial hypothesis or research question (Grover & Mehra, 2008), but that is not what you will be doing. You will be looking at a data set that is focused on an initial research question or hypothesis in order to visually analyze patterns or trends. With a critical eye, you can determine if there are possible patterns in the data that signify a relationship between different things so that you can make data-based decisions about educational interventions. Be careful to remember that the goal of looking for a pattern or trend in the data is not to determine causation but only a relationship.

So what is a pattern? Look for common features of the data gathered about a particular behavior. These features may involve a common location, common time of day, or common social interaction between peers. Use these commonalities to determine a possible relationship between the behavior and a variable in the environment, which may lead you to determine a function for the behavior. Consider the following example:

Linda is a seventh-grade student who has had behavioral issues in the classroom. She shuts down and becomes noncompliant, refusing to complete classroom tasks or follow teacher directives. She is not aggressive toward staff or peers but is still noncompliant. Ms. Johnson has begun collecting data about these behaviors. She has scatterplot data in order to determine time of day that the behavior is occurring. She has frequency data to determine exactly how many times a day the behavior occurs and has duration data that will provide information about how long each of the incidents lasts.

While continuing to collect data, Ms. Johnson begins looking for patterns. She asks herself a few questions:

- Does Linda's behavior occur only at certain times of the day or on certain days?
- Does Linda's behavior occur in certain subject area classes or when she is doing a specific type of task, such as one that involves writing, answering oral questions, or taking a test?
- Does her behavior occur when she interacts with a specific teacher or gender of teacher or with a certain group of peers?
- Does her behavior occur prior to lunch or around the time medications are given?
- What about the sensory environment? Is it very loud in the environments where the behavior occurs the most? Is Linda required to sit in the back of the classroom, where she is highly distracted by everything around her, and if so, is this where the behavior occurs most frequently?
- What about the duration of the episodes? Are they longer or shorter in certain environments or under certain circumstances?

Do you see how looking for patterns in your data is a great start to the analysis process? It could be a great brainstorming activity. This is where the puzzle of data analysis comes into play—the detective work! When a group of educators get together at a meeting and lay out the data that have been collected to begin looking at that data with a critical eye, the puzzle comes together. They also determine other questions that need answers. For instance, look again at the example of Derrick and the lunchroom discussed previously.

This is a compilation of the data that has been taken so far. The referral question was: Why is Derrick showing physical aggression, and what intervention can be put into place to decrease the behavior?

There were three types of data taken throughout the day.

- *Scatterplot:* These data show the physically aggressive behavior occurring around 9:30 and 11:45 a.m. and at 3:15 p.m.. There are no such behaviors or very few that occur at any other time during the day.

- *Frequency:* Even though there are some aggressive behaviors that occur at different times during the day, the frequency of the behaviors dramatically increases during the 11:45 time period.

- *Intensity:* Intensity of the behaviors increases during the 11:45 time period.

You can now brainstorm ideas to look for in the data in order to determine patterns. If you are in a meeting, this is when you will have a blank whiteboard and the data in front of you and will begin to toss out ideas as a team. Together, you will come up with the list of possible patterns or relationships that could be investigated further. Here are a few ideas of where to start the discussion:

- Does there seem to be a common pattern in the times of day in which the behavior is occurring most frequently?

- Are there common activities during the time period when the behavior occurs?

- Are there common people around, or is the size of the social group the same, during the time period when the behavior occurs?

- Are there common features in the sensory environment around the time period the behavior occurs?

These are just a few of the common patterns to look for in the data. After brainstorming ideas for what may be contributing to the behavior, the team can now look critically at existing data and determine what new data might need to be collected to clarify the relationship between the behavior and the environment.

Based on the initial data the team collected on Derrick's behaviors, here are the common patterns that were generated through the analysis:

- Derrick's behavior occurs during physical education and lunch and on the bus ramp getting on the bus in the afternoon.

- Most of the behaviors occur at lunch.

- All three of these environments are large-group environments with a high degree of sensory input.

The simple patterns in the data show that there are other questions that need answers and will require additional information. Here are a few:

- Are peers provoking the student?

- Does the student have a place to sit at lunch? Is there a group that is shunning him?

- Does the student have an aversion to large, loud, bright spaces with a lot of sensory input, such as smells?

- Does the student take medication around lunchtime?

- Is there a specific peer or peer group the student is interacting with during this time, and is this peer or peer group commonly present during other times when aggression occurs?

- Does the unstructured setting cause problems—not understanding the routine, not being able to communicate issues?

- Does the student have the money to buy lunch, or is there an issue concerning the purchase of lunch?

- Is a teacher involved who has relationship difficulties with the student?

- Does the student have medical issues with hypo- or hyperglycemia or diabetes?

Once team members have generated a list of questions, they can further investigate the environment. Do you see how determining common patterns within the data will assist you in getting to the core of the issue? You may find patterns using just one type of data, but in Derrick's case it took a combination of scatterplot, frequency, and intensity data to determine the issue. Some of the Quick-Graphs provided in this book will give you an easy way of collecting this information and provide you with a visual representation of the data for easy analysis.

Last but not least, is it important to look for trends in the data. There are statistical, computer-based ways to determine exact trendlines for the data, but the goal is not to turn you into a statistician. Rather, you will learn simple-to-understand ways to analyze data trends that allow the information to be redelivered to all. The end goal is to help you better interpret and use data for the good of your students.

To demonstrate visually how data are trending, include a best-fit straight line within the data. It will provide information on the direction data are moving. Here are three steps for creating a line that shows the direction of the data:

1. Look at the data values as a group (see Figure 7.10).

2. Circle the data, enclosing all of the data points. I suggest that you do this lightly with a pencil and as close to the data points and as evenly as possible. This should show a definite shape unique to the data set (see Figure 7.11).

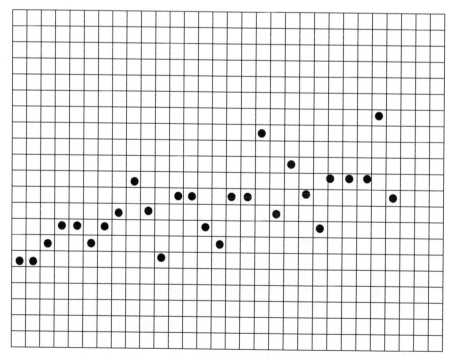

Figure 7.10. Step 1 to drawing a best-fit straight line.

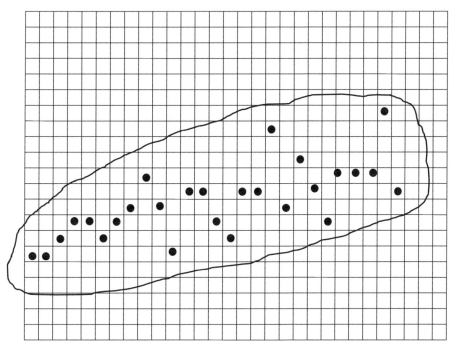

Figure 7.11. Step 2 to drawing a best-fit straight line.

3. Look within the circle, and divide the circle in half. Draw a line from one end to the other, and try to make the line cut the area into equal pieces (see Figure 7.12).

You can now erase the circle in order to show a clean line. The line should indicate the average of how the data is progressing. There are typically three descriptors used to analyze trends: increasing trend, decreasing trend, and no trend or zero trend. If the line

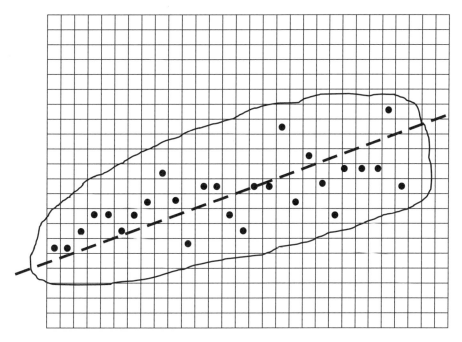

Figure 7.12. Step 3 to drawing a best-fit straight line.

you have drawn moves up, then there is an increasing trend. If the line you have drawn moves down, then the trend is decreasing. If the line moves straight across, then there is no trend or zero trend. It's that simple!

The way you would explain the data analysis from Figure 7.12 is "Even though the data values show a few outliers, the data set for this student shows an increasing trend." This is because the trendline you have drawn is moving up. You may notice there were a few hiccups or blips in the data, but trendlines are great for showing the overall trajectory in functioning over time. This is why you need to look at the data daily or every few days.

Step 6: Test Out Interventions While Continuing to Collect Data

How do you know that an intervention works? By collecting data to test out your intervention! Some teachers might collect data over a period of a few months but only graph and analyze the data once a year prior to the IEP meeting. This does not allow for ongoing evaluation of interventions, strategies, and supports to see what is working for the student and what changes might be needed. Rather, continual examination of the data is required in order to monitor the need for change. Tools such as the Quick-Graphs will help you examine your data on a regular basis by putting the data into a visual format for analysis.

After you have implemented an intervention, you will examine and compare the pre- and postintervention data to determine how effective the intervention was. After examining the data, you can determine that the intervention had one of three effects on the data:

- Positive effect

- Negative effect

- Neutral effect

What do you do when the intervention has a positive effect on the data? Keep it up! What about a negative effect? If you are sure the intervention is the contributing factor, and not other variables in the environment, then stop and modify the intervention. Base this decision on data and observation, not on your gut feeling, and do not keep doing something that has a negative impact on progress.

What if an intervention has a neutral effect? You may not have implemented the intervention long enough, so it may not have had time to have an impact. Perhaps the intervention was not implemented with integrity. Interventions that are implemented with integrity are done correctly and precisely as intended by all parties involved. If different people are working with the student on different days, they may all have a different understanding of how the intervention works.

Chapter 5 discussed compiling a Teaching Programs book. Teaching programs are written protocols to clarify how a certain intervention or teaching style should be implemented. The protocols are written so that everyone working with the student consistently implements the intervention or strategy according to plan. When everyone follows the teaching or implementation protocol, the intervention is implemented with integrity.

Before modifying an intervention, it is important to check for integrity, sometimes through observations by a lead teacher. In turn, an integrity check by the teacher may lead to training or retraining on the part of the staff. In summary, when using data to test interventions, the key word is follow-up! Continually revisit and analyze your data so that you can monitor progress and make modifications to interventions if necessary.

REVIEW OF THE FACTS AND A PEEK AHEAD

This chapter brought the importance of data analysis to the forefront. Too many times teachers collect data but find the task of analysis so daunting that they stop the process there. This chapter outlined several ways to make analysis easy. The acronym *COVERT* will help you remember the most important steps. This chapter also provided easy-to-use forms and tips on how to discuss the analysis with a layperson. The most important aspect of the data collection process is the change it brings to student achievement. After data are properly compiled and analyzed, you can make data-driven decisions, which will drive appropriate changes to the educational interventions used with students to enhance achievement. This topic is discussed in Chapter 8.

QUICK QUIZ

1. When analyzing data, the data can be compared to which of the following?
   a. Mastery level set by IEP committee
   b. Baseline data
   c. Both a and b, plus other ways

2. A new teaching method you are testing is an example of
   a. A control
   b. An independent variable
   c. A dependent variable

3. If a student's data points are scattered, the variability is considered to be
   a. Unusable
   b. Extremely variable
   c. Stable

4. An intervention is documented on a graph by a dotted vertical line.
   a. True
   b. False

5. Correlation is an easy way to determine the cause of a student's behavior.
   a. True
   b. False

CHAPTER 8

Data-Based Decision Making

 MISSION: To learn how to make educational decisions based on your data

QUESTIONS TO INVESTIGATE

- How can I explain analyzed data to parents or IEP team members?
- How do I make decisions based on the data I have collected?

DEFINITIONS OF TERMS AND ABBREVIATIONS

ABC Antecedent, behavior, consequence; this method of collecting observational data outlines the information collected into the antecedent (what is happening before or at the time the behavior occurs), behavior (the behavior that occurs), and consequence (what happens after the behavior occurs). The analysis of ABC data is an integral part of an FBA. It allows for a more thorough description of the behavior and a better idea of the function, which leads to more appropriate interventions (Heward, 2013).

Data-based decision making The process by which an educator examines and analyzes data for the purpose of making decisions about educational design in order to enhance student achievement (Mandinach & Jackson, 2012).

FBA Functional behavioral assessment; FBA is the process of examining behavior that involves observation and data collection. In an FBA, the antecedent and environmental conditions that trigger the behavior and consequences that reinforce the behavior are examined to uncover the function of the behavior.

Functional analysis Functional analysis involves the manipulation of independent variables to determine the function of a behavior.

Referral question The presenting question that guides the team in the educational investigation, data collection, and analysis. This question outlines the initial issue that triggered an academic or behavioral investigation and can be used in any setting.

Once data have been analyzed and interpreted, the final step is to use those data to inform educational decisions that will support individual students as well as the classroom as a whole. Oftentimes, decisions about teaching methods, interventions, and supports are made in collaboration with other professionals and parents, particularly during the IEP process, which requires by law that the family and education team come together to

125

support the child with special needs. For this reason, this chapter provides tools and tips for explaining data to others in clear, understandable ways so that the team can recommend next steps. There are practical suggestions for how to make decisions, implement interventions, and modify these interventions based on the data collected. The following Eyewitness Account describes a common challenge.

 Eyewitness Account

Brian is our youngest child and is in third grade. He seems to be struggling in a few academic areas, and we have been trying to help him with homework since the beginning of the year, but he does not seem to be making any progress. Brian's teacher contacted us to let us know that she shared our concerns and had data that may better explain Brian's academic levels. We met with the teacher, and she began sharing the data that had been collected on Brian's academic progress. As the teacher was explaining baseline, percentages, raw scores, and trendlines, our eyes glazed over with all the numbers presented to us. How did all this information answer the question we had about what to do for Brian? It was great information, but we just wanted to know how to help our child.

—*Mr. and Mrs. Richardson,*
Parents

HOW CAN I EXPLAIN ANALYZED DATA TO PARENTS OR IEP TEAM MEMBERS?

Analyzed data tell a story of what is happening with a student, and you should be able to share this story in clear language that everyone understands. Unless you are speaking to and sharing the data with other professionals who are familiar with educational terminology, be sure to use layman's terms when describing your data so that the information is accessible to all. Make sure that everyone in the meeting or on the committee has access to the data. Do not go into a meeting with only one copy of the data and graphs. If you have access to a projector, then use it to display the graphs and data on a screen so that everyone is focused on the same thing. If you are new to presenting data to a group, it helps to have a structure to follow.

In order to make the process of explaining data to others easier for you, this chapter includes two helpful forms, the ABC Data Summary (Narrative) and the Detailed Data Analysis Outline, that you can use to discuss data with education team members. You can add these photocopiable forms to your data collection notebook to help you conduct student observations; see also the About the Forms and Tools page at the beginning of this book for instructions on downloading printable copies.

The ABC Data Summary (Narrative) form is a two-page form (see Figure 8.1a-b) based on the analysis of behavioral data, particularly ABC (antecedent, behavior, consequence) data. Recall that an important and common way of addressing challenging behavior is to complete an FBA, the process of examining behavior that involves careful observation and data collection. In an FBA, the antecedent (A) that triggers the behavior (B) and consequences (C) that reinforce the behavior are examined to uncover the behavior's function. Thus, when analyzing ABC data, your goal is to use the data to determine the function of the behavior and guide you in choosing appropriate interventions and supports.

The ABC Data Summary (Narrative) provides a narrative summary of the behavior to help guide team discussions (see Page 1) and space to write recommendations for next steps (see Page 2). Page 1 should be completed using the data from your ABC Data Form. (See Form 20Ba-b in Toolkit B of Section IV: Your Classroom Data Toolkit for a blank photocopiable

ABC Data Summary (Narrative) (Front)

The data indicate that the behavior is happening _____

.

Name: _____

School year: _____

Grade: _____

IEP date: _____

IN THIS TYPE OF ENVIRONMENT
_____
_____
_____

IN THIS TYPE OF GROUP AND WITH WHOM
_____
_____
_____

AT THIS TIME OF DAY OR WEEK OR IN THIS CLASS
_____
_____
_____

DURING THESE ACTIVITIES OR WITH THIS DIRECTIVE
_____
_____
_____

WITH THESE SENSORY EVENTS OCCURRING OR NOT OCCURRING
_____
_____
_____

WE BELIEVE THAT THE FUNCTION OF THE BEHAVIOR IS TO
_____
_____
_____

Figure 8.1a–b. ABC Data Summary (Narrative) (Front and Back).

ABC Data Summary (Narrative) (Back)

Page 2 of 2

Based on the data, our recommendations are to modify the

ENVIRONMENT
by
_____
_____
_____

GROUP
by
_____
_____

ACTIVITIES, TASK,
or DIRECTIVES
by
_____
_____

SENSORY
ENVIRONMENT
by
_____
_____

_____
by
_____
_____

WE WILL CONTINUE TO TAKE DATA WITH THESE FOLLOW-UP PROCEDURES:			

Name: _____ **School year:** _____ **Grade:** _____ **IEP date:** _____

Figure 8.1a–b. *(continued)*

The Data Collection Toolkit: Everything You Need to Organize, Manage, and Monitor Classroom Data, by Cindy Golden.
Copyright © 2018 Paul H. Brookes Publishing Co. All rights reserved.

version; see also the About the Forms and Tools page at the beginning of this book for instructions on downloading a printable copy). On Page 2, the team writes recommendations for modifying the environment to reduce the challenging behavior and records follow-up procedures for continuing data collection. Use this form as a jumping-off point and a way to structure the decision-making process for behavioral interventions based on data.

You might be wondering how to structure a discussion about other types of behavioral data in a meeting (e.g., frequency, duration, intensity). Begin with the question or issue, then systematically review each piece of data and what the information might mean for the student. Consider how one team presented behavioral data during an IEP meeting:

It is time to review Bobby's data. The referral question asked us to determine the reason or function of Bobby's verbal outbursts in class and to look into the types of interventions that may be appropriate to use to help reduce this behavior. Based on the referral information and the referral question, our goal is to decrease Bobby's number of verbal outbursts in class and increase his use of more appropriate behavior.

Looking at the baseline data that was kept prior to interventions being implemented, Bobby's baseline functioning showed a stable rate of behavior, with the frequency being about one outburst every 5 minutes. That is at a high level. The scatterplot baseline showed that most of the behavior occurred in the first and last hours of the day.

Let's take a closer look at the behavioral data. The teacher implemented an intervention that involved moving Bobby's seat to the front of the room in all classes. Frequency and scatterplot data were kept for 3 weeks. The frequency data indicated a mild to moderate level of variability, or that most of the data points were consistent but there was some scatter or spread. This means that Bobby's behavior is pretty much the same most days but that a couple of days during the week there were significant differences. Looking at the scatterplot, the behaviors tend to occur in the morning and the afternoon, specifically the first and last hour of the day. This is during reading with Mr. Steinberg and math with Ms. Turner. Have we looked at Bobby's academic functioning in these areas?

The frequency data graph shows data at a high level and shows a consistent spike in the occurrences of outbursts on Mondays and Thursdays. It looks like we need to determine what is different about those two days. The frequency is low on Fridays. What might be different then? Our data show us that we need answers to some questions in order to determine the exact reason for Bobby's behavior:

1. Does this intervention seem to be working to reduce the behavior?
2. What are Bobby's academic levels in the areas of reading and math as compared to the other areas?
3. What is different about class on Monday, Thursday, and Friday?
4. Are there differences in the teaching styles of Mr. Steinberg and Ms. Turner compared to Bobby's other teachers?
5. Are there certain students in those two classes who are not in the other classes?
6. Does Bobby have medical issues, or is he taking medication during the school day?
7. What does the classroom look like, and what about sensory issues? Is it noisier in those classrooms, or is his desk in the same place in both rooms?
8. What goes on right before or after those classes?
9. Parents, does something different go on at home on those days?
10. Has anyone talked to Bobby to ask him about his behaviors or about those particular classes?

We have a lot of questions to answer. The initial scatterplot data we collected helped us determine when the behaviors occur. Now, knowing what we do, what type of intervention can we implement while we are continuing to collect data? Also, in addition to continuing with frequency data, do we need to collect any other type of data? Let's decide who will do which tasks and when are we going to follow up.

Notice how discussing the analysis of the data leads to other questions. The data may not give you a definitive conclusion or solution right away, but they guide you in your continued journey toward an answer to the referral question. The data may guide you to an initial intervention, but it is important to continue your data collection to ensure your choice for an intervention is the appropriate one. This same process holds true when you explain and present academic data, which is meant to move you toward finding appropriate interventions for academic needs. When presenting data (academic or behavioral), consider the following talking points to guide your discussion:

- *Reason:* Why were data collected? Discuss the referral or target question and the goals for the data collection process. Make sure your data answer the question presented.

- *Baseline:* Review the standard on which you are making a comparison.

- *Trend/variability:* What does the trendline look like, and was there variability in the data?

- *Level:* Was the level of data high, moderate, or low?

- *Comparison:* Compare the data to the baseline data or to the standard you have chosen. Do the data meet the IEP goal mastery level? How do the data compare to the baseline prior to the intervention?

- *Analysis:* What do the data tell? Pick the data apart, and do not make statements that assume a cause. Rather, form a correlation or connection.

- *Questions:* The analysis of data typically brings forth new questions. Discuss and document them. Follow-up questions can be listed on the form shown in Figure 8.2, the Detailed Data Analysis Outline.

- *Interventions:* Do the data show a positive effect from the intervention that is being used? Determine if the intervention needs to be modified. Also, clarify how continued data collection and follow-up will be handled.

Figure 8.2, the Detailed Data Analysis Outline, is a form to organize and guide your discussion of data and a helpful reminder of important things to cover. This form also allows you to document follow-up questions to be answered and tasks to be completed (and, for accountability purposes, who will be responsible for seeing those tasks through to completion).

HOW DO I MAKE DECISIONS BASED ON THE DATA I HAVE COLLECTED?

Now that you know how to analyze, present, and disseminate data to families or the education team, let's look more deeply into how to use data to make educational decisions. Remember that when solving a case, detectives must persevere and not give up too soon; they must treat everything as evidence and follow every lead. The same goes for teachers who are collecting information to help students.

When you are involved in situations where data are required, do not stop data collection too soon, and make sure that some kind of change or new strategy is in place once you have determined that there is a problem to solve. If the strategy or intervention does not seem to answer the question or solve the problem the first time you collect data, then regroup and try again. As an example, consider the following scenario:

You have a student, Larissa, who is struggling with being able to write a paragraph with four sentences. Writing the four-sentence paragraph is one of Larissa's IEP goals, and data are being collected on her performance. You try to help her by implementing a standard intervention used with other struggling students. All of the other students are progressing slowly, but Larissa continues to have difficulty. You analyze the data and see that this intervention is not

Detailed Data Analysis Outline

Name: _____ Grade: _____ School year: _____ IEP date: _____

Reason	Let us review the data for **(student name)**. The referral question asked us to **(what did the referral question ask for?)**. Based on the referral information, our goal was to **(what did the referral ask you to find out?)**.
Baseline	Looking at the baseline data, which is **(the data prior to any interventions being implemented or the current functioning coming into this IEP)**, it appears that **(give summary of baseline data—including trends/patterns and information about variability)**. We are going to compare the current data we collected to **(e.g., baseline, IEP mastery level)** in order to establish a standard of functioning.
Trend/ variability	Now look at the graphs of our data. **(The type of data collected)** was taken for **(student name)**, and the data indicated a variability that was **(stable or variable)**. This means that the behavior **(was/was not)** very consistent or the same each day. The data graphs show a(an) **(increasing/decreasing or zero)** trendline which means the data are **(moving up/down or remaining about the same)**.
Level	In looking at the graphs, the **(type of data)** data appear to be at a **(high, moderate, low)** level.
Comparison	Comparing the data after the intervention was implemented to the baseline before using an intervention, it seems that the intervention is having a **(positive, negative, or neutral)** effect on functioning. OR Comparing the data to the expected mastery level of functioning, **(student name)** appears to **(have/have not)** mastered the goal.
Analysis	In looking at the data, what else could be happening that would be affecting progress on **(e.g., behavior/goals/progress)**?
Questions	What types of questions do we still have based on the data? Is there anything else that we need to determine or information that we need to gather? How are we going to find the answers?
Intervention	Through the analysis of this data, does it appear that we should continue with this intervention or modify it? We are going to continue with the data collection—How should we follow up?

Follow-up tasks	Person responsible
1	
2	
3	
4	
5	

Follow-up questions
1
2
3
4
5
6
7
8

Figure 8.2. Detailed Data Analysis Outline.

increasing Larissa's ability to do the task. Larissa struggles through the writing assignment every morning without making any progress, and in fact, there appears to be regression. She is becoming increasingly frustrated and soon starts exhibiting challenging behaviors during this time of day. You might continue the intervention because it works with other students, but Larissa is becoming discouraged, and you are as well.

What should you do in this situation? Do you keep going with the current intervention in the hopes that it will eventually have some positive effect on Larissa's writing skills? Do you move on to a different intervention? Or do you just give up on teaching Larissa this writing task and assume that nothing more can be done? One of the most heartbreaking things you will hear coming from the classroom is "nothing was working, so we just gave up and moved on to something else."

Looking back at the steps to data analysis, the final step is to test interventions while continuing to collect data. This does not mean that you change the interventions you are using every other day in the hopes that they will make a bigger or more immediate impact. It means you are constantly examining the day-to-day data so that you can notice patterns and trends and determine the impact an intervention is having on the behavior or progress. A pattern has to be established over time—just one or two data points do not signify a pattern or trend. Analyzing patterns in the data will help you determine whether the intervention is having a positive, negative, or neutral effect on the behavior. If the intervention is having a negative impact on the behavior, then of course you should not continue to implement it. This is when you regroup and examine the data to determine how the intervention should be modified.

You should never give up and simply resume "business as usual" in your classroom or learning environment, continuing on as you had before the issue came to light. Your student's education, well-being, and self-esteem are all at stake. In Larissa's case, the data showed that the intervention to improve her writing was not effective and actually caused more problems, so it was clearly time to try something else.

Our example of Larissa involved collecting data on an academic goal. Consider what steps to take after collecting data on behavior. The goal in behavioral intervention is to decrease the inappropriate behaviors while increasing appropriate behaviors (Bambara, Janney, & Snell, 2015). The intervention should not only be aimed at reducing the behavior you do not want to see occur but should also include replacing the inappropriate behavior with one that is appropriate. Remember that behavior is communication. The student is attempting to communicate something to you or to get a need met.

If you do not teach a more appropriate behavior that will serve the same purpose for the student after the inappropriate behavior is extinguished, then the student will try to come up with another way to get his or her needs met, sometimes through a different, or more extreme, inappropriate behavior. So, it is important to determine an appropriate behavior that will serve the same function and teach it to the student as a replacement behavior. You should also implement supports and strategies to help meet the student's needs. Strengthening the desired behavior is key (Sugai et. al., 2000). Table 8.1 lists some common functions of, or reasons for, challenging behavior in the classroom, with suggested interventions, supports, and strategies that can lead to improvement.

Posing the following questions can be helpful when discussing the need to modify an intervention, either academic or behavioral:

- Does the student understand the intervention the way it is presented?

- Is the student's cognitive ability affecting the intervention?

- Are you convinced that the intervention (and not something else) is having a negative effect on the student's behavior or progress?

Table 8.1. Common functions of challenging behavior in the classroom, with suggested interventions, supports, and strategies

If the student is exhibiting the behaviors to	Then
Communicate academic frustration	Examine the academic tasks and the student's ability level. Do a task analysis, and teach the task in discrete, small steps to a mastery level. Also consider modifying the task or presenting it in a way the student can better understand. Assist the student in getting organized if this is causing an issue.
Communicate sensory overload	Examine the sensory environment, and determine what input is overwhelming. Consider ways to lessen this input, such as moving the student's desk, offering the use of earplugs, and spacing out desks so the student has more room. Brainstorm with the student and/or parents to determine other ways of lessening the overload.
Get attention	Make sure the student has a way of communicating the need in an appropriate manner. Provide enough attention that is not contingent on behavior.
Escape a hard task	If the behavior is due to academic frustration, then see above. If it is due to the student's fear of failure, then slowly break down the task into chunks and try a modified errorless teaching approach. This will set up the environment so that the student is successful with small steps of the task until he or she feels comfortable. Also consider the use of choice; provide the student with the choice of a few tasks that meet the same goal.
Gain access to an object, activity, or person	Create a way for the student to communicate wants and desires. Include a way of earning the desired object, activity, or time with the person after appropriate behaviors have been displayed.
Communicate a need for sensory input	Examine sensory needs, and schedule sensory activities that are not contingent on behavior.
Communicate a social frustration, such as having difficulty making friends, being bullied, or not knowing how to fit in	Proactively teach appropriate social skills. Also consider the use of peer mentors.
Communicate a thought, need, or other concern	Create a way for the student to communicate.

- Should the intervention be tried a bit longer?

- Is the person implementing the intervention affecting the student's behavior?

- Is the intervention being implemented with integrity?

- Does the variability of data indicate that the intervention may not always be implemented consistently?

These questions can and should be answered through careful examination of your data. Analyze trends, patterns, levels, variability, and everything else that is pertinent. Give a classroom intervention time, and then, if things are still not progressing, modify the intervention, continue to collect and analyze new data, and keep moving forward toward a solution.

REVIEW OF THE FACTS AND A PEEK AHEAD

This chapter provided you with guidelines for making data-based decisions. It described how to explain data to others and collaborate on educational decision making as well as how to modify interventions and follow up with data collection. You have now learned all the steps for collecting data in the classroom!

Remember that you first need to determine the needs of your classroom in terms of collecting data and building a data collection system. You will typically collect data in the classroom to measure behavior, academic progress, and progress toward IEP goals or objectives. The steps to data collection presented in this book apply to any setting, whether you need the data for a homeschool program, an FBA or BIP, a general education setting, or a special education classroom.

So, determine the reason for the data collection, set your target, and select your tools! Every educator can create an easy-to-use and effective data collection system for his or her classroom, whatever setting that may be. Now that you have learned the basics, it's just a matter of getting started!

In Section IV: Your Classroom Data Toolkit, you will find data collection forms and handouts to collect information on all types of behavioral needs, track progress on academic skills, collect data on IEP goals or objectives, and organize your data collection system.

QUICK QUIZ

1. The terms FBA (functional behavioral assessment) and functional analysis refer to the same process and can be used interchangeably.
   a. True
   b. False

2. A referral question refers to
   a. The presenting issue that triggered a more thorough investigation
   b. The question that guides the data collection process
   c. Both a and b

3. In data collection, the acronym ABC stands for
   a. Analysis, behavior, consequence
   b. Assessment, behavior, context
   c. Antecedent, behavior, consequence
   d. None of the above

4. As the undesired behavior decreases, it is important to teach a more appropriate replacement behavior that serves the same function.
   a. True
   b. False

5. When explaining data, you should discuss
   a. Trendline and variability of data
   b. Comparison to baseline data
   c. Level (Did the behavior occur at a high, moderate, or low level?)
   d. All of the above

Your Classroom Data Toolkit

This section provides the essential tools you need to set up your own data collection program. You will find easy-to-use data materials, forms, and Quick-Graphs in the areas of academics, behavior, IEPs, and data organization. As you dive into looking at the photocopiable/printable data sheets in Toolkits A–D, you will notice that many of these forms have been designed to do two things at once. These forms are called Quick-Graphs because at the same time you are collecting raw data, you are also creating a visual representation of the data in the form of a graph. No fancy computer program or app is needed—just the data form and some colored pencils!

Chapters 1–8 showed you examples of the printable forms in this book and briefly discussed their purposes. This section offers blank photocopiable/printable versions with practical, step-by-step instructions for each form's use. The section is organized as follows:

- Toolkit A: Academic and Progress Monitoring Forms

- Toolkit B: Behavior Forms

- Toolkit C: IEP Forms

- Toolkit D: Organizational Tools: Establishing a Data Collection System

Each blank data form in Section IV is also available for download. See the About the Forms and Tools page at the beginning of this book for instructions on downloading printable copies.

TOOLKIT A

Academic and Progress Monitoring Forms

- Form 1A: Academic Progress Monitoring Quick-Graph
- Form 2A: Writing Rubric Quick-Graph
- Form 3A: Academic Rubric Quick-Graph
- Form 4A: Task Analysis Quick-Graph (Predetermined Levels)
- Form 5A: Task Analysis Quick-Graph (Blank Levels)
- Form 6A: Yes/No Quick-Graph
- Form 7A: Prompt Levels Quick-Graph (Predetermined Prompt Levels)
- Form 8A: Prompt Levels Quick-Graph (Blank Prompt Levels)
- Form 9A: Discrete Trial Quick-Graph (Predetermined Levels)
- Form 10A: Discrete Trial Quick-Graph (Blank Levels)

FORM 1A: ACADEMIC PROGRESS MONITORING QUICK-GRAPH

Steps for completing the Academic Progress Monitoring Quick-Graph are as follows. (Refer to Figure 3.1 for a completed example.)

1. Complete the student information.

2. Determine the subject area you will monitor.

3. Determine the date you will begin collecting data.

4. Pretest, and enter the student's score.

5. Take preintervention baseline data prior to the implementation of an intervention designed to improve academic functioning. Determine how you will assess the skill (i.e., percentage correct on a test). Each time you assess the skill, plot the percentages the student obtained, connecting the dots on the graph with a line.

6. Determine an appropriate intervention, and mark the date the intervention began with a dotted vertical line. Document the type of intervention that was used.

7. As you continue to monitor progress after the intervention is implemented, place dots, and connect with a line. Do not connect the line between pre- and postintervention. Begin a new line connecting the data dots after the vertical intervention line because this is considered a new batch of data and is a way to monitor the student's response to the intervention.

8. Also remember to draw a horizontal line on the graph indicating your goal for the student and what would be considered mastery of the skill. This mastery line will provide the visual you need for comparing the student's performance and functioning to the intended goal.

Academic Progress Monitoring Quick-Graph

Percentage											
100											
95											
90											
85											
80											
75											
70											
65											
60											
55											
50											
45											
40											
35											
30											
25											
20											
15											
10											
5											
0											
Task	Pretest										GOAL
Date											

Name: _____

Subject area: _____

Grade: _____

Begin date: _____

End date: _____

Intervention 1: _____

Intervention 2: _____

FORM 2A: WRITING RUBRIC QUICK-GRAPH

Steps for completing the Writing Rubric Quick-Graph are as follows. (Refer to Figure 3.2 for a completed example.)

1. Complete the student information.

2. Describe the writing assignment, and write in the dates for the pretest and the posttest.

3. Determine the different aspects of the writing assignment that you will assess (see left column). For each aspect of the writing assignment being assessed, provide a detailed and specific description for what constitutes a score of 0—*no response,* 1—*minimal,* 2—*adequate,* 3—*strong,* and 4—*outstanding.*

4. Assess the student's ability to complete aspects of the assignment (i.e., introduction, body, conclusion, grammar, and mechanics), and color in the dot beside the level that best fits the student's performance in that area (no response, minimal, adequate, strong, outstanding).

5. Continue with the scoring until you have evaluated all five areas of the written assignment. You can now determine the score for the pretest based on a maximum of 20 points.

6. After an intervention or after a set period of time, do a posttest on another similar writing assignment. Score the posttest the same way, but color in the dot in the posttest column in a different color.

7. In order to complete the visual, turn the graph to a portrait orientation. Connect the pre- and posttest scores in each of the five areas with a line. This creates a visual so that you can easily share the progress made between the pre- and posttesting. Remember that it is not appropriate to link areas of functioning together with one line if the areas are not connected. For example, when scoring a writing assignment, the areas scored by the rubric are not connected because the student may score high in the area of mechanics but not in the area of grammar. This Quick-Graph allows you to graph these distinctions.

Writing Rubric Quick-Graph

		0 — No response	1 — Minimal	2 — Adequate	3 — Strong	4 — Outstanding
Introduction	Pre	O	O	O	O	O
	Post	O	O	O	O	O
Body	Pre	O	O	O	O	O
	Post	O	O	O	O	O
Conclusion	Pre	O	O	O	O	O
	Post	O	O	O	O	O
Grammar	Pre	O	O	O	O	O
	Post	O	O	O	O	O
Mechanics	Pre	O	O	O	O	O
	Post	O	O	O	O	O

Name: _____

Pretest date: _____   **Pretest total points:** _____

Posttest date: _____   **Posttest total points:** _____

Topic or directions for assignment:

FORM 3A: ACADEMIC RUBRIC QUICK-GRAPH

This form is similar to the Writing Rubric Quick-Graph, but it is intended for a variety of academic assignments and has customizable scoring criteria. Steps for completing the Academic Rubric Quick-Graph are as follows:

1. Complete the student information.

2. Describe the academic assignment, and write in the dates for the pretest and the posttest.

3. Determine up to five areas of the assignment to assess, and write these in the Scoring Area column.

4. For each aspect of the assignment being assessed, provide a detailed and specific description for what constitutes a score of 0—*no response,* 1—*minimal,* 2—*adequate,* 3—*strong,* and 4—*outstanding.*

5. Assess the student's ability to complete the assignment (i.e., performance in each of the scoring areas), and color in the dot below the level that best fits the student's performance in each area (no response, minimal, adequate, strong, outstanding).

6. Continue with the scoring until you have evaluated all five scoring areas of the assignment. You can now determine the score for the pretest based on a maximum of 20 points.

7. After an intervention or a set period of time, do a posttest on a similar academic assignment. Score the posttest the same way, but color in the dot in the posttest column in a different color.

8. In order to complete the visual, turn the graph to a portrait orientation. Connect the pre- and posttest scores in each of the five areas with a line. This creates a visual so that you can easily share the progress made between the pre- and posttest scores in each of the scoring areas. Only connect the pre- and posttest scores; do not link scores in different scoring areas.

Academic Rubric Quick-Graph

Scoring area		0 — No response	1 — Minimal	2 — Adequate	3 — Strong	4 — Outstanding
	Pre	O	O	O	O	O
	Post	O	O	O	O	O
	Pre	O	O	O	O	O
	Post	O	O	O	O	O
	Pre	O	O	O	O	O
	Post	O	O	O	O	O
	Pre	O	O	O	O	O
	Post	O	O	O	O	O
	Pre	O	O	O	O	O
	Post	O	O	O	O	O

Directions for assignment:

Name: _____

Pretest date: _____ **Pretest total points:** _____

Posttest date: _____ **Posttest total points:** _____

FORM 4A: TASK ANALYSIS QUICK-GRAPH (PREDETERMINED LEVELS)

This Task Analysis Quick-Graph has predetermined levels for how independently a student completes each step of a task. Steps for completing this Quick-Graph are as follows. (Refer to Figure 3.4 for a completed example.)

1. Complete the demographic information.

2. Record the objective skill, and write in the dates for the pretest and the posttest.

3. Analyze the task by breaking it into discrete steps, and list the steps from left to right at the bottom of the form.

4. For the pretest, assess the student during an observation of the task. Place a dot on the middle line of the row for the student's level of independence in completing each step of the task.

5. For the posttest, plot the level of independence in performing each step in a different color. Connect the dots, drawing a line between Pre and Post. You will have small connecting lines that will assist you in showing progress within each discrete skill. The different skills are not connected to each other, so the lines should not connect across skills.

Task Analysis Quick-Graph (Predetermined Levels)

Prompt level

Prompt level	Pre	Post	Pre	Post	Pre	Post	Pre	Post	Pre	Post	Pre	Post	Pre	Post	Pre	Post	Pre	Post
Independent with no assistance required — LEVEL 4																		
Semi-independent & requires sporadic assistance — LEVEL 3																		
Requires **consistent** verbal assistance — LEVEL 2																		
Requires **full** verbal & physical assistance — LEVEL 1																		
No attempt, even with prompts — LEVEL 0																		

Discrete task steps →

Pretest date: _____

Posttest date: _____

Name: _____ School year: _____ Grade: _____

Objective skill: _____

FORM 5A: TASK ANALYSIS QUICK-GRAPH (BLANK LEVELS)

This Task Analysis Quick-Graph has customizable levels to describe how independently a student completes each step of a task, with room to write a description of each level. Steps for completing this Quick-Graph are as follows:

1. Complete the demographic information.

2. Determine the levels of functioning that you choose to use, and write a description for each of the Levels 0–4.

3. Record the objective skill, and write in the dates for the pretest and the posttest.

4. Analyze the task by breaking it into discrete steps, and list the steps from left to right.

5. For the pretest, assess the student during an observation of the task. Place a dot on the middle line of the row for the student's level of independence in completing each step of the task.

6. For the posttest, plot the level of independence in performing each step in a different color. Connect the dots, drawing a line between Pre and Post. You will have small connecting lines that will assist you in showing progress within each discrete skill. The different skills are not connected to each other, so the lines should not connect across skills.

Task Analysis Quick-Graph (Blank Levels)

Name: _____

School year: _____

Grade: _____

Objective skill:

Prompt level	Pre	Post	Pre	Post	Pre	Post	Pre	Post	Pre	Post	Pre	Post	Pre	Post	Pre	Post	Pre	Post	Pre	Post
LEVEL 4																				
LEVEL 3																				
LEVEL 2																				
LEVEL 1																				
LEVEL 0																				

Discrete task steps

Pretest date: _____

Posttest date: _____

FORM 6A: YES/NO QUICK-GRAPH

Steps for completing the Yes/No Quick-Graph are as follows. (Refer to Figure 3.6 for a completed example.)

1. Complete the demographic information.

2. Document the overall objective or goal for the student.

3. Either analyze a task by breaking it into discrete steps and listing them or list the specific objectives to be achieved (e.g., specific words from the word list).

4. As you work with the student each day on the objectives (e.g., vocabulary words, math facts, successful completion of tasks or steps), circle either Y (*the student was able to provide a correct response independently*) or N (*the student did not provide the correct response at an independent level*). No prompting is involved. Notice that dates are listed across the top of the graph, and there is enough room on one data sheet for 2 weeks of daily data (10 days).

5. Each day you document the student's response, also shade in the Y or N on the side bar graph so that you can visually see and compare the number of correct and incorrect responses. It is easier to use different colors for Y and N. At the end of the 10 days, you will have a bar graph of yes/no data.

Yes/No Quick-Graph

Name: _____

School year: _____

Date range: _____

Overall objective/goal: _____

Objective/task	Date										Total count of yes/no by objective										
											Bar graphs of data summaries										
											1	2	3	4	5	6	7	8	9	10	
											Y	N									
1	Y N	Y N	Y N	Y N	Y N	Y N	Y N	Y N	Y N	Y N											
2	Y N	Y N	Y N	Y N	Y N	Y N	Y N	Y N	Y N	Y N											
3	Y N	Y N	Y N	Y N	Y N	Y N	Y N	Y N	Y N	Y N											
4	Y N	Y N	Y N	Y N	Y N	Y N	Y N	Y N	Y N	Y N											
5	Y N	Y N	Y N	Y N	Y N	Y N	Y N	Y N	Y N	Y N											
6	Y N	Y N	Y N	Y N	Y N	Y N	Y N	Y N	Y N	Y N											
7	Y N	Y N	Y N	Y N	Y N	Y N	Y N	Y N	Y N	Y N											
8	Y N	Y N	Y N	Y N	Y N	Y N	Y N	Y N	Y N	Y N											
9	Y N	Y N	Y N	Y N	Y N	Y N	Y N	Y N	Y N	Y N											

FORM 7A: PROMPT LEVELS QUICK-GRAPH (PREDETERMINED PROMPT LEVELS)

This Prompt Level Quick-Graph comes with prompt levels provided. Steps for completing this Quick-Graph are as follows. (Refer to Figure 3.8 for a completed example.)

1. Complete the demographic information.

2. Record the subject area or task.

3. Either analyze the task by breaking it into discrete steps and listing them or list the separate tasks you are teaching.

4. As you work with the student on tasks, document on the graph the level of prompt that was required (i.e., the student did not respond, even with prompting; the student needed full physical, gestural, or verbal prompts; or the student independently completed the task). To create a bar graph, shade in the boxes that correspond to the level of prompting required each day. To create a line graph, place a dot in the center of the box indicating the level of prompt used, then connect the data points to form a line graph.

5. Continue collecting data and analyzing progress toward independent completion of tasks, adding data sheets as needed.

Prompt Levels Quick-Graph
(Predetermined Prompt Levels)

Page ___ of ___

Prompt level key

I	Independent
V	Verbal
G	Gesture
FP	Full physical
0	No response, even with prompting

Name:

Subject area or overall task:

Date range:

Objective	Prompt level	Dates											
	I												
	V												
	G												
	FP												
	0												
	I												
	V												
	G												
	FP												
	0												
	I												
	V												
	G												
	FP												
	0												
	I												
	V												
	G												
	FP												
	0												

FORM 8A: PROMPT LEVELS QUICK-GRAPH (BLANK PROMPT LEVELS)

This Prompt Levels Quick-Graph comes with a blank Prompt Level Key that allows you to modify the prompts as needed (e.g., you may not use gestural prompts with the student, but you might use partial physical prompts). Steps for completing this Quick-Graph are as follows:

1. Complete the demographic information.

2. Record the subject area or task.

3. Fill out the Prompt Level Key, describing the range of specific prompts used with the student and noting how each will be abbreviated. Place that abbreviation in the Prompt Level column of the graph.

4. Either analyze the task by breaking it into discrete steps and listing them or list the separate tasks you are teaching.

5. As you work with the student on tasks, indicate the level of prompt required on the graph, according to the Prompt Level Key. To create a bar graph, shade in the boxes that correspond to the level of prompting required each day. To create a line graph, place a dot in the center of the box indicating the level of prompt used, then connect the data points to form a line graph.

6. Continue collecting data and analyzing progress toward independent completion of tasks, adding data sheets as needed.

Prompt Levels Quick-Graph
(Blank Prompt Levels)

Prompt level key

Name: _____

Date range: _____

Subject area or overall task: _____

Objective	Prompt level	Dates														

FORM 9A: DISCRETE TRIAL QUICK-GRAPH (PREDETERMINED LEVELS)

This Discrete Trial Quick-Graph has prompt levels provided. Steps for completing this Quick-Graph are as follows. (Refer to Figure 3.9 for a completed example.)

1. Complete the demographic information.

2. Record the subject area, task, or overall goal.

3. Remember that when a larger, more complicated skill is broken into smaller steps, these steps are considered discrete skills. Analyze the larger skill, task, or goal for the student by breaking it into discrete skills for the student to master. These discrete skills are considered your targets and should be listed on the Quick-Graph. For some tasks, you may need to keep several sheets on one larger skill. For instance, you may have two data sheets for a total of 10 discrete skills that make up the larger task. The purpose of discrete trial training (DTT) is to teach each target to mastery, collecting data on the student's level of independence across sessions. Doing so allows you to focus on those targets that may be stumbling blocks for the student.

4. Determine the criteria for mastery. These criteria may have been decided at the individualized education program (IEP) meeting. If not, you may consider setting the criteria as "three consecutive independent responses." (The mastery level is typically an independent response and involves more than one independent response in a row to ensure that the student has truly mastered the skill.)

5. Assess the student's baseline functioning. Assess the skill, and record at which prompt level the student was able to correctly respond. Document this in the Baseline column by either marking a dot or shading in the box. (Use dots if you want to create a line graph; use shaded boxes to create a bar graph.)

6. Begin working with the student at the baseline level. As you assess the student over discrete trial sessions, continue with data collection as you did at baseline—by either marking a dot or shading in the box.

7. As you document the sessions, make sure to record the dates of the sessions across the top.

8. When the student meets criteria for mastery (usually a number of independent responses), draw a green horizontal line through the independent responses. This will clearly indicate that the child has met mastery for that target.

Discrete Trial Quick-Graph
(Predetermined Levels)

Prompt level key

I	Independent
PP	Partial physical
FP	Full physical
0	No response

Criteria for mastery

Baseline date: _____

Subject area or overall goal area:

Name: _____

Target	Prompt level	BASELINE	Dates/sessions												
	I														
	PP														
	FP														
	0														
	I														
	PP														
	FP														
	0														
	I														
	PP														
	FP														
	0														
	I														
	PP														
	FP														
	0														
	I														
	PP														
	FP														
	0														

FORM 10A: DISCRETE TRIAL QUICK-GRAPH (BLANK LEVELS)

This Discrete Trial Quick-Graph allows you to customize prompt levels for discrete trial sessions. Steps for completing this Quick-Graph are as follows:

1. Complete the demographic information.

2. Record the subject area, task, or overall goal.

3. Fill in the Prompt Level Key, describing the types of prompts that will be used during discrete trial sessions and an abbreviation that will be used for each. Designate the prompt levels on the Prompt Level column of the Quick-Graph using the abbreviation.

4. Remember that when a larger, more complicated skill is broken into smaller steps, these steps are considered discrete skills. Analyze the larger skill, task, or goal for the student by breaking it into discrete skills for the student to master. These discrete skills are considered your targets and should be listed on the Quick-Graph. For some more complicated tasks, you may need to keep several sheets on one skill. For instance, you may have two data sheets for a total of 10 discrete skills that make up the larger task. The purpose of DTT is to teach each target to mastery, collecting data on the student's level of independence across sessions. Doing so allows you to focus on those targets that may be stumbling blocks for the student.

5. Determine the criteria for mastery. These criteria may have been decided at the IEP meeting. If not, you may consider setting the criteria as "three consecutive independent responses." (The mastery level is typically an independent response and involves more than one independent response in a row to ensure that the student has truly mastered the skill.)

6. Assess the student's baseline functioning. Assess the skill, and record at which prompt level the student was able to correctly respond. Document this in the Baseline column by either marking a dot or shading in the box. (Use dots if you want to create a line graph; use shaded boxes to create a bar graph.)

7. Begin working with the student at the baseline level. As you assess the student over discrete trial sessions, continue with data collection as you did at baseline—by either marking a dot or shading in the box.

8. As you document the sessions, make sure to record the dates of the sessions across the top.

9. When the student meets criteria for mastery (usually a number of independent responses), draw a green horizontal line through the independent responses. This will clearly indicate that the child has met mastery for that target.

Discrete Trial Quick-Graph
(Blank Levels)

Page ___ of ___

Prompt level key

Criteria for mastery

Name: _____

Subject area or overall goal area: _____

Baseline date: _____

Target	Prompt level	BASELINE	Dates/sessions												

TOOLKIT B
Behavior Forms

- Form 1B: Frequency Quick-Graph 1
- Form 2B: Frequency Quick-Graph 2
- Form 3B: Frequency Quick-Graph 3
- Form 4B: Frequency/Intensity Quick-Graph 1
- Form 5B: Frequency/Intensity Quick-Graph 2
- Form 6B: Frequency Rate Data Sheet
- Form 7B: Frequency Rate Graph
- Form 8B: Duration Data Quick-Graph 1
- Form 9B: Duration Data Quick-Graph 2
- Form 10Ba-b: Duration/Intensity Quick-Graph
- Form 11B: Duration Percentage Data Sheet
- Form 12B: Duration Percentage Data Graph
- Form 13Ba-b: Intensity Quick-Graph
- Form 14Ba-b: Intensity Level Percentage Data Sheet
- Form 15Ba-b: Intensity Level Percentage Graph
- Form 16B: Time Interval Scatterplot Quick-Graph
- Form 17Ba-b: Time Interval/Intensity Scatterplot Quick-Graph
- Form 18B: Scatterplot Percentage Data Sheet
- Form 19B: Scatterplot Percentage Graph
- Form 20Ba-b: ABC Data Sheet and Quick-Graph

FORM 1B: FREQUENCY QUICK-GRAPH 1

Steps for completing Frequency Quick-Graph 1 are as follows. (Refer to Figure 4.2 for a completed example.)

1. Complete the demographic information.

2. Define the target behavior, and write the definition on the form. (See Chapter 2 for more information on how to determine and define the target behavior.) To save time, you can fill in the definition of the behavior and then copy the form so you will only have to do this step once.

3. Determine the date you will begin collecting data. Begin filling in the dates, but remember that on this form, you will need to record every consecutive day that you take data, even though there may be no behaviors exhibited that day. Zero needs to be reflected on the form. Make sure to fill in the page number at the top, and continue adding pages as the dates continue.

4. As you observe a behavior, place a slash mark in the numbered row, beginning with 1. You can also shade the box or use an X. Continue to count the behaviors that occur, checking off the numbers as indicated on the graph. This graph allows you to tally up to 25 instances of the behavior on one sheet.

5. At the end of the day, place a dot on the top line of the last numbered row you marked, indicating the total number of behaviors observed. It is helpful if you do this with a colored pencil for visual contrast. If there were no behaviors, then place a dot indicating 0.

6. After a few days, you can connect the dots, forming a line graph.

7. If you begin a new intervention or something occurs, indicate that event with a vertical dotted line. This will allow you to compare data between interventions or circumstances that may occur. Make sure to document what the dotted line represents.

Frequency Quick-Graph 1

Page ___ of ___

Name: ___

School year: ___

Grade: ___

Behavior Definition:

25													
24													
23													
22													
21													
20													
19													
18													
17													
16													
15													
14													
13													
12													
11													
10													
9													
8													
7													
6													
5													
4													
3													
2													
1													
0													

Frequency

Dates

The Data Collection Toolkit: Everything You Need to Organize, Manage, and Monitor Classroom Data, by Cindy Golden.

FORM 2B: FREQUENCY QUICK-GRAPH 2

This form is nearly identical to Frequency Quick-Graph 1; it simply provides a different way to tally and visualize the number of behaviors. Steps for completing Frequency Quick-Graph 2 are as follows. (Refer to Figure 4.3 for a completed example.)

1. Complete the demographic information.

2. Define the target behavior, and write the definition on the form. (See Chapter 2 for more information on how to determine and define the target behavior.)

3. Determine the date you will begin collecting data. Begin filling in the dates, but remember that on this form, you will need to record every consecutive day that you take data, even though there may be no behaviors exhibited that day. Zero needs to be reflected on the form. Make sure to fill in the page number at the top, and continue adding pages as the dates continue.

4. As you observe a behavior, place a slash mark in the numbered row, beginning with 1. You can also shade the box or use an X. Continue to count the behaviors that occur, checking off the numbers as indicated on the graph. This graph allows you to tally up to 25 instances of the behavior on one sheet.

5. At the end of the day, place a dot on the top line of the last numbered row you marked, indicating the total number of behaviors observed. It is helpful if you do this with a colored pencil for visual contrast. If there were no behaviors, then place a dot indicating 0.

6. After a few days, you can connect the dots, forming a line graph.

7. If you begin a new intervention or something significant occurs, indicate that event with a vertical dotted line. This will allow you to compare data between interventions or circumstances that may occur. Make sure to document what the dotted line represents.

Frequency Quick-Graph 2

Page ____ of ____

Frequency

25	25	25	25	25	25	25	25	25	25	25	25	25	25
24	24	24	24	24	24	24	24	24	24	24	24	24	24
23	23	23	23	23	23	23	23	23	23	23	23	23	23
22	22	22	22	22	22	22	22	22	22	22	22	22	22
21	21	21	21	21	21	21	21	21	21	21	21	21	21
20	20	20	20	20	20	20	20	20	20	20	20	20	20
19	19	19	19	19	19	19	19	19	19	19	19	19	19
18	18	18	18	18	18	18	18	18	18	18	18	18	18
17	17	17	17	17	17	17	17	17	17	17	17	17	17
16	16	16	16	16	16	16	16	16	16	16	16	16	16
15	15	15	15	15	15	15	15	15	15	15	15	15	15
14	14	14	14	14	14	14	14	14	14	14	14	14	14
13	13	13	13	13	13	13	13	13	13	13	13	13	13
12	12	12	12	12	12	12	12	12	12	12	12	12	12
11	11	11	11	11	11	11	11	11	11	11	11	11	11
10	10	10	10	10	10	10	10	10	10	10	10	10	10
9	9	9	9	9	9	9	9	9	9	9	9	9	9
8	8	8	8	8	8	8	8	8	8	8	8	8	8
7	7	7	7	7	7	7	7	7	7	7	7	7	7
6	6	6	6	6	6	6	6	6	6	6	6	6	6
5	5	5	5	5	5	5	5	5	5	5	5	5	5
4	4	4	4	4	4	4	4	4	4	4	4	4	4
3	3	3	3	3	3	3	3	3	3	3	3	3	3
2	2	2	2	2	2	2	2	2	2	2	2	2	2
1	1	1	1	1	1	1	1	1	1	1	1	1	1

Dates

Behavior Definition:

Name: _____ **School year:** _____ **Grade:** _____

The Data Collection Toolkit: Everything You Need to Organize, Manage, and Monitor Classroom Data, by Cindy Golden.
Copyright © 2018 Paul H. Brookes Publishing Co. All rights reserved.

FORM 3B: FREQUENCY QUICK-GRAPH 3

Frequency Quick-Graph 3 allows you to tally up to 50 instances of a behavior on one sheet. Steps for completing Frequency Quick-Graph 3 are as follows:

1. Complete the demographic information.

2. Define the target behavior, and write the definition on the form. (See Chapter 2 for more information on how to determine and define the target behavior.)

3. Determine the date you will begin collecting data. Begin filling in the dates, but remember that on this form, you will need to record every consecutive day that you take data, even though there may be no behaviors exhibited that day. Zero needs to be reflected on the form. Make sure to fill in the page number at the top, and continue adding pages as the dates continue.

4. As you observe a behavior, place a slash mark in the numbered row, beginning with 1. You can also shade the box or use an X. Continue to count the behaviors that occur, checking off the numbers as indicated on the graph. This graph allows you to tally up to 50 instances of the behavior on one sheet.

5. At the end of the day, place a dot on the top line of the last numbered row you marked, indicating the total number of behaviors observed. It is helpful if you do this with a colored pencil for visual contrast. If there were no behaviors, then place a dot indicating 0.

6. After a few days, you can connect the dots, forming a line graph.

7. If you begin a new intervention or something significant occurs, indicate that event with a vertical dotted line. This will allow you to compare data between interventions or circumstances that may occur. Make sure to document what the dotted line represents.

Name: _____

School year: _____

Grade: _____

Behavior Definition:

Frequency

50	50	50	50	50	50	50	50	50	50	50	50	50	50	50
49	49	49	49	49	49	49	49	49	49	49	49	49	49	49
48	48	48	48	48	48	48	48	48	48	48	48	48	48	48
47	47	47	47	47	47	47	47	47	47	47	47	47	47	47
46	46	46	46	46	46	46	46	46	46	46	46	46	46	46
45	45	45	45	45	45	45	45	45	45	45	45	45	45	45
44	44	44	44	44	44	44	44	44	44	44	44	44	44	44
43	43	43	43	43	43	43	43	43	43	43	43	43	43	43
42	42	42	42	42	42	42	42	42	42	42	42	42	42	42
41	41	41	41	41	41	41	41	41	41	41	41	41	41	41
40	40	40	40	40	40	40	40	40	40	40	40	40	40	40
39	39	39	39	39	39	39	39	39	39	39	39	39	39	39
38	38	38	38	38	38	38	38	38	38	38	38	38	38	38
37	37	37	37	37	37	37	37	37	37	37	37	37	37	37
36	36	36	36	36	36	36	36	36	36	36	36	36	36	36
35	35	35	35	35	35	35	35	35	35	35	35	35	35	35
34	34	34	34	34	34	34	34	34	34	34	34	34	34	34
33	33	33	33	33	33	33	33	33	33	33	33	33	33	33
32	32	32	32	32	32	32	32	32	32	32	32	32	32	32
31	31	31	31	31	31	31	31	31	31	31	31	31	31	31
30	30	30	30	30	30	30	30	30	30	30	30	30	30	30
29	29	29	29	29	29	29	29	29	29	29	29	29	29	29
28	28	28	28	28	28	28	28	28	28	28	28	28	28	28
27	27	27	27	27	27	27	27	27	27	27	27	27	27	27
26	26	26	26	26	26	26	26	26	26	26	26	26	26	26
25	25	25	25	25	25	25	25	25	25	25	25	25	25	25
24	24	24	24	24	24	24	24	24	24	24	24	24	24	24
23	23	23	23	23	23	23	23	23	23	23	23	23	23	23
22	22	22	22	22	22	22	22	22	22	22	22	22	22	22
21	21	21	21	21	21	21	21	21	21	21	21	21	21	21
20	20	20	20	20	20	20	20	20	20	20	20	20	20	20
19	19	19	19	19	19	19	19	19	19	19	19	19	19	19
18	18	18	18	18	18	18	18	18	18	18	18	18	18	18
17	17	17	17	17	17	17	17	17	17	17	17	17	17	17
16	16	16	16	16	16	16	16	16	16	16	16	16	16	16
15	15	15	15	15	15	15	15	15	15	15	15	15	15	15
14	14	14	14	14	14	14	14	14	14	14	14	14	14	14
13	13	13	13	13	13	13	13	13	13	13	13	13	13	13
12	12	12	12	12	12	12	12	12	12	12	12	12	12	12
11	11	11	11	11	11	11	11	11	11	11	11	11	11	11
10	10	10	10	10	10	10	10	10	10	10	10	10	10	10
9	9	9	9	9	9	9	9	9	9	9	9	9	9	9
8	8	8	8	8	8	8	8	8	8	8	8	8	8	8
7	7	7	7	7	7	7	7	7	7	7	7	7	7	7
6	6	6	6	6	6	6	6	6	6	6	6	6	6	6
5	5	5	5	5	5	5	5	5	5	5	5	5	5	5
4	4	4	4	4	4	4	4	4	4	4	4	4	4	4
3	3	3	3	3	3	3	3	3	3	3	3	3	3	3
2	2	2	2	2	2	2	2	2	2	2	2	2	2	2
1	1	1	1	1	1	1	1	1	1	1	1	1	1	1
0	0	0	0	0	0	0	0	0	0	0	0	0	0	0

DATES

FORM 4B: FREQUENCY/INTENSITY QUICK-GRAPH 1

You will need a set of colored pencils to complete Frequency/Intensity Quick-Graph 1. Steps for completing this Quick-Graph are as follows. (Refer to Figure 4.4a-b for a completed example.)

1. Both pages of this form should stay together. Print the form on the front and back of one page or have the second page of the form (with the detailed Intensity Key and defined target behavior) available at all times.

2. Complete the demographic information.

3. Define the target behavior on the back sheet.

4. Determine the colors you will use to code intensity levels, and define each level of intensity in specific and observable terms.

5. On the front sheet, color in the blocks on the Intensity Key, indicating which color corresponds to which intensity level.

6. Determine the date you will begin collecting data. Begin filling in the dates, but remember that on this form, you will need to record every consecutive day that you take data, even though there may be no behaviors exhibited that day. Zero needs to be reflected on the form. Make sure to fill in the page number at the top, and continue adding pages as the dates continue.

7. As you observe a behavior, place a slash mark in the numbered row, beginning with 1. You can also shade the box or use an X. Make these marks in the color corresponding to the intensity level of the behavior.

8. Continue to count the behaviors that occur, checking off the numbers as indicated on the graph in the color corresponding to each behavior's intensity. This graph allows you to tally up to 25 instances of the behavior on one sheet.

9. At the end of the day, place a dot on the top line of the last numbered row you marked, indicating the total number of behaviors observed. If there were no behaviors, then place a dot indicating 0.

10. After a few days, you can connect the dots, forming a line graph.

11. If you begin a new intervention or something significant occurs, indicate that event with a vertical dotted line. It will provide additional information so that you can compare data between interventions or circumstances that may occur. Make sure to document what the dotted line represents.

Frequency/Intensity Quick-Graph 1—Front

Frequency

25	25	25	25	25	25	25	25	25	25	25	25	25	25
24	24	24	24	24	24	24	24	24	24	24	24	24	24
23	23	23	23	23	23	23	23	23	23	23	23	23	23
22	22	22	22	22	22	22	22	22	22	22	22	22	22
21	21	21	21	21	21	21	21	21	21	21	21	21	21
20	20	20	20	20	20	20	20	20	20	20	20	20	20
19	19	19	19	19	19	19	19	19	19	19	19	19	19
18	18	18	18	18	18	18	18	18	18	18	18	18	18
17	17	17	17	17	17	17	17	17	17	17	17	17	17
16	16	16	16	16	16	16	16	16	16	16	16	16	16
15	15	15	15	15	15	15	15	15	15	15	15	15	15
14	14	14	14	14	14	14	14	14	14	14	14	14	14
13	13	13	13	13	13	13	13	13	13	13	13	13	13
12	12	12	12	12	12	12	12	12	12	12	12	12	12
11	11	11	11	11	11	11	11	11	11	11	11	11	11
10	10	10	10	10	10	10	10	10	10	10	10	10	10
9	9	9	9	9	9	9	9	9	9	9	9	9	9
8	8	8	8	8	8	8	8	8	8	8	8	8	8
7	7	7	7	7	7	7	7	7	7	7	7	7	7
6	6	6	6	6	6	6	6	6	6	6	6	6	6
5	5	5	5	5	5	5	5	5	5	5	5	5	5
4	4	4	4	4	4	4	4	4	4	4	4	4	4
3	3	3	3	3	3	3	3	3	3	3	3	3	3
2	2	2	2	2	2	2	2	2	2	2	2	2	2
1	1	1	1	1	1	1	1	1	1	1	1	1	1

Dates

Intensity Key

Mild	Moderate	Intense

Behavior Definition:

Name: _____

School year: _____

Grade: _____

Frequency/Intensity Quick-Graph 1 — Back

Target behavior

Intensity key

FORM 5B: FREQUENCY/INTENSITY QUICK-GRAPH 2

Frequency/Intensity Quick-Graph 2 allows you to tally up to 50 instances of a behavior on one sheet. You will need a set of colored pencils to complete this form. Steps for completing Frequency/Intensity Quick-Graph 2 are as follows:

1. Both pages of this form should stay together. Print the form on the front and back of one page or have the second page of the form (with the detailed Intensity Key and defined target behavior) available at all times.

2. Complete the demographic information.

3. Define the target behavior on the back sheet.

4. Determine the colors you will use to code intensity levels, and define each level of intensity in specific and observable terms.

5. On the front sheet, color in the blocks on the Intensity Key, indicating which color corresponds to which intensity level.

6. Determine the date you will begin collecting data. Begin filling in the dates, but remember that on this form, you will need to record every consecutive day that you take data, even though there may be no behaviors exhibited that day. Zero needs to be reflected on the form. Make sure to fill in the page number at the top, and continue adding pages as the dates continue.

7. As you observe a behavior, place a slash mark in the numbered row, beginning with 1. You can also shade the box or use an X. Make these marks in the color corresponding to the intensity level of the behavior.

8. Continue to count the behaviors that occur, checking off the numbers as indicated on the graph in the color corresponding to each behavior's intensity. This graph allows you to tally up to 50 instances of the behavior on one sheet.

9. At the end of the day, place a dot on the top line of the last numbered row you marked, indicating the total number of behaviors observed. If there were no behaviors, then place a dot indicating 0.

10. After a few days, you can connect the dots, forming a line graph.

11. If you begin a new intervention or something significant occurs, indicate that event with a vertical dotted line. It will provide additional information so that you can compare data between interventions or circumstances that may occur. Make sure to document what the dotted line represents.

Frequency/Intensity Quick-Graph 2—Front

Page ___ of ___

Name: _____

Behavior Definition:

School year: _____

Beginning date: _____

Grade: _____

Frequency

50	50	50	50	50	50	50	50	50	50	50	50	50	50	50
49	49	49	49	49	49	49	49	49	49	49	49	49	49	49
48	48	48	48	48	48	48	48	48	48	48	48	48	48	48
47	47	47	47	47	47	47	47	47	47	47	47	47	47	47
46	46	46	46	46	46	46	46	46	46	46	46	46	46	46
45	45	45	45	45	45	45	45	45	45	45	45	45	45	45
44	44	44	44	44	44	44	44	44	44	44	44	44	44	44
43	43	43	43	43	43	43	43	43	43	43	43	43	43	43
42	42	42	42	42	42	42	42	42	42	42	42	42	42	42
41	41	41	41	41	41	41	41	41	41	41	41	41	41	41
40	40	40	40	40	40	40	40	40	40	40	40	40	40	40
39	39	39	39	39	39	39	39	39	39	39	39	39	39	39
38	38	38	38	38	38	38	38	38	38	38	38	38	38	38
37	37	37	37	37	37	37	37	37	37	37	37	37	37	37
36	36	36	36	36	36	36	36	36	36	36	36	36	36	36
35	35	35	35	35	35	35	35	35	35	35	35	35	35	35
34	34	34	34	34	34	34	34	34	34	34	34	34	34	34
33	33	33	33	33	33	33	33	33	33	33	33	33	33	33
32	32	32	32	32	32	32	32	32	32	32	32	32	32	32
31	31	31	31	31	31	31	31	31	31	31	31	31	31	31
30	30	30	30	30	30	30	30	30	30	30	30	30	30	30
29	29	29	29	29	29	29	29	29	29	29	29	29	29	29
28	28	28	28	28	28	28	28	28	28	28	28	28	28	28
27	27	27	27	27	27	27	27	27	27	27	27	27	27	27
26	26	26	26	26	26	26	26	26	26	26	26	26	26	26
25	25	25	25	25	25	25	25	25	25	25	25	25	25	25
24	24	24	24	24	24	24	24	24	24	24	24	24	24	24
23	23	23	23	23	23	23	23	23	23	23	23	23	23	23
22	22	22	22	22	22	22	22	22	22	22	22	22	22	22
21	21	21	21	21	21	21	21	21	21	21	21	21	21	21
20	20	20	20	20	20	20	20	20	20	20	20	20	20	20
19	19	19	19	19	19	19	19	19	19	19	19	19	19	19
18	18	18	18	18	18	18	18	18	18	18	18	18	18	18
17	17	17	17	17	17	17	17	17	17	17	17	17	17	17
16	16	16	16	16	16	16	16	16	16	16	16	16	16	16
15	15	15	15	15	15	15	15	15	15	15	15	15	15	15
14	14	14	14	14	14	14	14	14	14	14	14	14	14	14
13	13	13	13	13	13	13	13	13	13	13	13	13	13	13
12	12	12	12	12	12	12	12	12	12	12	12	12	12	12
11	11	11	11	11	11	11	11	11	11	11	11	11	11	11
10	10	10	10	10	10	10	10	10	10	10	10	10	10	10
9	9	9	9	9	9	9	9	9	9	9	9	9	9	9
8	8	8	8	8	8	8	8	8	8	8	8	8	8	8
7	7	7	7	7	7	7	7	7	7	7	7	7	7	7
6	6	6	6	6	6	6	6	6	6	6	6	6	6	6
5	5	5	5	5	5	5	5	5	5	5	5	5	5	5
4	4	4	4	4	4	4	4	4	4	4	4	4	4	4
3	3	3	3	3	3	3	3	3	3	3	3	3	3	3
2	2	2	2	2	2	2	2	2	2	2	2	2	2	2
1	1	1	1	1	1	1	1	1	1	1	1	1	1	1
0	0	0	0	0	0	0	0	0	0	0	0	0	0	0

Dates

Frequency/Intensity Quick-Graph 2—Back

Target behavior

Intensity key

The Data Collection Toolkit: Everything You Need to Organize, Manage, and Monitor Classroom Data, by Cindy Golden.

FORM 6B: FREQUENCY RATE DATA SHEET

Steps for completing the Frequency Rate Data Sheet are as follows. (Refer to Figure 4.5 for a completed example.)

1. Complete the demographic information.

2. Define the target behavior.

3. Write in the date at the bottom.

4. Determine the time intervals for observation, and place them on the left side of the form.

5. Collect frequency data during these time periods. (You may use tally marks, as shown in Figure 4.5.)

6. Total the number of behaviors, and place that number in the Total by Time Interval column.

7. Determine the total number of minutes for the time interval.

8. Divide the total number of behaviors for each interval (total frequency count) by the total minutes for that interval. This step determines the rate of behaviors per minute during that time period.

9. Use additional sheets as needed, numbering them at the top.

Frequency Rate Data Sheet

Page _____ of _____

$$\frac{\text{Number of behaviors}}{\text{Total minutes}} = \text{Rate of behavior per interval of time}$$

Time intervals	Frequency (F) data		TOTAL by time interval	TOTAL F count / TOTAL minutes	Rate per minute

Date: _____

Name: _____ **School year:** _____ **Grade:** _____

Behavior Definition:

The Data Collection Toolkit: Everything You Need to Organize, Manage, and Monitor Classroom Data, by Cindy Golden.
Copyright © 2018 Paul H. Brookes Publishing Co. All rights reserved.

FORM 7B: FREQUENCY RATE GRAPH

The Frequency Rate Graph serves as a companion to the Frequency Rate Data Sheet. Steps for completing the Frequency Rate Graph are as follows. (Refer to Figure 4.6 for a completed example.)

1. Complete the demographic information.

2. Define the target behavior.

3. Document the date you will begin collecting data. Begin filling in the dates, but remember that on this form, you will need to record every consecutive day that you take data, even though there may be no behaviors exhibited that day. Zero needs to be reflected on the form. Make sure to fill in the page number at the top, and continue adding pages as the dates continue.

4. Determine frequency rates using the Frequency Rate Data Sheet. Next, determine the scale you want to use to graph your frequency rate (e.g., rate per minute).

5. Place dots on the graph indicating the frequency rate for each day data were collected. Connect the dots, forming a line graph of the rate of the behavior over time.

6. If you begin a new intervention or something significant occurs, indicate that event with a vertical dotted line. It will provide additional information so that you can compare data between interventions or other important circumstances that may occur. Make sure to document what the dotted line represents.

Frequency Rate Graph

Page ___ of ___

Name: _____ **School year:** _____ **Grade:** _____

Behavior Definition:

Rate per minute

| 0.40 |
| 0.38 |
| 0.36 |
| 0.34 |
| 0.32 |
| 0.30 |
| 0.28 |
| 0.26 |
| 0.24 |
| 0.22 |
| 0.20 |
| 0.18 |
| 0.16 |
| 0.14 |
| 0.12 |
| 0.10 |
| 0.08 |
| 0.06 |
| 0.04 |
| 0.02 |
| 0 |

Time intervals

KEY: Date

FORM 8B: DURATION DATA QUICK-GRAPH 1

Steps for completing the Duration Data Quick-Graph 1 are as follows. (Refer to Figure 4.7 for a completed example.)

1. Complete the demographic information.

2. Define the target behavior.

3. Fill in the dates that you collect duration data.

4. Document the time a behavioral event starts and ends.

5. Determine the total amount of time the behavior occurred—the duration (e.g., total minutes).

6. Turn the paper to portrait orientation. Plot the data points on the middle, darker line, with each data point placed to correspond to the number of minutes equaling the duration of each behavioral event. It is helpful if you make these dots in red.

7. Draw lines between the data points on the graph, connecting each one. This will form your line graph indicating duration.

8. If you begin a new intervention or something significant occurs, indicate that event with a vertical dotted line. It will provide additional information so that you can compare data between interventions and baseline or other circumstances that may occur. Make sure to document what the dotted line represents.

9. Use additional sheets as needed, numbering them at the top.

Duration Data Quick-Graph 1

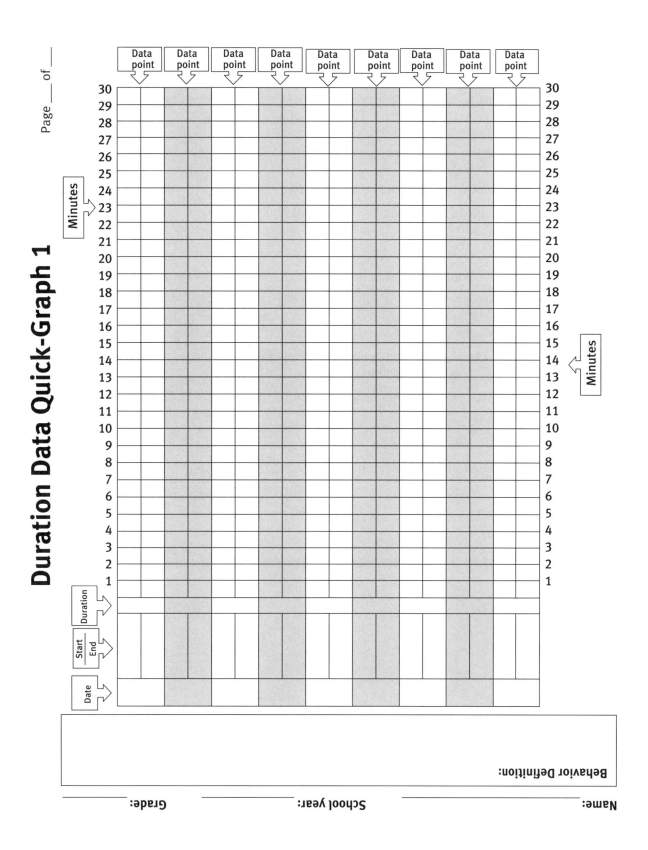

Behavior Definition:

Name: _____ **School year:** _____ **Grade:** _____

FORM 9B: DURATION DATA QUICK-GRAPH 2

Duration Data Quick-Graph 2 allows you to customize the sequence of minutes you use when measuring and graphing duration. For instance, you could use 2-minute increments or even 5-minute increments. Steps for completing Duration Data Quick-Graph 2 are as follows:

1. Complete the demographic information.

2. Define the target behavior.

3. Fill in the dates that you collect duration data.

4. Determine the increments of time you would like to use for your duration graph, and write in the corresponding minutes horizontally across the top of the form.

5. Document the time a behavioral event starts and ends.

6. Determine the total amount of time the behavior occurred—the duration.

7. Turn the paper to portrait orientation. Plot the data points on the middle, darker line, with each data point placed to correspond to the number of minutes equaling the duration of each behavioral event. It is helpful if you make these dots in red.

8. Draw lines between the data points on the graph, connecting each one. This will form your line graph indicating duration.

9. If you begin a new intervention or something significant occurs, indicate that event with a vertical dotted line. It will provide additional information so that you can compare data between interventions and baseline or other circumstances that may occur. Make sure to document what the dotted line represents.

10. Use additional sheets as needed, numbering them at the top.

Duration Data Quick-Graph 2

		Data point	Data point	Data point	Data point	Data point	Data point	Data point	Data point	Data point

Minutes

Date	Start / End	Duration

Behavior Definition:

Name: ____   **School year:** ____   **Grade:** ____

FORM 10Ba-b: DURATION/INTENSITY QUICK-GRAPH

Steps for completing the Duration/Intensity Quick-Graph are as follows. (Refer to Figure 4.8a-b for a completed example.)

1. Both pages of this form should stay together. Print the form on the front and back of one page or have the second page of the form (with the detailed Intensity Key and defined target behavior) available at all times.

2. Complete the demographic information.

3. Define the target behavior on the back sheet.

4. Determine the colors you will use to code intensity levels, and define each level of intensity in specific and observable terms.

5. On the front sheet, color in the blocks on the Intensity Key, indicating which color corresponds to which intensity level.

6. Document the time a behavioral event starts and ends.

7. Determine the total amount of time the behavior occurred—the duration.

8. Using colored pencils, shade in the box indicating the duration in minutes, using the color that corresponds to the intensity level of the behavior.

9. Place dots on each shaded block of time, and draw lines to connect the data points. This will form a line graph of behavior duration. You can make comparisons with this line graph that will indicate the ebb and flow of the duration of behaviors, but you must make a more detailed analysis about the intensity of each behavior. For example, if the duration of behaviors increases or remains constant but the intensity of those behaviors decreases, then you should keep in mind that progress is still being made.

10. If you begin a new intervention or something significant occurs, indicate that event with a vertical dotted line. It will provide additional information so that you can compare data between interventions or circumstances that may occur.

11. Use additional sheets as needed, numbering them at the top.

Duration/Intensity Quick-Graph—Front

Page ___ of ___

Minutes →

	30	30
	29	29
	28	28
	27	27
	26	26
	25	25
	24	24
	23	23
	22	22
	21	21
	20	20
	19	19
	18	18
	17	17
	16	16
	15	15
	14	14
	13	13
	12	12
	11	11
	10	10
	9	9
	8	8
	7	7
	6	6
	5	5
	4	4
	3	3
	2	2
	1	1

Date → Start/End → Duration →

INTENSITY KEY

Intense	Moderate	Mild

Behavior Definition:

Name: _____

School year: _____

Grade: _____

The Data Collection Toolkit: Everything You Need to Organize, Manage, and Monitor Classroom Data, by Cindy Golden.
Copyright © 2018 Paul H. Brookes Publishing Co. All rights reserved.

Duration/Intensity Quick-Graph — Back

Page ___ of ___

Intensity key

Target behavior

FORM 11B: DURATION PERCENTAGE DATA SHEET

Steps for completing the Duration Percentage Data Sheet are as follows. (Refer to Figure 4.9 for a completed example.)

1. Complete the demographic information.

2. Define the target behavior.

3. Fill in the dates that you collect duration data.

4. Determine the total time interval for each day, and write it in the row directly below each date.

5. Each time the behavior occurs, collect duration data and indicate (by date) the start and end times and the total duration of the behavior.

6. Each day, total the number of minutes the student was involved in a behavior at the bottom of the column in the place indicated.

7. Each day, total the number of minutes for the day or the observation period, and write this number in the place indicated. In some instances, the student may only attend half of the day or a class period. In other words, the total number of minutes represents the total time for observation.

8. Divide the total number of minutes the student was involved in the behavior by the number of minutes in the observation period and multiply by 100. This will determine the percentage of time the student was involved in the behavior that day.

9. Use additional sheets as needed, numbering them at the top.

Duration Percentage Data Sheet

Behavior Definition:

Name: _____

School year: _____

Grade: _____

Date and total time

Start

End

Total duration / Total time

Percentage

× 100

× 100

× 100

× 100

× 100

FORM 12B: DURATION PERCENTAGE DATA GRAPH

The Duration Percentage Data Graph serves as a companion to the Duration Percentage Data Sheet. Steps for completing the Duration Percentage Data Graph are as follows. (Refer to Figure 4.10 for a completed example.)

1. Complete the demographic information.

2. Define the target behavior.

3. Determine the date you will begin collecting data. Begin filling in the dates, but remember that on this form, you will need to record every consecutive day that you take data, even though there may be no behaviors exhibited that day. Zero needs to be reflected on the form. Make sure to fill in the page number at the top, and continue adding pages as the dates continue.

4. Determine duration percentages using the Duration Percentage Data Sheet.

5. Plot the percentage for each day. After a few days, you can connect the dots, forming a line graph.

6. If you begin a new intervention or something significant occurs, indicate that event with a vertical dotted line. It will provide additional information so that you can compare data between interventions or circumstances that may occur.

Duration Percentage Data Graph

Percentage													
100													
95													
90													
85													
80													
75													
70													
65													
60													
55													
50													
45													
40													
35													
30													
25													
20													
15													
10													
5													
0													

Dates

Name: _____

School year: _____

Grade: _____

Behavior Definition:

FORM 13Ba-b: INTENSITY QUICK-GRAPH

Steps for completing the Intensity Quick-Graph are as follows. (Refer to Figure 4.11a-b for a completed example.)

1. Complete the demographic information.

2. Define the target behavior.

3. Define each level of intensity in behavioral terms. The data form outlines intensity in four levels, but it is certainly not necessary to use them all.

4. Determine the date you will begin collecting data. However, on this form, you will only need to put the dates of a behavioral event. You may want to put the beginning and ending date of data collection for your reference, even though there may not be a behavior on every date. One reason that you would do this is because you may have 3 or 4 days at the end of the observation period with no behaviors. This is good information to have.

5. As a behavior occurs, place a dot or an X on the middle line of the box corresponding to the intensity level.

6. After a few days, you can connect the dots, forming a line graph.

7. If you begin a new intervention or something significant occurs, indicate that event with a vertical line. It will provide additional information so that you can compare data between interventions or circumstances that may occur.

8. If you add data sheets, make sure to fill in the page number at the top of the sheet.

Intensity Quick-Graph

Intensity level

Date/time

Name: _____

School year: _____

Grade: _____

Target behavior:

FORM 14Ba-b: INTENSITY LEVEL PERCENTAGE DATA SHEET

Steps for completing the Intensity Level Percentage Data Sheet are as follows. (Refer to Figure 4.12a-b for a completed example.)

1. Complete the demographic information.

2. Define the target behavior.

3. On the back sheet, color-code each of the intensity levels. You may decide you need fewer than four levels; however, you have the option of coding up to four. On the front sheet, shade in each intensity level in the designated color.

4. Define each intensity level in behavioral, objective, specific terms.

5. As a behavior occurs, place that day's date at the top of the sheet.

6. As the behavior takes place, determine at what level it occurs, and put a check mark in the column corresponding to the intensity level (1, 2, 3, or 4).

7. Continue to record each instance of the behavior throughout the day, checking off the appropriate column to designate intensity.

8. At the end of the day, total the number of behaviors in each intensity column, recording the sum of behaviors at each level in the Total row.

9. Determine the total sum of behaviors for that day, and place it in the Sum of Behaviors row.

10. Divide the total behaviors at each intensity level by the sum of all behaviors throughout the day. Multiply each answer by 100 to obtain the percentage of behaviors at each intensity level.

Intensity Level Percentage Data Sheet—Front

Intensity levels

DATE	1	2	3	4	1	2	3	4	1	2	3	4	1	2	3	4	1	2	3	4
Behavior incidents																				
Total																				
/Sum of behaviors																				
× 100 = %																				

Target Definition:

Name: _____

School year: _____

Grade: _____

Intensity Level Percentage Data Sheet—Back

Intensity key

| 4 | 3 | 2 | 1 |

Target behavior

FORM 15Ba-b: INTENSITY LEVEL PERCENTAGE GRAPH

The Intensity Level Percentage Graph serves as a companion to the Intensity Level Percentage Data Sheet. Steps for completing the Intensity Level Percentage Graph are as follows. (Refer to Figure 4.13a-b for a completed example.)

1. Both pages of this form should stay together. Print the form on the front and back of one page or have the second page of the form (with the Intensity Key and defined target behavior) available at all times.

2. Complete the demographic information.

3. Define the target behavior

4. On the back sheet, determine the colors you will use to code intensity levels, and define each level of intensity in specific and observable terms.

5. On a date when there are behavior incidents, use colored pencils to plot the intensity level percentages that were calculated for each intensity level, marking dots in colors corresponding to the Intensity Key. Remember that you are graphing the intensity levels across days—not the intensity levels over 1 day.

6. The next date when the behavior occurs, plot the data points in the same way. Once you have collected several days of data, begin to connect the dots made on the graph. Connect the same-colored dots to form several colored line graphs that correspond to different intensity levels.

7. If you begin a new intervention or something significant occurs, indicate that event with a dashed vertical line. It will provide additional information so that you can compare data between interventions or circumstances that may occur.

8. Use additional sheets as needed, numbering them at the top.

Intensity Level Percentage Graph—Front

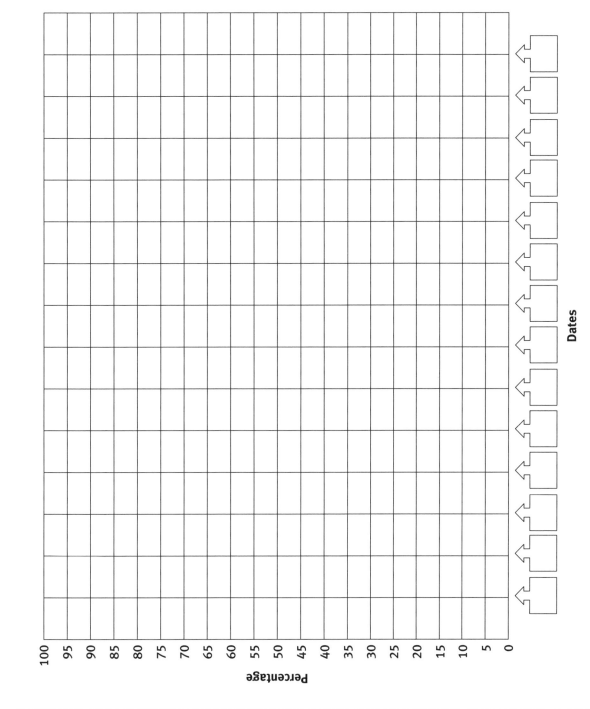

Page _____ of _____

Percentage

100
95
90
85
80
75
70
65
60
55
50
45
40
35
30
25
20
15
10
5
0

Dates

Name: _____   School year: _____   Grade: _____

Behavior definition:

Intensity Level Percentage Graph—Back

Target behavior

Intensity key

| 4 | 3 | 2 | 1 |

FORM 16B: TIME INTERVAL SCATTERPLOT QUICK-GRAPH

Steps for completing the Time Interval Scatterplot Quick-Graph are as follows. (Refer to Figure 4.14 for a completed example.)

1. Complete the demographic information.

2. Define the target behavior.

3. Divide the day out evenly, and place the time intervals in the far left column. Dividing the day by 15- or 20-minute intervals typically works well. The intervals should be consistent.

4. As a behavior occurs, indicate it with a slash mark or X in the block corresponding to the time period in which it takes place.

5. Make sure to indicate dates at the bottom of the form.

6. Analyze the scatterplot data to see when the behaviors most frequently occur.

Time Interval Scatterplot Quick-Graph

Time intervals

Dates

Target behavior:

Name: _____

School year: _____

Grade: _____

FORM 17Ba-b: TIME INTERVAL/INTENSITY SCATTERPLOT QUICK-GRAPH

Steps for completing the Time Interval/Intensity Scatterplot Quick-Graph are as follows. (Refer to Figure 4.15a-b for a completed example.)

1. Complete the demographic information.

2. Define the target behavior.

3. Divide the day out evenly, and place the time intervals in the far left column. Dividing the day by 15- or 20-minute intervals typically works well. The intervals should be consistent.

4. Use the back sheet to color-code and specifically define each of the intensity levels.

5. As a behavior occurs, shade the block corresponding to the time period, using the color associated with the intensity level of the behavior.

6. Make sure to indicate dates at the bottom of the form.

Time Interval/Intensity Scatterplot Quick-Graph—Front

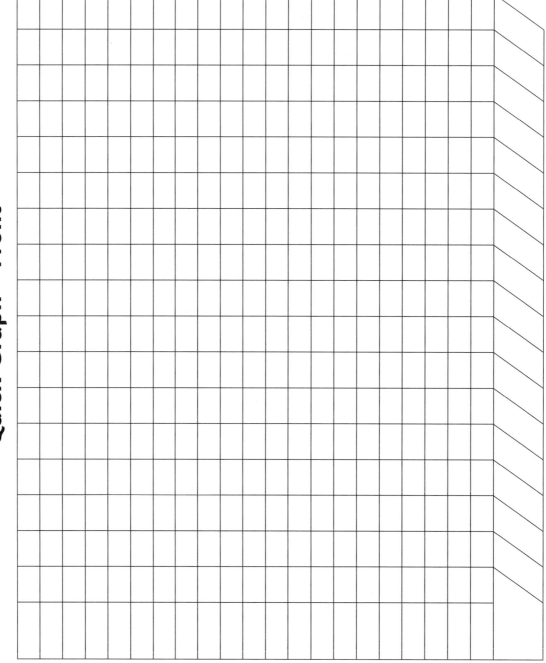

Time Intervals

Dates

Page ___ of ___

Name: _____

School year: _____

Grade: _____

Target behavior:

The Data Collection Toolkit: Everything You Need to Organize, Manage, and Monitor Classroom Data, by Cindy Golden.
Copyright © 2018 Paul H. Brookes Publishing Co. All rights reserved.

Time Interval/Intensity Scatterplot Quick-Graph—Back

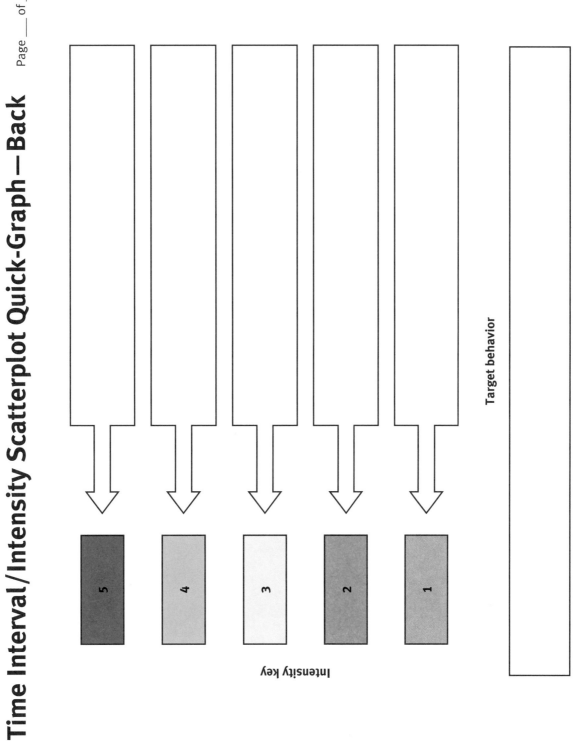

Target behavior

Intensity key

FORM 18B: SCATTERPLOT PERCENTAGE DATA SHEET

Steps for completing the Scatterplot Percentage Data Sheet are as follows. (Refer to Figure 4.16 for a completed example.)

1. Complete the demographic information.

2. Define the target behavior.

3. Divide the day out evenly, and place the time intervals on the far left column.

4. Record the dates when a behavior occurs at the top of the form.

5. As you observe a behavior, place a slash mark or *X* in the box corresponding to the time interval during which the behavior occurs. If more than one instance of the behavior occurs during that same time interval, only mark the box once.

6. As behaviors occur throughout the day, continue marking the boxes indicating when they are taking place.

7. At the end of the day, count the total number of intervals in which a behavior occurred, and record that total number in the Number of Intervals with Behaviors row.

8. Count the total segments of time possible throughout the day, and record that number in the Total Intervals row.

9. Divide these two numbers, and multiply by 100 to yield a percentage for that date.

Scatterplot Percentage Data Sheet

Dates →

Number of intervals with behaviors											
TOTAL INTERVALS											
× 100 = PERCENTAGE											

Time Intervals

Target behavior:

Name: _____ **School year:** _____ **Grade:** _____

FORM 19B: SCATTERPLOT PERCENTAGE GRAPH

Steps for completing the Scatterplot Percentage Graph are as follows. (Refer to Figure 4.17 for a completed example.)

1. Define the target behavior.

2. List the dates at the bottom that correspond to the dates on the Scatterplot Percentage Data Sheet.

3. Plot the scatterplot percentages derived for each day.

4. After a few days, you can connect the dots, forming a line graph.

5. If you begin a new intervention or something significant occurs, indicate that event with a vertical dotted line. It will provide additional information so that you can compare data between interventions or circumstances that may occur.

Scatterplot Percentage Graph

Page ____ of ____

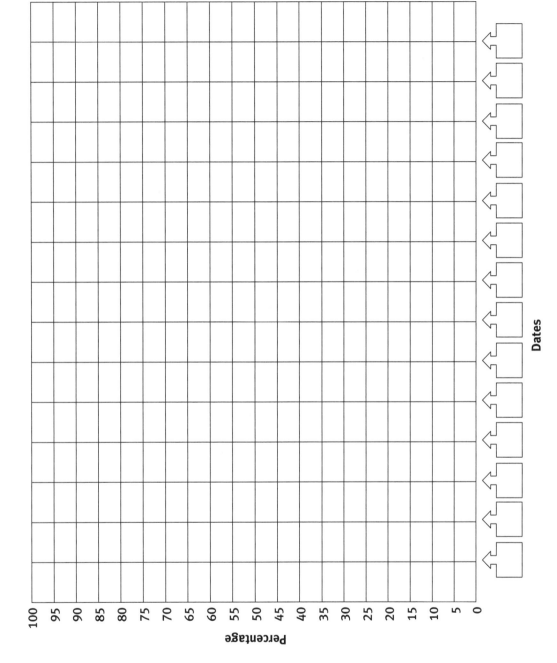

Percentage

Dates

Name: ____ **School year:** ____ **Grade:** ____

Behavior definition:

The Data Collection Toolkit: Everything You Need to Organize, Manage, and Monitor Classroom Data, by Cindy Golden.

FORM 20Ba-b: ABC DATA SHEET AND QUICK-GRAPH

Steps for completing The ABC Data Sheet and Quick-Graph are as follows. (Refer to Figure 4.18a-b for a completed example.)

1. Complete the demographic information on the ABC Data Sheet and ABC Data Quick-Graph.

2. Document each behavioral event on the ABC Data Sheet by giving information about the context; antecedent; behavior observed; types of behavioral data collected, if applicable (i.e., frequency, duration, and intensity); and consequence(s) following the behavior.

3. To the best of your ability, determine the possible function of (reason for) the behavior. Possible functions include to gain access, to gain attention, to communicate a want or need, to escape a challenging demand or task, or to regulate sensory input. Sometimes, a behavior may be caused by sickness or pain. All of these possible functions are listed on the ABC Data Form, in addition to an "other" option to specify any other possible functions.

4. On the ABC Data Sheet, find the antecedent and possible function for Behavior 1. On the Quick-Graph, document each by finding the function from the large shaded areas and, beginning in Column 1, put a slash mark or X in the grid/column that corresponds to the antecedent. Move to the next column for the second behavior and so forth.

5. This will provide a visual of which functions are playing the biggest role in each environment or context.

ABC Data Sheet

Name: _____ School year: _____ Grade: _____ Date range: _____

Incident	Context Give info about the following:	Antecedent What directive or action occurred before the behavior?	Behavior What did the student do?	Data — Intensity	Data — Duration	Data — Frequency count	Consequence What did staff do?	Possible function Why did it happen?
1	Date Time Setting Activity People Group size Subject	☐ Transition ☐ Denied access ☐ Directive ☐ New task ☐ Told no ☐ Waiting ☐ Unstructured time ☐ High sensory input ☐ Low sensory input ☐ No attention ☐		☐ Low ☐ Medium ☐ High	☐ <1 min. ☐ 1–5 min. ☐ 5–10 min. ☐ 10–30 min.			Access Attention Communication Escape Sensory Sickness/pain Other
2	Date Time Setting Activity People Group size Subject	☐ Transition ☐ Denied access ☐ Directive ☐ New task ☐ Told no ☐ Waiting ☐ Unstructured time ☐ High sensory input ☐ Low sensory input ☐ No attention ☐		☐ Low ☐ Medium ☐ High	☐ <1 min. ☐ 1–5 min. ☐ 5–10 min. ☐ 10–30 min.			Access Attention Communication Escape Sensory Sickness/pain Other
3	Date Time Setting Activity People Group size Subject	☐ Transition ☐ Denied access ☐ Directive ☐ New task ☐ Told no ☐ Waiting ☐ Unstructured time ☐ High sensory input ☐ Low sensory input ☐ No attention ☐		☐ Low ☐ Medium ☐ High	☐ <1 min. ☐ 1–5 min. ☐ 5–10 min. ☐ 10–30 min.			Access Attention Communication Escape Sensory Sickness/pain Other

ABC Data Quick-Graph

Access

6	6	6	6	6	6	6	6	6	6	6	6
5	5	5	5	5	5	5	5	5	5	5	5
4	4	4	4	4	4	4	4	4	4	4	4
3	3	3	3	3	3	3	3	3	3	3	3
2	2	2	2	2	2	2	2	2	2	2	2
1	1	1	1	1	1	1	1	1	1	1	1

Attention

6	6	6	6	6	6	6	6	6	6	6	6
5	5	5	5	5	5	5	5	5	5	5	5
4	4	4	4	4	4	4	4	4	4	4	4
3	3	3	3	3	3	3	3	3	3	3	3
2	2	2	2	2	2	2	2	2	2	2	2
1	1	1	1	1	1	1	1	1	1	1	1

Communication

6	6	6	6	6	6	6	6	6	6	6	6
5	5	5	5	5	5	5	5	5	5	5	5
4	4	4	4	4	4	4	4	4	4	4	4
3	3	3	3	3	3	3	3	3	3	3	3
2	2	2	2	2	2	2	2	2	2	2	2
1	1	1	1	1	1	1	1	1	1	1	1

Escape

6	6	6	6	6	6	6	6	6	6	6	6
5	5	5	5	5	5	5	5	5	5	5	5
4	4	4	4	4	4	4	4	4	4	4	4
3	3	3	3	3	3	3	3	3	3	3	3
2	2	2	2	2	2	2	2	2	2	2	2
1	1	1	1	1	1	1	1	1	1	1	1

Sensory

6	6	6	6	6	6	6	6	6	6	6	6
5	5	5	5	5	5	5	5	5	5	5	5
4	4	4	4	4	4	4	4	4	4	4	4
3	3	3	3	3	3	3	3	3	3	3	3
2	2	2	2	2	2	2	2	2	2	2	2
1	1	1	1	1	1	1	1	1	1	1	1

Sickness/pain

6	6	6	6	6	6	6	6	6	6	6	6
5	5	5	5	5	5	5	5	5	5	5	5
4	4	4	4	4	4	4	4	4	4	4	4
3	3	3	3	3	3	3	3	3	3	3	3
2	2	2	2	2	2	2	2	2	2	2	2
1	1	1	1	1	1	1	1	1	1	1	1

Other: _____

Transition	Denied access	Directive	New task	Told no	Waiting	Unstructured time	High sensory input	Low sensory input	No attention		
6	6	6	6	6	6	6	6	6	6	6	6
5	5	5	5	5	5	5	5	5	5	5	5
4	4	4	4	4	4	4	4	4	4	4	4
3	3	3	3	3	3	3	3	3	3	3	3
2	2	2	2	2	2	2	2	2	2	2	2
1	1	1	1	1	1	1	1	1	1	1	1

Other: _____

Transition	Denied access	Directive	New task	Told no	Waiting	Unstructured time	High sensory input	Low sensory input	No attention		
6	6	6	6	6	6	6	6	6	6	6	6
5	5	5	5	5	5	5	5	5	5	5	5
4	4	4	4	4	4	4	4	4	4	4	4
3	3	3	3	3	3	3	3	3	3	3	3
2	2	2	2	2	2	2	2	2	2	2	2
1	1	1	1	1	1	1	1	1	1	1	1

Name: _____ School year: _____ Date range: _____

Target behavior: _____

IEP Forms

- Form 1C: IEP Goal Data Sheet
- Form 2C: IEP Goal Mastery Quick-Graph
- Form 3C: Academic Needs Checklist
- Form 4C: Teaching Programs

FORM 1C: IEP GOAL DATA SHEET

Steps for completing the IEP Goal Data Sheet are as follows. (See Figure 5.3 for completed example.)

1.   Complete the demographic information.

2.   Number and write out the IEP goals or objectives you are tracking.

3.   In the Method of Measurement column, note how each goal should be measured (e.g., rate, percentage, prompt).

4.   Write the criteria for mastery (e.g., 80% weekly average, correct responses for 4 out of 5 consecutive days) in the Mastery column.

5.   Collect data on IEP goals for each day of the week according to how each goal should be measured (i.e., percentage correct, number of prompts required, rate of correct responses).

6.   At the end of the week, calculate a week total, and compare it to the criteria for mastery to track the student's weekly progress toward goals.

IEP Goal Data Sheet

#	Goals/objectives	Method of measurement	Dates					Week total / Mastery

Name: _____

School year: _____

IEP date: _____

FORM 2C: IEP GOAL MASTERY QUICK-GRAPH

The IEP Goal Mastery Quick-Graph is a companion to the IEP Goal Data Sheet. Steps for completing the Quick-Graph are as follows. (See Figure 5.4 for a completed example.)

1. Number and write out the IEP goals or objectives you are tracking.

2. Write in the week-ending dates.

3. Using the IEP Goal Data Sheet, shade in Yes or No to indicate whether the student achieved mastery of the goal at the end of the week.

IEP Goal Mastery Quick-Graph

Name: _____

School year: _____

Grade: _____

IEP date: _____

#	Goals/objectives	Mastered	Dates (Week ending)										
		Yes											
		No											
		Yes											
		No											
		Yes											
		No											
		Yes											
		No											
		Yes											
		No											

FORM 3C: ACADEMIC NEEDS CHECKLIST

The Academic Needs Checklist will help you organize your students' IEP information according to the supports, services, and environments they need to meet their goals. The form can be customized to match the needs of your classroom. Steps for completing the Academic Needs Checklist are as follows. (See Figure 5.5 for a completed example.)

1. List all your students; make as many copies of the form as needed to do this.

2. For the first student, list either the subject areas you teach or the subject areas linked to IEP goals.

3. List any specific teaching materials needed to support the student in each subject area.

4. Check off the type of grouping or learning environment where the student should be taught for each subject (e.g., small group, regular classroom). (Note that two customizable boxes allow you to list any learning arrangements not specified on the form.)

5. Repeat Steps 2–4 for the remaining students.

Academic Needs Checklist

Teacher: _____

School year: _____

Student	Subject	Specific materials	Grouping					
			Regular class	Coteaching			Small group	Individual

FORM 4C: TEACHING PROGRAMS

Steps for completing the Teaching Programs form are as follows. (See Figure 5.6 for a completed example):

1. Record the student's name, school year, and subject area.

2. List the materials needed for the lesson.

3. Circle the grouping that will be used for the lesson or activity (i.e., individual, small group, large group).

4. Circle whether the student is working on an IEP goal. If so, write the goal in the space provided.

5. Describes the teaching methods or protocols that will be used with the student in precise detail (i.e., the directive to be given, how the teacher should respond to the student, any additional instructions). This ensures the integrity of both teaching methods and data collection.

6. Indicate whether data were taken.

Teaching Programs

Materials

Student name: _____

School year: _____ Subject area: _____

Grouping (circle): individual   small group   large group   IEP goal (circle) Yes   No

⭐ **IEP GOAL:** _____

_____

Method

Teacher directive

_____
_____
_____

For correct response

_____
_____
_____
_____
_____

For no response or incorrect response

_____
_____
_____
_____
_____

Additional information

_____
_____
_____
_____

⭐ Were data taken? (Circle.)   YES   NO

TOOLKIT D

Organizational Tools
Establishing a Data Collection System

- Form 1D: Round Robin Organization Chart
- Form 2D: Round Robin Organization Chart (Customizable Stations)
- Form 3D: Round Robin Center Bookmarks
- Form 4D: Cold Probe Data Sheet 1 (Individual Student)
- Form 5D: Cold Probe Data Sheet 2 (Daily—Multiple Students)
- Form 6D: Cold Probe Data Sheet 3 (Daily—Multiple Students)
- Form 7D: Cold Probe Data Sheet 4 (3 Days—Multiple Students)
- Form 8D: Work Sample Analysis Stickers

FORM 1D: ROUND ROBIN ORGANIZATION CHART

The Round Robin Organization Chart will assist you in organizing a data collection system in the classroom that involves collecting various kinds of data on students as they rotate through a sequence of stations or activities. Round robin data collection can be set up so that each of the stations in the classroom involves a method of data collection. This version of the Round Robin Organization Chart is precoded with shapes in order to help organize center movement for the students. If you want the flexibility of coding using colors, numbers, or even stickers, see Form 2D: Round Robin Organization Chart (Customizable Stations).

Steps for completing the Round Robin Organization Chart are as follows. (See Figure 6.1 for completed example.)

1. Determine the total length of center time. Divide this number by the number of centers to get the amount of time per center. Fill this information in the box at the top left.

2. List the student names in the second column, next to the numerals.

3. Divide the students into the centers using the predetermined code.

4. If you want to divide a session in half, indicate that.

5. Give the students bookmark strips (see Form 3D: Round Robin Center Bookmarks) so they can independently navigate the centers.

Round Robin Organization Chart

Indicates ½ time sessions

Time sessions

	1	2	3	4	5	6	7	8	9	10
1										
2										
3										
4										
5										
6										
7										
8										
9										
10										
11										
12										

Students

Total time	Time per center	✔
60 min.		
90 min.		
120 min.		

STATIONS							
○	◆	✕	★	▽	□	B	Break

FORM 2D: ROUND ROBIN ORGANIZATION CHART (CUSTOMIZABLE STATIONS)

The Round Robin Organization Chart (Customizable Stations) allows you to customize how you code different stations or activities (e.g., through pictures, symbols, or colors). Steps for completing the form are as follows.

1. Fill in the coding for the number of centers or stations you want. You could use shapes, colors, letters, or numbers. Be creative! You could even use tiny stickers that would help you organize stations for younger students.

2. Determine the total length of center time. Divide this number by the number of centers to get the amount of time per center. Fill this information in the box at the top left.

3. List the student names in the second column, next to the numerals.

4. Divide the students into the centers using the predetermined code.

5. If you want to divide a session in half, indicate that.

6. Give the students bookmark strips (see Form 3D: Round Robin Center Bookmarks) so they can independently navigate the centers.

Round Robin Organization Chart (Customizable Stations)

	Indicates _____

Total time	Time per center	✓
60 min.		
90 min.		
120 min.		

Time sessions

Students		1	2	3	4	5	6	7	8	9	10
1											
2											
3											
4											
5											
6											
7											
8											
9											
10											
11											
12											

STATIONS

FORM 3D: ROUND ROBIN CENTER BOOKMARKS

When coordinating a round robin activity for your students, consider providing them with a bookmark with shapes, colors, or images indicating the order of the stations they will visit. Steps for completing the Round Robin Organization Chart are as follows. (See Figure 6.2 for an example.)

1. Fill in student names in the first column.

2. Using the codes for centers, fill in the order of centers down the bookmark for each child, splitting the box into two when applicable.

3. Print or photocopy the bookmarks on cardstock.

4. Cut on the dotted line.

5. Use the bookmark strips so the students can independently navigate the centers.

Round Robin Center Bookmarks

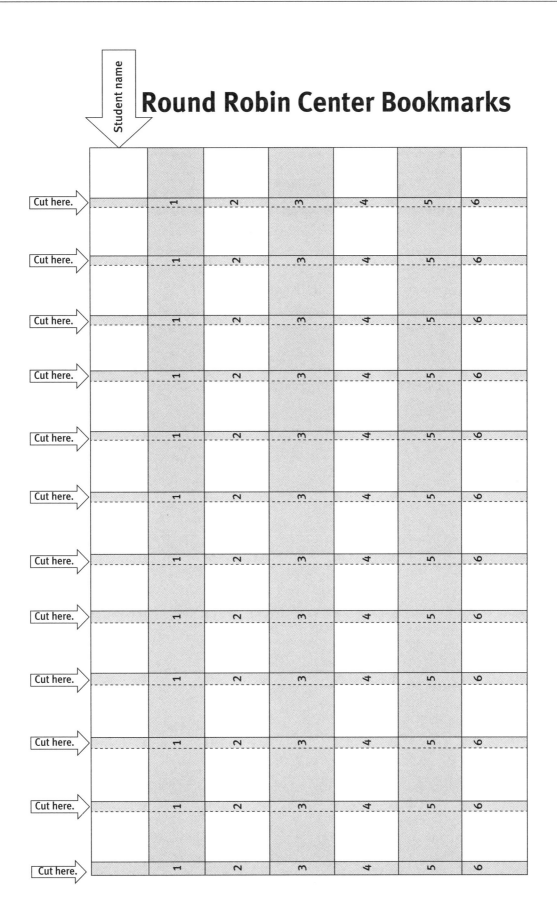

Student name

Cut here.	1	2	3	4	5	6
Cut here.	1	2	3	4	5	6
Cut here.	1	2	3	4	5	6
Cut here.	1	2	3	4	5	6
Cut here.	1	2	3	4	5	6
Cut here.	1	2	3	4	5	6
Cut here.	1	2	3	4	5	6
Cut here.	1	2	3	4	5	6
Cut here.	1	2	3	4	5	6
Cut here.	1	2	3	4	5	6
Cut here.	1	2	3	4	5	6

FORM 4D: COLD PROBE DATA SHEET 1 (INDIVIDUAL STUDENT)

Cold Probe Data Sheet 1 collects cold probe data for an individual student. Cold probes are data collected during the first trial of a task. They occur with no reinforcement for appropriate responses and no practice of the skill, so they are a great way of discerning true skill mastery. Steps for completing the Cold Probe Data Sheet 1 (Individual Student) are as follows (See Figure 6.4 for a completed example.)

1. Fill out the student information, subject area, and dates that you will be collecting data.

2. List the specific tasks, objectives, or skills being assessed for that subject or goal area.

3. Determine the criteria for mastery (i.e., number of consecutive "yes" responses to whether the student demonstrated the skill).

4. Conduct cold probes by assessing whether the student can complete the task, objective, or skill, circling either Y or N. Do not reinforce the student or practice the skill beforehand.

5. Continue with this procedure each day, recording when the student has achieved mastery based on the mastery criteria in the Date Mastered column. Add data sheets as needed.

Cold Probe Data Sheet 1
(Individual Student)

Name: _____

School year: _____

Beginning date: _____

Subject area:

Criteria for mastery:

Objective/task	Dates													Date mastered
1		Y N	Y N	Y N	Y N	Y N	Y N	Y N	Y N	Y N	Y N	Y N	Y N	
2		Y N	Y N	Y N	Y N	Y N	Y N	Y N	Y N	Y N	Y N	Y N	Y N	
3		Y N	Y N	Y N	Y N	Y N	Y N	Y N	Y N	Y N	Y N	Y N	Y N	
4		Y N	Y N	Y N	Y N	Y N	Y N	Y N	Y N	Y N	Y N	Y N	Y N	
5		Y N	Y N	Y N	Y N	Y N	Y N	Y N	Y N	Y N	Y N	Y N	Y N	
6		Y N	Y N	Y N	Y N	Y N	Y N	Y N	Y N	Y N	Y N	Y N	Y N	
7		Y N	Y N	Y N	Y N	Y N	Y N	Y N	Y N	Y N	Y N	Y N	Y N	
8		Y N	Y N	Y N	Y N	Y N	Y N	Y N	Y N	Y N	Y N	Y N	Y N	
9		Y N	Y N	Y N	Y N	Y N	Y N	Y N	Y N	Y N	Y N	Y N	Y N	

FORM 5D: COLD PROBE DATA SHEET 2 (DAILY—MULTIPLE STUDENTS)

Cold Probe Data Sheet 2 is a daily data sheet for collecting cold probe data for groups of students. Students are listed vertically, and tasks, objectives, or skills are listed horizontally. Steps for completing the Cold Probe Data Sheet 2 (Daily—Multiple Students) are as follows. (See Figure 6.5 for a completed example.)

1. List the names of students for which you will be collecting cold probe data. This is a daily sheet—one sheet will be used per day.

2. Indicate the subject area.

3. Write out the tasks, objectives, or skills to be assessed for that subject or goal area.

4. Determine the criteria for mastery (i.e., number of consecutive "yes" responses to whether the students correctly demonstrate the skill).

5. Conduct cold probes by assessing whether the students in your class can complete the task, objective, or skill; record the data for each student by circling either Y or N. Do not reinforce the students or practice the skill beforehand.

6. Compare daily data sheets to monitor whether each of your students has achieved mastery based on the mastery criteria.

Cold Probe Data Sheet 2 (Daily—Multiple Students)

Class: _____

School year: _____

Data taken by: _____

Subject area: _____

Criteria for mastery: _____

DATE										
Objectives/tasks										

Students	Y N	Y N	Y N	Y N	Y N	Y N	Y N	Y N	Y N	Y N
1										
2										
3										
4										
5										
6										
7										
8										
9										
10										

FORM 6D: COLD PROBE DATA SHEET 3 (DAILY—MULTIPLE STUDENTS)

Cold Probe Data Sheet 3 is a daily data sheet for collecting cold probe data for groups of students. Students are listed horizontally, and tasks, objectives, or skills are listed vertically. Steps for completing the Cold Probe Data Sheet 3 (Daily—Multiple Students) are as follows. (See Figure 6.6 for a completed example.)

1. List the names of students for which you will be collecting cold probe data. This is a daily sheet—one sheet will be used per day.

2. Indicate the subject area.

3. Write out the tasks, objectives, or skills to be assessed for that subject or goal area.

4. Determine the criteria for mastery (i.e., number of consecutive "yes" responses to whether the students correctly demonstrate the skill).

5. Conduct cold probes by assessing whether the students in your class can complete the task, objective, or skill; record data for each student by circling either Y or N. Do not reinforce the students or practice the skill beforehand.

6. Compare daily data sheets to monitor whether each of your students has achieved mastery based on the mastery criteria.

Cold Probe Data Sheet 3
(Daily—Multiple Students)

Page ____ of ____

DATE																
Student																

Objectives/tasks: 1, 2, 3, 4, 5, 6, 7, 8, 9, 10 (Y/N per entry)

Class: _____

School year: _____

Data taken by: _____

Subject area: _____

Criteria for mastery: _____

The Data Collection Toolkit: Everything You Need to Organize, Manage, and Monitor Classroom Data, by Cindy Golden.
Copyright © 2018 Paul H. Brookes Publishing Co. All rights reserved.

FORM 7D: COLD PROBE DATA SHEET 4 (3 DAYS—MULTIPLE STUDENTS)

Cold Probe Data Sheet 4 is a data sheet for collecting cold probe data for groups of students that tracks up to 3 days of data. Steps for completing the Cold Probe Data Sheet 4 (3 Days—Multiple Students) are as follows.

1. List the names of students for which you will be collecting cold probe data.

2. Indicate the subject area.

3. Write out the tasks, objectives, or skills to be assessed for that subject or goal area.

4. Determine the criteria for mastery (i.e., number of consecutive "yes" responses to whether the students correctly demonstrate the skill).

5. Conduct cold probes each day by assessing whether the students in your class can complete the task, objective, or skill; record data for each student by circling either Y or N. Do not reinforce the students or practice the skill beforehand. This form tracks up to 3 days of cold probe data for a group or classroom of students; add data sheets as needed.

6. Continue to collect data on your students over time, recording when each student achieves mastery based on the mastery criteria. To manage and monitor data that spans multiple forms, note the number of consecutive Ys from the previous data form for each student in the # of Consecutive YES Carryover column.

Cold Probe Data Sheet 4
(3 Days—Multiple Students)

Task/objectives	Date												
Student		Y	N	Y	N	Y	N	Y	N	Y	N	Y	N
1													
2													
3													
4													
5													
6													
7													
8													

consecutive YES: carry over

Class: _____

Data Taken by: _____

School Year: _____

Subject Area: _____

Criteria for Mastery: _____

FORM 8D: WORK SAMPLE ANALYSIS STICKERS

Use the Work Sample Analysis Stickers to analyze work samples and permanent products. Steps for completing the stickers are as follows. (See Figure 6.10 for a completed example.)

1. Print the template on mailing label paper so that you can easily write on the stickers, pull them off, and stick them on the work sample for instant analysis.

2. Check off the level of prompting that is required for the student to complete the task.

3. If there were significant behavioral issues during the task, make sure to indicate this on the sticker. If the student was given extended time or needed multiple attempts to complete the assignment or task, checking these boxes also.

4. If the task was directly related to an IEP goal, check the IEP Goal/Objective box or put the number of the IEP goal in the box.

WORK SAMPLE ANALYSIS	Date: _____		
Prompt level	✓	**Additional analysis**	✓
Independent		Multiple attempts	
Verbal		Extended time	
Gesture		Behavioral issues	
Modeling			
Partial physical		**IEP goal/objective**	
Full physical		**Percentage correct**	

WORK SAMPLE ANALYSIS	Date: _____		
Prompt level	✓	**Additional analysis**	✓
Independent		Multiple attempts	
Verbal		Extended time	
Gesture		Behavioral issues	
Modeling			
Partial physical		**IEP goal/objective**	
Full physical		**Percentage correct**	

WORK SAMPLE ANALYSIS	Date: _____		
Prompt level	✓	**Additional analysis**	✓
Independent		Multiple attempts	
Verbal		Extended time	
Gesture		Behavioral issues	
Modeling			
Partial physical		**IEP goal/objective**	
Full physical		**Percentage correct**	

WORK SAMPLE ANALYSIS	Date: _____		
Prompt level	✓	**Additional analysis**	✓
Independent		Multiple attempts	
Verbal		Extended time	
Gesture		Behavioral issues	
Modeling			
Partial physical		**IEP goal/objective**	
Full physical		**Percentage correct**	

WORK SAMPLE ANALYSIS	Date: _____		
Prompt level	✓	**Additional analysis**	✓
Independent		Multiple attempts	
Verbal		Extended time	
Gesture		Behavioral issues	
Modeling			
Partial physical		**IEP goal/objective**	
Full physical		**Percentage correct**	

WORK SAMPLE ANALYSIS	Date: _____		
Prompt level	✓	**Additional analysis**	✓
Independent		Multiple attempts	
Verbal		Extended time	
Gesture		Behavioral issues	
Modeling			
Partial physical		**IEP goal/objective**	
Full physical		**Percentage correct**	

WORK SAMPLE ANALYSIS	Date: _____		
Prompt level	✓	**Additional analysis**	✓
Independent		Multiple attempts	
Verbal		Extended time	
Gesture		Behavioral issues	
Modeling			
Partial physical		**IEP goal/objective**	
Full physical		**Percentage correct**	

WORK SAMPLE ANALYSIS	Date: _____		
Prompt level	✓	**Additional analysis**	✓
Independent		Multiple attempts	
Verbal		Extended time	
Gesture		Behavioral issues	
Modeling			
Partial physical		**IEP goal/objective**	
Full physical		**Percentage correct**	

WORK SAMPLE ANALYSIS	Date: _____		
Prompt level	✓	**Additional analysis**	✓
Independent		Multiple attempts	
Verbal		Extended time	
Gesture		Behavioral issues	
Modeling			
Partial physical		**IEP goal/objective**	
Full physical		**Percentage correct**	

WORK SAMPLE ANALYSIS	Date: _____		
Prompt level	✓	**Additional analysis**	✓
Independent		Multiple attempts	
Verbal		Extended time	
Gesture		Behavioral issues	
Modeling			
Partial physical		**IEP goal/objective**	
Full physical		**Percentage correct**	

References

Bambara, L. M., Janney, R., & Snell, M. E. (2015). *Teachers' guides to inclusive practices: Behavior support* (3rd ed.). Baltimore, MD: Paul H. Brookes Publishing Co.

Batsche, G., Elliott, J., Graden, J. L., Grimes, J., Kovaleski, J. F., Prasse, D., Schrag, J., Tilly III, W. D. (2005). *Response to intervention: Policy considerations and implementation.* Alexandria, VA: National Association of State Directors of Special Education.

Brigance, A. H., & French, B. F. (2013). *Brigance Inventory for Early Development III.* North Billerica, MA: Curriculum Associates.

Cooper, J. O., Heron, T. E., & Heward, W. L. (2007). *Applied behavior analysis* (2nd ed.). Upper Saddle River, NJ: Prentice Hall.

Centers for Disease Control and Prevention. (2016). *Developmental milestones.* Retrieved from https://www.cdc.gov/ncbddd/actearly/milestones/

Fisher, D., & Frey, N. (2013). Implementing RTI in a high school: A case study. *Journal of Learning Disabilities, 46*(2), 99–114.

Fuchs, D., & Fuchs, L. S. (2006). Introduction to response to intervention: What, why, and how valid is it? *Reading Research Quarterly, 41*(1), 92–99.

Gay, L. R., Mills, G. E., & Airasian, P. (2015). *Educational research: Competencies for analysis and applications* (11th ed.). Upper Saddle River, NJ: Pearson Education.

Gickling, E. E., Shane, R. L., & Croskery, K. M. (1989). Developing math skills in low-achieving high school students through curriculum-based assessment. *School Psychology Review, 18,* 344–345.

Golden, C. (2012). *The special educator's toolkit: Everything you need to organize, manage, and monitor your classroom.* Baltimore, MD: Paul H. Brookes Publishing Co.

Grigg, N. C., Snell, M. E., & Lloyd, B. H. (1989). Visual analysis of student evaluation data: A qualitative analysis of teacher decision making. *Journal of The Association for Persons with Severe Handicaps, 14,* 23–32.

Grover, L. K., & Mehra, R. (2008). The lure of statistics in data mining. *Journal of Statistics Education, 16*(1). Punjab, India: Guru Nanak Dev University, BBK DAV College for Women, India Institution of Authors.

Heward, W. L. (2000). *Exceptional children: An introduction to special education* (6th ed.). Upper Saddle River, NJ: Merrill/Prentice Hall.

Heward, W. L. (2013). *Exceptional children: An introduction to special education* (10th ed.). Boston, MA: Pearson.

Individuals with Disabilities Education Improvement Act (IDEA) of 2004, PL 108-446, 20 U.S.C. §§ 1400 *et seq.*

Jimenez, B. A., Mims, P. J., & Browder, D. M. (2012). Data-based decision guidelines for teachers of students with severe intellectual and developmental disabilities. *Education and Training in Autism and Developmental Disabilities, 47*(4), 407–413.

Kansas MTSS. (2008). *Kansas Multi-Tier System of Support.* Retrieved from http://www.ksde.org/Portals/0/CSAS/Content%20Area%20(M-Z)/School%20Counseling/School_Coun_Resource/Kansas%20Multi-Tiered%20System%20of%20Support.pdf

Keller-Margulis, M. A., Mercer, S. H., & Shapiro, E. S. (2014). Differences in growth on math curriculum-based measures using triannual benchmarks. *Assessment for Effective Intervention, 39*(3), 146–155.

Kurz, A., Elliott, S. N., & Roach, A. T. (2015). Addressing the missing instructional data problem: Using a teacher log to document Tier 1 instruction. *Remedial and Special Education, 36*(6), 361–373.

Lane, J. D., & Ledford, J. R. (2014). Using interval-based systems to measure behavior in early childhood special education and early intervention. *Topics in Early Childhood Special Education, 34*(2), 83–93.

Lindsley, O. R. (1991). From technical jargon to Plain English for application. *Journal of Applied Behavior Analysis, 24,* 449–458.

Love, N., Stiles, K. E., Mundry, S., & DiRanna, K. (2008). *A data coach's guide to improving learning for all students. Unleashing the power of collaborative inquiry.* Thousand Oaks, CA: Corwin.

Mandinach, E. B., & Jackson, S. S. (2012). *Transforming teaching and learning through data-driven decision making.* Thousand Oaks, CA: Corwin.

Mertler, C. A. (2016). *Introduction to educational research.* Thousand Oaks, CA: SAGE.

O'Reilly, M., Dogra, N., & Ronzoni, P. D. (2013). *Research with children: Theory and practice.* Thousand Oaks, CA: SAGE.

Partington, J. W. (2006). *The Assessment of Basic Language and Learning Skills–Revised (ABLLS-R).* Walnut Hill, CA: Behavior Analysts.

Rowe, D. A., & Test, D. W. (2013). Effects of simulation to teach students with disabilities basic finance skills. *Remedial and Special Education, 34*(4), 237–248.

Smith, K. A., Ayres, K. M., Mechling, L. C., Alexander, J. L., Mataras, T. K., & Shepley, S. B. (2013). Evaluating the effects of a video prompt in a system of least prompts procedure. *Career Development and Transition for Exceptional Individuals, 38*(1), 39–49.

Stecker, P. M., Fuchs, D., & Fuchs, L. S. (2008). Progress monitoring as essential practice within response to intervention. *Rural Special Education Quarterly, 27*(4), 10–17.

Stronge, J. H., Ward, T. J., & Grant, L. W. (2011). What makes good teachers good? A cross-case analysis of the connection between teacher effectiveness and student achievement. *Journal of Teacher Education, 62*(4), 339–355.

Sugai, G., Horner, R. H., Dunlap, G., Hieneman, M., Lewis, T. J., Nelson, C. M., … Ruef, M. (2000). Applying positive behavioral support and functional behavioral assessment in schools. *Journal of Positive Behavior Interventions, 2,* 131–143.

Winterman, K. G., & Rosas, C. E. (2014). *The IEP checklist: Your guide to creating meaningful and compliant IEPs.* Baltimore, MD: Paul H. Brookes Publishing Co.

Witt, J. C., VanDerHeyden, A. M., & Gilbertson, D. (2004). Troubleshooting behavioral interventions: A systematic process for finding and eliminating problems. *School Psychology Review, 33,* 363–383.

Building Your Data Collection Notebook

Handouts, Embellishments, and Extras

In this appendix, you will find a few handouts and photocopiable materials that can help you design and organize your own data collection notebook or miniguide to data collection for your classroom or learning environment. Not only can you use a data collection notebook as a place to store the tools of the trade—your data sheets and Quick-Graphs—but also as a place where you can reference helpful reminders related to the data collection process. Included in this appendix is a cover sheet for your notebook, two reminder handouts, and two printable bookmarks related to IEP goals. Use these extra materials to build your own data collection notebook for the classroom or to craft a quick guide to data collection for the purpose of training staff. The following materials are included in this appendix:

• The Basics of Data Collection (data collection notebook cover sheet)

• Steps to Data Collection (handout)

• "Now, What Kind of Behavioral Data Do I Need?" (handout)

• Writing IEP Goals and Setting Criteria (bookmarks)

The Basics of Data Collection

Steps to Data Collection

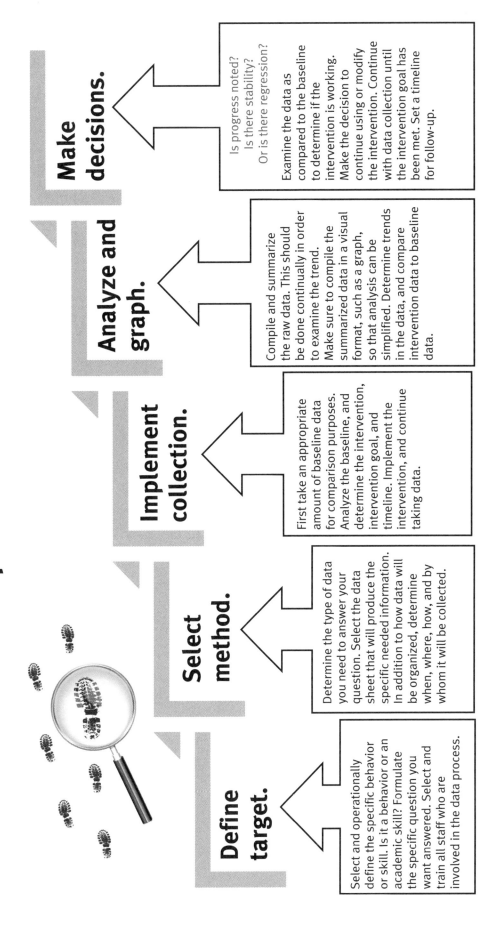

Define target.

Select and operationally define the specific behavior or skill. Is it a behavior or an academic skill? Formulate the specific question you want answered. Select and train all staff who are involved in the data process.

Select method.

Determine the type of data you need to answer your question. Select the data sheet that will produce the specific needed information. In addition to how data will be organized, determine when, where, how, and by whom it will be collected.

Implement collection.

First take an appropriate amount of baseline data for comparison purposes. Analyze the baseline, and determine the intervention, intervention goal, and timeline. Implement the intervention, and continue taking data.

Analyze and graph.

Compile and summarize the raw data. This should be done continually in order to examine the trend. Make sure to compile the summarized data in a visual format, such as a graph, so that analysis can be simplified. Determine trends in the data, and compare intervention data to baseline data.

Make decisions.

Is progress noted?
Is there stability?
Or is there regression?

Examine the data as compared to the baseline to determine if the intervention is working. Make the decision to continue using or modify the intervention. Continue with data collection until the intervention goal has been met. Set a timeline for follow-up.

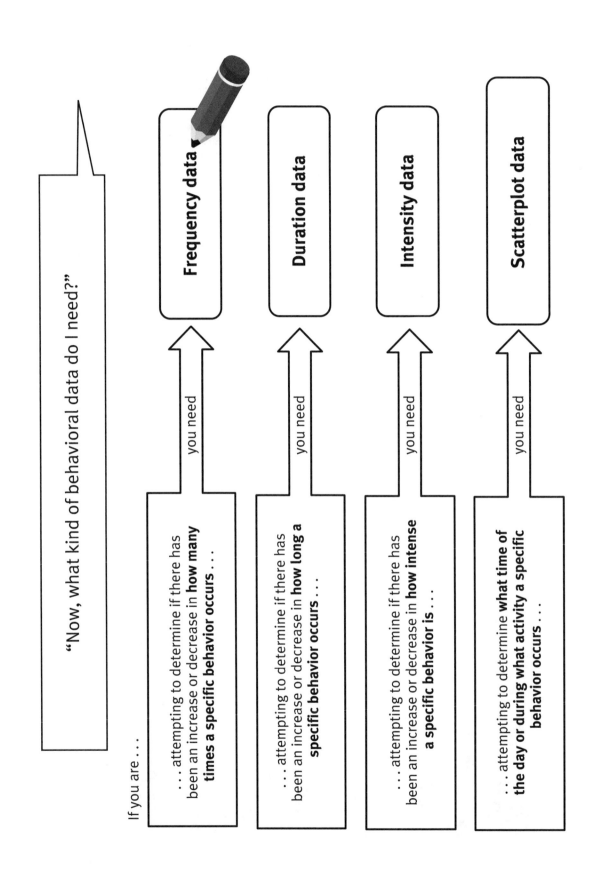

"Now, what kind of behavioral data do I need?"

If you are . . .

. . . attempting to determine if there has been an increase or decrease in **how many times a specific behavior occurs** . . .

you need → **Frequency data**

. . . attempting to determine if there has been an increase or decrease in **how long a specific behavior occurs** . . .

you need → **Duration data**

. . . attempting to determine if there has been an increase or decrease in **how intense a specific behavior is** . . .

you need → **Intensity data**

. . . attempting to determine **what time of the day or during what activity a specific behavior occurs** . . .

you need → **Scatterplot data**

Writing IEP Goals

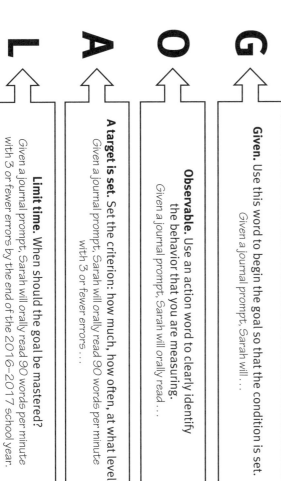

G — **Given.** Use this word to begin the goal so that the condition is set.
Given a journal prompt, Sarah will . . .

O — **Observable.** Use an action word to clearly identify the behavior that you are measuring.
Given a journal prompt, Sarah will orally read . . .

A — **A target is set.** Set the criterion: how much, how often, at what level.
Given a journal prompt, Sarah will orally read 90 words per minute with 3 or fewer errors . . .

L — **Limit time.** When should the goal be mastered?
Given a journal prompt, Sarah will orally read 90 words per minute with 3 or fewer errors by the end of the 2016–2017 school year.

Setting Criteria

Rate — Time — Percentage

Rate: The task or behavior must be repeated to show mastery.
Tarik will correctly complete 4 out of 5 assignments.

Time: The task must be completed within a time limit.
Danae will correctly answer 15 single-digit addition facts within 5 minutes.

Percentage: Level of performance is measured relative to 100%.
Anna will give her correct phone number in 90% of the opportunities.

Answers to Quick Quizzes

Chapters	Answers
Chapter 1	A, B, C, A, B
Chapter 2	C, C, B, A
Chapter 3	A, B, A, C, B
Chapter 4	B, A, A, A, C
Chapter 5	B, C, A, D
Chapter 6	B, A, A, D, C
Chapter 7	C, B, B, A, B
Chapter 8	B, C, C, A, D

Index

Page numbers followed by *f* and *t* indicate figures and tables, respectively.

ABC (antecedent, behavior, consequence) data, 66–67, 68*f*–69*f*, 125
ABC Data Quick-Graph, 67, 69*f*, 204, 206*f*
ABC Data Sheet, 67, 68*f*, 204, 205*f*
ABC Data Summary, 126, 127*f*–128*f*, 129
ABLLS-R, *see* Assessment of Basic Language and Learning Skills–Revised
Academic data collection, 25–39
Academic forms, 137–158
Academic Needs Checklist, 76, 78*f*, 212, 213*f*
Academic Progress Monitoring Quick-Graph, 27–28, 28*f*, 138, 139*f*
Academic Rubric Quick-Graph, 142, 143*f*
Analysis, 3
   task, 4, 6, 25, 29–32
   see also Data analysis
Antecedents, 67
Assessment
   curriculum-based, 25, 27
   functional behavior, 3, 14–15, 125
   standardized, 113
   statewide, 26–27
Assessment of Basic Language and Learning Skills–Revised (ABLLS-R), 113–114

Bar graphs, 109, 110*f*, 112*f*
Baseline data, 11, 107–108, 108*f*, 110–111, 113
BCBA, *see* Board Certified Behavior Analyst
Behavior
   antecedents, 67
   challenging, 132–133, 133*t*
   off-task, 19–20, 19*t*
   replacement, 11, 14–15, 15*t*, 16*t*
   target, 4, 7, 7*f*, 13–16, 15*t*, 16*t*, 19
Behavior forms, 159–206
Behavior intervention plan (BIP), 3, 4, 41
Behavioral data, 41–70, 240*f*
   ABC, 66–67, 68*f*–69*f*, 125
   duration data, 41, 43, 50–54, 55, 59
   frequency data, 16, 41, 43–50, 51, 56, 59, 119
   intensity data, 43, 51, 54–59, 119
   interval data sampling, 65–66
   latency data, 41, 65
   scatterplot data, 41, 43*f*, 44, 51, 56, 59, 62–64, 119
   types of, 42, 43*f*, 64–67
Benchmarks, 110–111, 113–114
Best-fit straight line, 120–122, 120*f*, 121*f*
BIP, *see* Behavior intervention plan
Board Certified Behavior Analyst (BCBA), 3

Causal link, 105
Causation, 114
CBA, *see* Curriculum-based assessment
Challenging behaviors, 132–133, 133*t*
Classroom environment, data collection in, 6
Clipboards, 99, 101*f*
CBM, *see* Curriculum-based measurement
Cold Probe Data Sheet, 93–94
   3 days—multiple students, 97*f*, 230, 231*f*
   daily—multiple students, 95*f*, 96*f*, 226, 227*f*, 228, 229*f*
   individual student, 93*f*, 224, 225*f*
Cold probes, 83, 92–94, 92*f*, 93*f*
Control group, 105
Correlation, 105, 114
Curriculum-based assessment (CBA), 25, 27
Curriculum-based measurement (CBM), 27

Data, 3
   ABC, 66–67, 68*f*–69*f*, 125
   academic, 25–39
   baseline, 11, 107–108, 108*f*, 110–111, 113
   behavioral, 41–70, 240*f*
   cold probe, 92–94, 92*f*, 93*f*
   duration, 41, 43, 43*f*, 50–55, 59
   frequency, 16, 41, 43–51, 43*f*, 56, 59, 119
   graphing, *see* Graphs/graphing
   IEP, 71–81
   intensity, 43, 43*f*, 51, 54–59, 119
   interval data sampling, 65–66
   latency, 41, 65
   organization of, 108–109
   presentation of, 9
   prompt-level, 34–35, 38
   qualitative, 25, 29
   quantitative, 25, 29
   raw, 83, 105
   scatterplot, 41, 43*f*, 44, 51, 56, 59, 62–64, 119
   yes/no, 32–34, 32*f*
Data analysis, 8–9, 105–123
   checklist, 115*f*
   explaining to parents and IEP team members, 126, 129–130
   levels, 115, 116*f*
   looking for trends or patterns, 114–122
   meaning of, 106–107
   process, 107–122
   variability, 115–118, 117*f*
Data collection
   academic data, 25–39
   applications of, 19–20

Data collection—*continued*
  data analysis and, 107–108
  defining target behavior and, 13–14
  environments for, 6
  IPE goals and objectives, 71–81
  issue determination for, 12–13
  materials and paperwork, 94–102
  need for, 5
  organization of, 86–102
  organizational tools, 217–233
  reasons for, 5
  round robin, 88–90, 89f, 91f
  step-by-step process, 3–10, 7f, 13, 239f
  system, 83–102
  technology for, 84–86, 84t
  testing interventions and, 122
  time management and, 87–94
  tools, 8
Data collection days, 87–88
Data crates, 95
Data dredging, 118
Data mining, 118
Data notebooks, 96–99, 237–241
Data sheets
  ABC Data Sheet, 67, 68f, 204, 205f
  Cold Probe Data Sheet, 93–94, 93f, 95f, 96f, 97f, 224,
    225f, 226, 227f, 228, 229f, 230, 231f
  Duration Percentage Data Sheet, 54, 55f, 183, 184f
  Frequency Rate Data Sheet, 48–49, 49f, 172, 173f
  IEP Goal Data Sheet, 75–76, 208, 209f
  Intensity Level Percentage Data Sheet, 58, 60f, 189,
    190f–191f
  Scatterplot Percentage Data Sheet, 64, 65f, 200, 201f
  self-graphing, 83, 86
Data-based decision making, 8, 106–107, 125–134
Dead Man Test, 14, 15
Decision making, data-based, 8, 106–107, 125–134
Dependent variables, 105
Detailed Data Analysis Outline, 130, 131f
Developmental milestones, 113
Discrete Trial Quick-Graph, 35, 37f, 154, 155f, 156, 157f
Discrete trial training (DTT), 20, 25, 35
Duration data, 41, 50–54
  calculating duration percentages, 52, 54
  recording and graphing, 51–52, 52f
  when to use, 43, 43f, 51, 55, 59
Duration Data Quick-Graph, 51, 52f, 176, 177f,
    178, 179f
Duration Percentage Data Graph, 54, 56f, 185, 186f
Duration Percentage Data Sheet, 54, 55f, 183, 184f
Duration/Intensity Quick-Graph, 51–52, 53f, 180,
    181f–182f

Environments, for data collection, 6

FBA, *see* Functional behavior assessment
Frequency data, 16, 41, 43–50, 119
  calculating frequency rates, 46, 48–49
  recording and graphing, 45f, 46f, 445
  when to use, 43f, 44, 51, 56, 59

Frequency Quick-Graph, 44–45, 45f, 46f, 160, 161f, 162,
    163f, 164, 165f
Frequency Rate Data Sheet, 48–49, 49f, 172, 173f
Frequency Rate Graph, 48, 49, 50f, 174, 175f
Frequency/Intensity Quick-Graph, 47f, 166, 167f–168f,
    169, 170f–171f
Functional analysis, 125
Functional behavior assessment (FBA), 3,
    14–15, 125

Generalization, 11
Global evaluation tools, 26–27
Graphs/graphing, 8, 56f
  bar graphs, 109, 110f, 112f
  duration data, 51–52, 52f
  frequency data, 44–45, 45f, 46f
  intensity data, 57, 58f
  line graphs, 109–110, 111f, 112f
  scatterplot, 62f
  scatterplot data, 59, 62
  see also Quick-Graphs

IEP, *see* Individualized education program
IEP data, 71–81
IEP forms, 207–215
IEP Goal Data Sheet, 75–76, 208, 209f
IEP Goal Mastery Quick-Graph, 77f, 210, 211f
IEP goals, 71
  data collection for, 72–73
  system for measuring, 75–76
  writing measurable, 73–75, 74f, 241f
IEP objectives, 71
  data collection for, 72–73
  system for measuring, 75–76
IEP-related information, 76, 78, 80
Independent variables, 105
Individual progress measurement, 19–20
Individualized education program (IEP), 4, 6, 71,
    106, 125
Intensity data, 54–59, 119
  calculating intensity level percentages, 57–59
  recording and graphing, 57
  when to use, 43, 43f, 51, 56, 59
Intensity Level Percentage Data Sheet, 58, 60f, 189,
    190f–191f
Intensity Level Percentage Graph, 58, 61f, 192,
    193f–194f
Intensity Quick-Graph, 57, 58f, 187, 188f
Interval data sampling, 65–66
Interventions
  evaluation of, 5
  modifying, 132–133
  testing, 122
Issue determination, 12–13

Last documented functioning level, 114
Latency data, 41, 65
Level of functioning, 115, 116f
Line graphs, 109–110, 111f, 112f

Mastery standards, 111, 113–114
Momentary time sampling, 66
Multi-tiered system of supports (MTSS), 4, 9, 26, 27, 87

Observation, 11
  neutral observer, 11
  Student Observation Form, 17f–18f, 19
  write-up, 15–16, 15f
Off-task behavior, 19–20, 19t
Operationally defined, 11
Organizational tools, 217–233

Paperwork, organization of, 94–102, 101f
Partial interval, 66
Patterns, 114–122
Progress monitoring, 11, 27–38
Progress monitoring forms, 137–158
Prompt Levels Quick-Graph, 34, 36f, 150, 151f, 152, 153f
Prompt-level data, 34–35, 38
Prompts, 25, 34
Prosocial skills, 113–114

Qualitative data, 25, 29
Quantitative data, 25, 29
Quick-Graphs
  ABC Data, 204, 206f
  Academic Progress Monitoring, 27–28, 28f, 138, 139f
  Academic Rubric, 142, 143f
  Discrete Trial, 35, 37f, 154, 155f, 156, 157f
  Duration Data, 51, 52f, 176, 177f, 178, 179f
  Duration/Intensity, 51–52, 53f, 180, 181f–182f
  Frequency, 44–45, 45f, 46f, 160, 161f, 162, 163f, 164, 165f
  Frequency/Intensity, 47f, 166, 167f–168f, 169, 170f–171f
  IEP Goal Mastery, 77f, 210, 211f
  Intensity, 57, 58f
  Prompt Levels, 34, 36f, 150, 151f, 152, 153f
  Task Analysis, 30, 31f, 32, 144, 145f, 146, 147f
  Time Interval Scatterplot, 59, 62f, 195, 196f
  Time Interval/Intensity Scatterplot, 62, 63f, 197, 198f–199f
  Writing Rubric, 29, 30f, 140, 141f
  Yes/No, 33–34, 33f, 148, 149f

Raw data, 83, 105
Referral question, 125
Replacement behavior, 11, 14–15, 15t, 16t
Response to intervention (RTI), 4, 8, 9, 26, 27, 87
Round Robin Center Bookmarks, 91f, 222, 223f
Round robin data collection, 88–90, 89f, 91f

Round Robin Organization Chart, 89f, 90, 218, 219f, 220, 221f
RTI, see Response to intervention
Rubrics, 25, 28–29

Scatterplot data, 41, 59, 62–64, 119
  calculating scatterplot percentages, 62, 64
  recording and graphing, 59, 62
  when to use, 43f, 44, 51, 56, 59
Scatterplot Percentage Data Sheet, 64, 65f, 200, 201f
Scatterplot Percentage Graph, 64, 66f, 202, 203f
Self-graphing data sheets, 83, 86
Skill mastery, 20
Social skills, 113–114
Spreadsheets, 84
Standardized assessment, 113
Statewide assessments, 26–27
Stations, 88, 90
Student Observation Form, 17f–18f, 19

Target behavior, 4, 7, 7f, 16t
  defining, 13–16, 19
  link between replacement behavior and, 15t
Task analysis, 4, 6, 25, 29–32
Task Analysis Quick-Graph, 30, 31f, 32, 144, 145f, 146, 147f
Teaching methods, 78, 78t, 80
Teaching Programs form, 76, 79f, 80, 122, 214, 215f
Technology, for data collection, 84–86, 84t
Time Interval Scatterplot Quick-Graph, 59, 62f, 195, 196f
Time Interval/Intensity Scatterplot Quick-Graph, 62, 63f, 197, 198f–199f
Time management, 87–94
Trendline, 105
Trends, 107–108, 114–122

Variability, 105, 115–118, 117f
Variables
  dependent, 105
  independent, 105
Visual analysis, 4

Whole interval, 66
Work sample analysis, 83, 96–99, 98f, 100f
Work Sample Analysis Stickers, 99, 232, 233f
Workstations, see Stations
Writing Rubric Quick-Graph, 29, 30f, 140, 141f

Yes/no data, 32–34, 32f
Yes/No Quick-Graph, 33–34, 33f, 148, 149f